ONE MAN'S UNSELFISH ATTEMPT TO SAVE THE COUNTRY HE LOVED

Fiercely dedicated to honor and justice, Leon Jaworski took on the job of Special Prosecutor fully aware that it might "destroy him." In the midst of a Washington corrupted by cynical men of uncontrolled ambition, Jaworski took a stand to uphold the inherent virtues and principles of his country.

The RIGHT and the POWER

The Prosecution of Watergate

by Leon Jaworski

A KANGAROO BOOK
PUBLISHED BY POCKET BOOKS NEW YORK

THE RIGHT AND THE POWER

Reader's Digest Press edition published 1976

POCKET BOOK edition published August, 1977

This POCKET BOOK edition includes every word contained in the original, higher-priced edition. It is printed from brand-new plates made from completely reset, clear, easy-to-read type.
POCKET BOOK editions are published by
POCKET BOOKS,
a Simon & Schuster Division of
GULF & WESTERN CORPORATION
1230 Avenue of the Americas,
New York, N.Y. 10020.
Trademarks registered in the United States
and other countries.

THIS WORK is gratefully dedicated to the members
of the staff of the Watergate Special Prosecution Force
who served from November 5, 1973,
to October 25, 1974, the period when I was
the Special Prosecutor.
Their loyalty, objectivity, and professionalism
made possible the public service
here recounted.

publisher's note

THE MANUSCRIPT on which this volume is based was written by Leon Jaworski and donated by him and Jeannette Adam Jaworski to the Leon Jaworski Foundation, a nonprofit organization, created on July 2, 1969, for charitable, religious, and educational purposes. The author's royalties and other proceeds will be received exclusively by the Foundation under contract between it and the Publisher.

acknowledgment

GRATEFUL ACKNOWLEDGMENT is due to Jack Donahue, author and journalist, for his editorial supervision. My thanks also to Volla Mathews Miller and Connie Dillon Hutchison for proficient secretarial services and to the many friends and believers whose prayers and expressions of faith undergirded the efforts described in this book.

contents

The Right and the Power

chapter one

"He Wants You"

I WAS WORKING at my desk on the morning of October 30, 1973, immersed in a stack of mail to which I was dictating replies, when my phone rang. It was a friend of mine, an attorney. He was speaking from New York.

"Leon," he said, "you're going to get a call shortly from General Alexander Haig at the White House. He's going to try to persuade you to accept the job of Watergate Special Prosecutor."

"After what happened to Archibald Cox?" I answered with a wry chuckle.

"He wants you, Leon."

"Perhaps," I replied. "But I was approached about the job before Cox took it. I told them at the time that the job didn't have enough independence to suit me. What happened to Cox is evidence that I was right."

"It doesn't make any difference," my friend said. "Haig, and the others at the White House, seem determined to get you. Hear him out, anyway."

I said I would, and settled back to wait for Haig's call.

Meanwhile, I thought about Archibald Cox. He had promised Congress that he would follow the intrigues of Watergate to a conclusion—even if the trail led into the Oval Office—and I had watched the resulting developments carefully. When Cox had subpoenaed tape recordings from the White House that were relevant to the case, he had been fired as the Watergate Special Prosecutor on orders from President Richard Nixon less than two weeks earlier. Attorney General Elliott Richardson, who had selected Cox for the job, refused to comply with Nixon's orders and resigned. His deputy, William Ruckelshaus, also refused to fire Cox and was himself discharged. Solicitor General Robert Bork was next in the line of succession. He had been appointed Acting Attorney General and he agreed to remove Cox from office. The events now were known as the "Saturday Night Massacre," and had produced protests and cries of outrage from across the nation. A majority of Americans, it appeared, interpreted the President's move as another—and the most violent— attempt to protect a number of his associates, and perhaps himself, from several investigations that were probing the very vitals of the Administration. There had to be more to Watergate than what met the eye. But at that moment, I knew little more about it than most other well-informed Americans.

Haig's call was not long in coming. I had never met Haig. I had read about him, of course, and knew that he had seen combat in both Korea and Vietnam, that he had leaped over more than two hundred senior generals to four-star rank to become Henry Kissinger's aide, that he had become the President's chief of staff after the resignation of H. R. Haldeman. From news reports it was obvious that the President leaned heavily on him.

He got right to the point; he wanted to discuss my taking the Special Prosecutor's job.

"Are you aware the job was mentioned to me before Cox took it?" I asked.

"No, but it makes no difference."

"It does to me, General. I didn't consider it at the time because I didn't think the independence to act was there."

"We can give you the independence."

"Cox probably thought he had it," I said.

Haig pressed on. "It has been discussed with the President," he said. "He's willing to let you exercise whatever independence you need. We'll find a way to get you what you want."

And so we talked, with Haig promising independence while I insisted that I couldn't fathom how it could be accomplished. I had felt the urgency in his voice at the beginning of our conversation. Now I sensed what might be desperation. "The least you can do is come to Washington and talk it out with us," he said. "I want you to talk with the President and some other people."

I still hesitated, and his voice warmed with friendly cajolery. "Oh, come on. If you leave Houston tomorrow morning, I promise to have you back home in time for dinner!"

So I said I would come to see him. However, I gave not the slightest indication that I would accept the job.

I FLEW TO WASHINGTON the next morning in the small Air Force jet Haig sent for me. The crew—pilot, co-pilot, navigator and steward—was in uniform. I was the only passenger, though the plane would have accommodated six or eight. We took off from Ellington Air Force Base, just outside town, and I saw no one I knew.

Gazing out the window, I analyzed Haig's dilemma. Public reaction to the "Saturday Night Massacre" must have been far more violent than the White House had anticipated. Congressmen had to be reporting to Haig and other Administration officials that their constituents were baffled and angry. The morning paper said there was talk in Congress of creating a Special Prosecutor's office outside the President's control. Obviously,

Haig and the President were trying to beat Congress to the punch.

It seemed reasonable that Haig and Bork, as well as William Saxbe, whom the President had designated as his choice to take over as Attorney General, had made calls around the country in a hunt for someone Congress and the public might accept. Haig said my name had surfaced more often than others. Haig, who had known little or nothing about me, now knew that I had begun my career as a trial lawyer when I was twenty years old, that I had been president of the American Bar Association and served on governmental commissions, and was no stranger either in Washington or the White House itself. And I felt certain he had been assured, "This guy won't be out after the President's scalp." So, as I puzzled out the moves in this great chess game of politics I concluded that Haig now thought I was the answer.

A limousine was waiting at Andrews Air Force Base. I was taken directly to the White House and escorted to Haig's office. He greeted me cordially in a soft voice and looked me straight in the eye as he did so. Haig is a handsome man, and civilian clothing does not hide his military bearing. He picked up the conversation where we had left it on the telephone, and it was immediately obvious that if he had not always been a diplomat, his work with Henry Kissinger had made him one. He was articulate and persuasive.

"Your name cropped up around the country," he said with a warm and friendly smile, "and the suggestion that you serve as Special Prosecutor was virtually unanimous." He talked on for a while in this vein, charming me, and then said, almost as an afterthought, "You're highly regarded, and it's no secret that you're high on the list for appointment to the Supreme Court."

4

I suppressed a smile. The remark could have been part flattery, part fact, but I suspected it was all bait. So I quickly told Haig, "My serving on the Supreme Court was discussed in the Lyndon Johnson Administration. I had no interest in it then and I have none now."

Haig moved right on, and his soft voice grew grave. "I'm putting the patriotic monkey on your back, Mr. Jaworski. The situation in this country is almost revolutionary. Things are about to come apart. The only hope of stabilizing the situation is for the President to be able to announce that someone in whom the country has confidence has agreed to serve."

I told him I was impressed with his argument, but I went back to my original contention: there just wasn't a strong enough guarantee that I could operate with independence. I pointed out that the charter and guidelines creating the job had appeared strong enough for Cox—until he was fired.

Haig said that President Nixon had authorized that the charter and guidelines be enlarged. He offered a new formula: assurance from the President of complete independence of action, and the stipulation that he would not discharge me (except for extraordinary improprieties) without first obtaining a supporting consensus from the leadership of both parties in the House and Senate as well as the leadership of both parties in the House Judiciary Committee and the Senate Judiciary Committee. This amounted to eight individuals. Consensus would be defined as six of the eight.

While I pondered, Haig decided to go talk to the President, and asked me if I wanted to come with him to talk it over with Mr. Nixon. I told him I didn't. He had asked me this several times during our discussion; each time I told him it would be a mistake for me to talk to the President because, *if* I took the assignment, the news media would surely draw incorrect inferences from the meeting.

Sitting alone, waiting for Haig to return, I was aware that many Americans would be suspicious of any new Special Prosecutor selected by the President, regardless of the freedom promised him to pursue the truth. And while Haig was urging me to take the job for patriotic reasons, I now knew he was in a hurry to fill it before Congress filled it for him. This did not disturb me. I believed I could work unhindered with the safeguards Haig offered. And I felt that Congress could not settle on a Special Prosecutor until after months of debate, and the country could not afford such a delay. Further, I had doubts about the constitutionality of such congressional action. It was not a prerogative of the Congress to appoint a member of the executive branch.

From what Haig had heard about me it was apparent that he had concluded that I was a political conservative and a member of the Establishment, as many considered me to be. But it was likely that Haig had never heard of a speech I delivered before the Jefferson County, Texas, Bar Association some six months earlier. It had been on Law Day, May 3, two weeks before Cox had been appointed Special Prosecutor.

Watergate had been on my mind, and to my fellow attorneys I had lauded Judge John Sirica for his "plain and unadulterated faithfulness to duty, which appears to be lacking in some other public servants. . . ." I had recommended that "with dispatch there should be instituted investigatory proceedings assuring a full and fair exposure of all aspects of this incredible affair. . . ." And I had praised the news media for "an alert and astute exposure that sounded a much-needed alarm to the American people. . . ."

My enthusiasm for Judge Sirica and the press obviously was not shared by those in the White House. Now I thought it proper that Haig and the President know my feelings about a "full and fair exposure" of Watergate and related affairs.

When Haig returned I told him: "I've taken a public position since this affair started that it should be thoroughly investigated and publicized. And I feel that every person criminally involved should be prosecuted. If I take this job, I'm going to work that way."

"That's just what we want," Haig said. The President, he said, had heartily approved the safeguards. "Is there any other assurance you need?" I told him I couldn't think of anything else.

He seemed like a salesman on the verge of "closing a deal." He brought in Acting Attorney General Bork and Attorney General Designate Saxbe to help clinch it. Both men urged me to accept the appointment. Bork said he had talked with the President and had been authorized to enlarge the charter and guidelines according to the formula Haig and I had agreed on.

After they left, in came Fred Buzhardt and Leonard Garment, both White House lawyers. They also urged me to take the job. They were followed by Melvin Laird and Bryce Harlow, advisors to the President, and the ceremony was repeated.

Finally Haig and I were alone again. The question now was this: Are you, Leon Jaworski, at sixty-eight and with a fair share of good fortune, willing to take on something that probably will be nothing but trouble?

For years I had been exhorting my fellow lawyers not to shun unpopular cases. So I decided that as hard as the Special Prosecutor's job was going to be—and it could destroy me—I would always feel better if I took it rather than letting it go by.

"I accept," I told Haig.

He appeared greatly relieved and said: "You're a great American!"

He said an announcement of my acceptance would be made the next day. "Remember," he said, "the key words in any news conference are that you've got the right to take the President to court."

"I'll remember," I said.

JACK-O'-LANTERNS WERE SHINING in windows as I drove home that evening from the airport in Houston and, late as it was, some neighborhood children in goblin garb were still trick-or-treating on lighted porches. But the people milling around in front of my house were not children observing Halloween. They were newspeople, from all the media, and they were there to let me know the news of my acceptance had "leaked out" in Washington.

And I also was to learn that while I was being importuned in Haig's office to take the job, Fred Buzhardt had told Judge Sirica that two of the nine tapes that Cox had subpoenaed did not exist.

JEANNETTE, MY WIFE of forty-two years, did not question my accepting the Special Prosecutor's job, though she suspected the work would be hard and the tenure probably long. She amused me when she told a reporter, "All I can say is that I just feel sorry for him." She shooed away the last newsman about one o'clock in the morning. But it seemed as if we had hardly closed our eyes when a fresh television crew awakened us with enough racket to raise up the Witch of Endor. It was 5 A.M. With as much civility as I could muster I told them to return at a more suitable hour. They graciously agreed, but by then Jeannette and I were fully awake, so we prepared to face the day.

I couldn't handle the number of newspeople who swarmed into the house after breakfast. Finally a friend suggested I hold one large news conference. I arranged for the auditorium in the Bank of the Southwest Building where my law firm had its office, and it appeared for a while that even that huge room would not be large enough. But a news conference finally was held, and I answered all the questions I considered proper.

That afternoon Jeannette and I slipped away to Austin, where we held a reception for members of the state constitutional revision committee, of which I had been a member. It was a commitment made some time back and one we were happy to fulfill. A number of state officials also were present. The talk, quite naturally, swung to my appointment, and a gift was presented to me. When I finally got the package opened and the paper unwound, I found two spools of blank recording tape.

The next day we went to our ranch, the Circle J. It is a working ranch, not far from Austin in the Texas Hill Country, where we were breeding quarter horses. On the acreage are the main house, a guest house, an office Jeannette built for me, and a hunting lodge. Here I had an important piece of work to do. I had to call Henry Ruth in Washington. Ruth had been Archibald Cox's deputy and at present was holding the staff together. I had met and grown to admire Ruth when I served as a member of the President's Crime Commission during the Johnson Administration and Ruth had been on the staff. I knew that he had been a professor of law and had been director of Mayor John Lindsay's Criminal Justice Coordinating Council in New York City. He was a slender, mild-mannered man, so unassuming that some people, on first meeting, were inclined to misjudge his talents.

Selfishly, I wanted Ruth to remain on as my deputy, and I promptly told him so when I got him on the phone. Ever succinct, Ruth said, "I'm grateful for your confidence." It was not a long conversation, but I hung up the phone with the feeling that I had done a good day's work.

The next day, Saturday, we were in Waco. It was Baylor University homecoming day and earlier I had been honored by being selected as the grand marshal of the homecoming day parade. In 1925 I had been graduated from Baylor Law School and ties with the old school had remained strong. It was a happy occasion, but I was restless.

It was time to go to work.

IT WOULD NOT BE TRUE to suggest that I hit Washington like a Texas tornado. I merely deplaned at Dulles Airport to be engulfed by what appeared to be a regiment of newspeople. I was beginning to feel like a lost goose in a snowstorm when a small man with merry eyes and a delightful smile took me in tow. He said he was Jim Doyle, my public relations chief, and he nodded toward a younger man whom he introduced as John Barker, his assistant. After I had answered what Doyle considered the proper number of questions, they whisked me away to a waiting automobile. So cheerful was Doyle, and so strong the aura of competence about him, that the newspeople seemed to accept him with both affection and regard. I was to learn shortly that he had won a Pulitzer Prize as a newsman for the Boston *Globe* and had later worked for the Washington *Star*.

The offices of the Special Prosecutor Force were in a twelve-story civilian building called One McPherson Square in Northwest Washington at 1425 K Street. It was like entering a fortress, and I sincerely doubt that James Bond could have gained surreptitious entry. We left the elevator on the ninth floor and were immediately picked up by three television cameras that followed us to a narrow waiting room where two armed guards awaited us. I was told that to go farther a visitor had to be issued a colored badge that he had to wear in plain sight at all times while inside. Staff members wore badges that bore their pictures. A staffer surrendered this badge when he left the office and was

10

given an identification card. The ID card was carried by the staffer at all times except when he exchanged it for the picture badge he wore in the office.

Headquarters took up most of the ninth floor and part of the eighth. Hypersensitive burglar alarms were hidden about like Easter eggs. Guards were in the offices around the clock. And, of course, there were shredders for confidential papers and safes designed to thwart the cleverest knob-knocker.

I was ushered into my office. It was of good size, it looked comfortable, and it was unpretentious. A security officer informed me that the blinds on the windows had to be closed at all times. I asked him why. "So anyone with a telescope in another building can't read anything on your desk," he said.

Since there was nothing on my desk I pulled back a blind and looked out. Across Vermont Avenue, at number 1024, I saw a low, ancient building. Signs declared that it housed a real estate firm, a café, and The Velvet Touch, which was a nice name for what I presumed to be a massage parlor. But I recognized that old building. I had lived there, on the third floor, when I was attending George Washington University in 1925 and 1926 for a postgraduate degree. The building had been grander then, the times simpler.

The staff worked in small offices like rabbits in a warren, and Henry Ruth summoned them forth like a magician. How he managed to arrange some seventy-five persons in positions to hear my voice I'll never understand.

Standing there before them, my eyes ranging around from face to face, I suddenly realized how very *young* these men and women were! Most of them appeared to be in their late twenties or early thirties. And I realized that they very well may have been saying to themselves, How *old* he is! There was a generation chasm, not a gap. But Henry Ruth had assured me that most of them were highly competent, some brilliant, and I had confidence in his judgment. They would have to find out if my sixty-eight years had dulled my faculties or dimmed my enthusiasm for the task at hand.

I began to speak. I told them I thought I could get the job done as Special Prosecutor, that I wanted them to reserve any doubts about me, that I had no doubts about them, and I felt we could work together.

"I believe we can get the job done," I said, "because I have greater independence than Archie Cox had, and . . ."

Ruth interrupted me. "You're not implying that Archie Cox didn't think he had independence, are you?"

"No! Not at all," I hastened to explain. "Being aware of Cox's experience, I wouldn't have taken this on without feeling I had the independence to get the job done, with your help." And I proceeded to explain carefully the changes in the charter and guidelines I had been promised.

They listened, intent on what I was saying, and I neither saw nor heard a restless movement. But their skepticism was palpable. They had been selected by Cox. With him they had challenged the mighty. He had fallen; had, in their minds, been betrayed. He was a law professor; he had pulled them together in these offices, a wise and friendly teacher gathering with his students for a bull session after classes. I was a career attorney with a big-law-firm background, a life-style many of them had eschewed. How could such a man as myself, with open paths to the seats of economic and political power, understand the motives that had nudged them into what they considered noble public service? The best they could hope from me was a professional approach. Well, I thought, professionalism is what they'll get.

I wound it up and told Ruth I had to be sworn in

to get on with the work. I went over to the U.S. Court of Claims where an old friend and fellow Texan, Judge Byron Skelton, gave me the oath in a simple ceremony witnessed by some photographers and a straggling of newspeople.

Now it was official. My salary would be $38,000 a year.

THAT NIGHT I INVITED Archibald Cox to dinner. I had been told that he would soon be leaving Washington to return to Harvard. I wanted to learn what I could from him, of course, but we had worked together years earlier during the Kennedy Administration, he as Solicitor General, I as a specially-appointed Assistant Attorney General in one particular case brought against then-Governor Ross Barnett of Mississippi. We had become friends: it was a friendship I had enjoyed through the years, and I wanted to renew it. I also felt that he might be lonely. He was a conscientious man, and he had to feel that he was leaving town with a job undone. He was out—and here I was, taking his place. I wanted him to know that I was doing so with nothing but respect and admiration for him.

Cox was his delightful self, but his usual dry humor was tinged with sadness and, perhaps, chagrin. He answered all of my questions about investigations in progress and volunteered information he thought might be useful. He wished me luck, but did not venture an opinion about my guarantees.

Henry Ruth dined with us, as did Philip Lacovara, who had served as counsel to the Special Prosecutor under Cox. Throughout the evening I was impressed by Lacovara. He was about thirty, a short, stocky man with long black hair and a handsome moustache. Facts and figures were at the tip of his tongue when needed in the conversation and he obviously possessed a volatile disposition. Just as obviously, he had a healthy

13

regard for his ability and mental agility and, as the evening wore on, I became inclined to agree with him. Such men, I had learned over the years, sometimes need assurances of their value more than do their lesser, plodding fellows. I determined to let Lacovara know as quickly as possible how much I wanted him to remain as counsel.

The opportunity soon appeared. Ruth came to me and said Lacovara was hinting that he might leave. I called him to my office. I told him he had done a fine job for Cox, that I wanted him to continue with me, that both I and the staff needed him. He said he would stay.

I WALKED TO WORK from my hotel the next morning with the wry knowledge that some of the nation's major newspapers were distinctly unhappy with my appointment. The Chicago *Sun-Times*, for example, didn't think much of my guarantees. Neither did the Milwaukee *Journal*, which said that my appointment meant that the executive branch was still investigating itself. One sentence from a New York *Times* editorial was graven in my mind: "Mr. Jaworski's personal integrity is not in doubt, but he is fatally handicapped from the outset because he enters the Watergate investigation as the President's man. . . ." It seemed on this lovely morning that my appointment was approved only by Texas publishers and those who brought out Polish-language newspapers.

The *Times,* the Washington *Post,* and others were calling for legislation that would allow Judge Sirica and other U.S. District Judges to appoint the Special Prosecutor. And a bill to do just that was being considered by the Senate Judiciary Committee. The House Judiciary Committee had not acted, and the newspapers were urging the members to do so. It was my feeling that Judge Sirica, and perhaps the other judges, would not relish such a task. And I was not the only person in Washington who believed such legislation was of doubtful constitutionality. Nevertheless, the lack of approval by the press was a small gray cloud over my head as I walked to work. I could only hope that Congress would assess the safeguards given me by the White House and find them as reassuring as I did.

At the office, Henry Ruth began a painstaking briefing of the events the Prosecutor's office had been investigating. In June, 1972, five men had been arrested in the Democratic National Committee Headquarters in the Watergate complex while repairing electronic surveillance equipment they had installed some three weeks earlier. Two other men with connections at the White House and the Committee to Re-elect the President (CREEP) also were arrested in the same criminal action. All seven were indicted by a federal grand jury three months later, in September. Their trials began the following January, 1973, and all seven were convicted. Judge John Sirica, who presided at their trial, made it plain that he did not believe the full story had come out in his courtroom. For this he blamed the Justice Department.

Meanwhile, the press had been digging into the story, especially the Washington *Post,* the New York *Times,* and the Los Angeles *Times.* Their stories suggested that the Watergate defendants had been promised money and clemency in return for not implicating others, and that the Watergate break-in had been financed by CREEP. Other reports pointed to secret cash funds controlled by high-ranking CREEP and White House officials that had been used to finance other shadowy political projects. The names of John Mitchell, Hugh Sloan, Maurice Stans, Jeb Magruder, H. R. Haldeman, John Ehrlichman, and Herbert Kalmbach were in the news almost daily. But the President had announced that his counsel, John Dean, had conducted an investigation of the affair and had reported that no one in the White House, or employed by the Administration, was involved.

Not everyone had believed this. The Senate unanimously passed a resolution creating the select Committee on Presidential Campaign Activities, which became known as the Senate Watergate Committee.

Meanwhile, in Los Angeles, Judge Matthew Byrne dismissed all charges against Daniel Ellsberg in the "Pentagon Papers" case when it was revealed that the Watergate burglars earlier had broken into the office of Ellsberg's psychiatrist. And Judge Byrne also announced that John Ehrlichman—while the Ellsberg trial was in progress—had suggested that Byrne was being considered as the new Director of the Federal Bureau of Investigation.

More shocking was the testimony developed by the Senate Watergate Committee. John Dean, the President's counsel, testified that President Nixon had known of the Watergate "cover-up" as early as September, 1972. And Herbert Kalmbach, Nixon's California attorney and Republican money-raiser, claimed that John Ehrlichman, the President's Domestic Advisor and confidant, had approved cash payments to the Watergate burglars.

But the most important testimony the committee heard came from Alexander Butterfield, an aide to H. R. Haldeman, who testified that the President had installed a voice-activated taping system in the Oval Office that recorded all conversations without the visitor's knowledge or consent. A similar system had been installed in the President's private room in the Executive Office Building, and in his cabin at Camp David. Three of the President's telephones also were equipped with recording devices.

Two of Nixon's closest associates—Haldeman and Ehrlichman—had resigned. Dean was fired. Former

Attorney General Mitchell had resigned earlier as chairman of CREEP and so had Hugh Sloan, CREEP's treasurer. Attorney General Richard Kleindienst, who had succeeded Mitchell, also resigned. Acting FBI Director L. Patrick Gray had been caught up in the situation and resigned. Mitchell and Maurice Stans, the chief fund-raiser for CREEP, were indicted in New York for attempting to impede a Securities and Exchange Commission investigation into what had become known as the Robert Vesco affair, and the case was being prosecuted by the U.S. Attorney in the Southern District of New York.

All of this had provided grist for the mill of the Special Prosecutor's office. The cases were broken down and divided among five task forces, each one concentrating on a separate area of investigation. After Ruth outlined the progress of each group, I asked him to schedule meetings with the men directing them. The Watergate Task Force was headed by Richard Ben-Veniste, a short man of thirty whose eyes danced with sardonic humor behind thick lenses. As he brought me up to date with his unit's activities I concluded he was a "stinger," a lawyer who could hang a barb in a reluctant witness's nose and bring him to taw. He had been an Assistant United States Attorney for the Southern District of New York, where he had tried—and won— a number of significant cases.

William Merrill headed the Plumbers Task Force. A tall, graying man of fifty, he was as soft-spoken as Ruth. Merrill had served for five years as Chief Assistant U.S. Attorney in Michigan, and he also had worked before and after this government service as a defense attorney in many and varied litigations. This was important. Almost all of the staff had little or no defense experience, including Ruth, who had the wit to recognize its value. A good prosecutor is generally one who has had to destroy a prosecutor's case from

17

the defendant's side of the table. A prosecution witness can shine before a grand jury, where there is no cross-examination, then completely fall apart when subjected to a defense attorney's questioning. So Merrill's background provided me some comfort and, as he talked, it grew into confidence.

The chief of the Campaign Contributions Task Force was Thomas F. McBride. He was a medium-sized man of forty-four. Long hair, getting gray, framed his sharp features. He described his group's work in what I would call a "careful" voice, making sure I understood his every nuance. I liked that; a careful man—not necessarily a cautious man—could serve as a gentle curb on the more impulsive . . . and it appeared I might have a few under my command. McBride's sharp features said he would be hard to fool. He had been an Assistant District Attorney in New York City and had worked in the Organized Crime Section of the Department of Justice. Interestingly, while with the Department of Justice, McBride had acted as advisor to the Home Ministry of India on investigation and prosecution of political corruption. He also had served for several years with the Peace Corps in Latin America. Later he was Deputy Chief Counsel for the House Select Committee on Crime and returned to the Justice Department in its Law Enforcement Assistance Administration. He had no defense experience.

Richard Davis, chief of the Political Espionage Task Force, was growing bald at twenty-seven and I fervently hoped, as the old saying went, that grass didn't grow on a busy street. He had been a brilliant student, a law clerk to a U.S. District Judge, and an Assistant U.S. Attorney in the Southern District of New York. Listening to him, weighing him, I sensed a strength of character to be admired. I marked him down as a team player. He might not always agree with my decisions, I felt, but he would accept them with good grace and

18

work to realize the ends I had chosen. He appeared so able, and conducted himself with such good manners, that I concluded he could handle any reasonable task set before him.

Heading up the ITT Task Force was Joseph Connolly. He was thirty-two. Like Davis, he had been a brilliant student. He had been an Assistant Solicitor General in the U.S. Justice Department and had served on the staff of Secretary of Defense Robert McNamara. He had come to the Special Prosecution Force after a short stint as a practicing attorney in Philadelphia. He was to resign some months later when I failed to accept his recommendation on an issue. On this day, explaining what his group had been doing, he impressed me as both intelligent and capable.

I disqualified myself immediately in the Associated Milk Producers, Inc. (AMPI) investigation because my law firm had represented the Independent Milk Producers Association in an antitrust suit against AMPI. It would later develop that Jake Jacobsen, with whom I had a long acquaintance, was involved in milk fund matters, and at his trial again I would disqualify myself. Still later, I would disqualify myself once more in the case when John Connally, former Secretary of the Treasury, would come under investigation. I had known Connally for many years, and had served at his urging as chairman of the Governor's Committee on Public School Education when he was the Texas chief executive. This case in its entirety was taken over by Henry Ruth.

Two other men on the staff were obvious standouts—Peter Kriendler, who had been Cox's executive assistant, and Carl Feldbaum, who held a similar post under Ruth. Kriendler was twenty-eight, Feldbaum thirty. Kriendler had practiced law in Washington, and he had been law clerk for both Supreme Court Justice William O. Douglas and Chief Judge Irving R. Kaufman of the U.S. Court of Appeals—jobs generally reserved for young men with exceptional ability. Feldbaum also had been a law clerk and had served as an Assistant District Attorney in Philadelphia. Both men had filing-cabinet minds; there was no facet of any of the various investigations to which they were not privy.

Late in the evening, alone, I sat with my notes and memory to sum up what the "young whippersnappers" had accomplished. (The columnists who called them "young whippersnappers" had written that the ages of the thirty-seven lawyers on the staff averaged out to a little less than thirty-one.) Their work had produced guilty pleas from John Dean, the former White House counsel; Jeb Magruder, deputy campaign director of CREEP and former aide to H. R. Haldeman; and Fred LaRue, also a CREEP deputy director and aide to John Mitchell, who headed CREEP. All had been charged with conspiring to obstruct justice in the alleged Watergate cover-up. And all had agreed to make full revelations of what they knew about the Watergate case and other operations under investigation.

Their work had also led Donald Segretti, a California attorney with connections in the White House, to plead guilty to charges of conspiracy and distributing campaign literature without properly identifying its source while conducting his "dirty tricks" operation. Like the others, he had agreed to talk. He had been sentenced to six months in prison on the day I was sworn in for my new job. Egil Krogh, Deputy Assistant to the President for Domestic Affairs and aide to John Ehrlichman, had been indicted for lying to the grand jury in testimony regarding the Plumbers' activities. The Plumbers had been involved in the burglary of the office of Dr. Lewis Fielding, Daniel Ellsberg's psychiatrist.

As a result of the work of the Campaign Contributions Task Force, Minnesota Mining and Manufacturing, American Airlines, and Goodyear Tire and Rubber had pleaded guilty to making illegal corporate contributions in the 1972 presidential election, and First Interoceanic Corporation had been charged with the same offense.

As I thought of the work each task force had done, I was convinced totally that any abrupt changes, either in the staff or in methods of operation, could disrupt the entire organization at the most or, at the least, interrupt its momentum. It was a risk I couldn't afford to run. Each of the task forces had gathered information that my new colleagues felt could lead to more indictments and guilty pleas—if hard, supporting evidence could be obtained. I realized, as did they, that this was a big "if," because what I had learned from the briefings made me aware that most of the evidence—and all of the best evidence—was to be found in the White House.

The staff was looking to me to get it.

chapter two

The Battle Line
Is Drawn

THE NEXT DAY the sounds emanating from Congress and the studied prose of the editorial pages made it appear likely that my stay in Washington could be a short one. There were a few warm spots, however. Stories of my boyhood in rural Texas were being unearthed by reporters, including one about my riding a donkey to school, while others dealt with my service as Trial Judge Advocate in Word War II and my prosecution of the first major war crimes trial in the European Theater. In some of these stories comments had been elicited from prominent attorneys and most of the comments were laudatory. I didn't believe they would influence Congress.

And there were other stories. One said the CIA had channeled funds through a foundation of which I had been a trustee. Another pointed out that my law firm was representing a corporation in an antitrust suit brought by the government and that I was a board member of the corporation. I had severed all my business connections after accepting the Special Prosecutor job, and had sold my interest in the law firm to my partners. I put these stories aside as of no consequence, and I felt confident Congress would do the same.

My course of action seemed clear. While Cox had subpoenaed only nine presidential tapes, he had been trying for months to obtain other evidence: tapes, logs, and documents dealing with the various areas under investigation. He had selected the nine tapes to subpoena because they dealt exclusively with the Watergate break-in and appeared to bear directly upon the President's claim of executive privilege—and Cox properly had wanted to test that claim. He had considered all of the tapes important, but he had a special interest in one particular tape—that of March 21, 1973. John Dean had told investigators and the Senate Watergate Committee that on that day he had brought the President fully up to date on Watergate cover-up developments and other covert activities. Those involved in the break-in and the cover-up had challenged Dean's veracity; the tape possibly could clear up the matter. Dean also had told investigators about other related incidents. It was important to determine if his word could be trusted.

The President, it will be recalled, had refused to turn over the tapes despite a court order. Instead, he had fired Cox. Three days later, apparently shocked by public reaction, he had said he would release the tapes. And, on the day I had accepted Haig's proposal, the President's lawyer, Fred Buzhardt, had notified the court two of the tapes did not exist. This had caused another uproar; the press generally referred to the "missing tapes," indicating that they did not believe Buzhardt or, for that matter, the President.

Buzhardt had said there was no tape for a presidential conversation on June 20, 1972, three days after the Watergate break-in. Cox had information that the President had talked with John Mitchell by telephone that day, and Mitchell was believed to have been involved in the crime. Buzhardt had explained that the conversation was held on a telephone not connected to the taping system. And, he had said, a conversation between Nixon and Dean on April 15, 1973, had not been recorded because an unattended machine ran out of tape.

Now Buzhardt was in the process of dribbling over the subpoenaed existing tapes to Judge Sirica. The judge was to study them for relevancy to Watergate before passing them to our office and the grand jury. We had not received any of them.

In the other material Cox had been trying to get from the White House were tapes and documents concerning the Plumbers' activities. Cox had felt the material was vital in pursuing the investigation of the break-in of Dr. Fielding's office. He had been put off repeatedly. President Nixon had said the Plumbers' work dealt with national security and must remain secret. The White House position seemed to be this: the material could not help but reveal everything the Plumbers had done and the country could not afford such a revelation.

Both Henry Ruth and Bill Merrill had told me at the staff briefings that the material was needed now more than ever. Egil Krogh, head of the Plumbers, had been indicted on charges of lying to the grand jury when examined about the Fielding break-in. Hearings on his motion to dismiss the charges were to be held soon. It seemed likely that he would argue that he had lied because to have been truthful would have disclosed information the President had labeled classified.

Krogh also had been indicted on state charges of conspiracy and burglary in Los Angeles County, where Dr. Fielding's office was located. Three other former White House aides—John Ehrlichman, G. Gordon Liddy, and David R. Young—also were under indictment in Los Angeles, as were some lesser lights. We had plans to ask for federal indictments against some of these people in the Fielding break-in, and possibly others—all the more reason the material was vital.

Assistant Attorney General Henry Petersen had

been overseeing the Special Prosecution Force in the interval between Cox's firing and my appointment. He also had requested the material in a letter to Buzhardt, and at the same time had asked for tapes and logs and records dealing with the Watergate cover-up and other actions under investigation.

I didn't want to hit anyone as dilatory as Buzhardt with a broadside. Neither did I want to appear slow of foot. So I immediately sent him a message requesting copies of recordings of talks between Nixon and some of his aides about the Administration's dealings with ITT (International Telephone and Telegraph Corporation).

Then, the next day, I requested the materials we wanted about the Plumbers. And I followed that with a request for copies of recordings of talks between Nixon and Charles Colson in early 1973 for use in the Watergate investigation. Colson was a former Special Counsel to the President and so-called White House hatchet man.

In each message I made it clear, without being arrogant about it, that I expected an early response. I didn't, knowing Buzhardt's track record, but I hoped that a firm expression of expecting action would prompt him to shuffle his feet in the tar pit in which they seemed mired.

As days passed I began to experience the frustration that must have acidized Cox's stomach. There were no deliveries of material from Buzhardt. And some newspapers and members of Congress continued their campaigns for a Special Prosecutor not selected by the White House. A House Judiciary subcommittee called for my appearance. Bork, the Acting Attorney General, had told this group about the safeguards guaranteed me, indicating that the job charter would be strengthened even more. And Bork hinted that he would quit government service if the White House tried to hobble me. "Should the investigations be compromised, I would regard my position as morally intolerable," he declared.

At the hearing I told the Congressmen the full story of my appointment and stressed that I felt I had a free hand. I quoted General Haig that I had the President's assurance that I had the absolute right to sue the President if necessary to procure the material our office felt it needed. And I let them know I already had requested tapes and documents from the White House. The Congressmen did not appear to be totally satisfied.

Uncertainty gnawed at me, but I tried to hide it as I went about my work. My staff did not exactly rally around, but I sensed that most of them had at least accepted that my intentions were good. I pitched in to help the Plumbers Task Force prepare its brief contesting Egil Krogh's motion to dismiss the charges of perjury against him.

The media considered the thrust of our brief a major story because it struck at the heart of the White House's national security contentions. Our brief held that "not even the highest office in the land" had the authority to break the law in the name of national security.

"Most frequently the claim has been made that the national security justifies warrantless wiretapping of domestic subversives, a claim that the Supreme Court has decisively rejected," our brief said. "Recently, however, the debate over what may be done in the name of 'national security' has taken a more ambitious turn. It has been advanced by low-level personnel to justify an illegal break-in for the installation of microphones in the offices of the Democratic National Committee."

We pointed out that John Ehrlichman advanced the claim in Senate testimony as a "legal umbrella" for the burglary of Dr. Fielding's office. "Now it seems that defendant [Krogh] will claim that national security justified lying under oath in a judicial proceeding.

"While the claim of national security gives these claims of legalized burglary and perjury a deceptively compelling ring, ultimately they rest on a wholesale rejection of the rule of law and espouse a doctrine that government officials may ignore the requirements of positive criminal statues when they feel the circumstances dictate. . . .

"No government office, not even the highest office in the land, carries with it the right to ignore the law's command, any more than the orders of a superior can be used by government officers to justify illegal behavior. . . ."

And we suggested that in Krogh's case "political and personal self preservation, rather than the national security, may have motivated his perjury. . . ."

The next day, while the hearing of Krogh's case still was in progress, I decided to go see Haig and Buzhardt. I wanted to jog Haig's memory about his promises of cooperation, I wanted to shake Buzhardt loose from his tar pit, and I wanted to satisfy myself about the "grave national security matters" the Plumbers had handled. I still had top-secret clearance from my war crimes prosecution days. We talked in Buzhardt's office in the Executive Office Building.

Haig was at his persuasive best. I could not help but admire the way he set about trying to channel my thinking. I listened. The national security matters he described didn't appear to be very grave to me. I concluded that if most of them were made public at that very moment the country would not be endangered.

Haig and Buzhardt moved directly to the Fielding break-in. Daniel Ellsberg *had* taken the Pentagon Papers and released them. The Pentagon Papers *did* have a bearing on the country's international affairs and thus security. Therefore, it *was* a matter of national security to break into Dr. Fielding's office to obtain more information about Ellsberg.

I didn't tell them that my staff had been told that any information about Ellsberg the burglars had hoped to find in Dr. Fielding's office was to have been used to smear and defame him before he came to trial in the Pentagon Papers case and discredit him as a Vietnam War critic. Colson, the hatchet man, was to have handled this "public relations" job. And I didn't think it necessary to tell them of our knowledge because the staff and I concluded that we could confine the Fielding break-in cases to the issues at hand: conspiracy, burglary, and perjury.

I told Haig and Buzhardt so. "Breaking into a man's office to get information about another is far removed from national security," I said. In this country we afford people their rights. We protect their liberty, regardless of what we think of their actions. One of the things we don't do is break down their doors. All we at our office are interested in are criminal matters. And we want the tapes and documents we need to pursue them."

I spoke firmly because I recognized that Haig had now become an adversary, not a supplicant.* He would be one without hate and, I thought, a candid one, but he had drawn the battle line, however faintly. Implicit in my little speech was the promise to move legally to get what was needed if it were not handed over voluntarily.

Haig seemed a trifle disappointed in me.

---

* In the many meetings with Haig which followed this one, some of them under strained conditions, I never found him less than honorable. Each of us recognized the other as a volatile being and, without design, we avoided extreme language in our discussions. On my part, I tried to be plainspoken, wanting to leave no doubt how I stood on various issues. I believe he did the same.

We talked on, and they finally agreed that I could have the material within ten days. I found that acceptable. To pin it down I went to the office and prepared a letter to the White House detailing again what we wanted.

Krogh's attorney also had been asking for some of the Plumbers material. The next day I was able to inform Judge Gerhard Gesell, the presiding judge, that I had been assured of access to it. This created a mild sensation in the press; the President, newspeople decided, had made an about-face on national security.

FRED BUZHARDT surprised me. He called and said he wanted to see me at my office. My first thought was that he was bringing me some material in advance of the ten-day promise. The staff also was surprised. Buzhardt had never been in the office before; Cox had always gone to the White House to see him.

But Buzhardt came bearing no gifts. Leonard Garment, another White House lawyer to whom Haig had introduced me, was with Buzhardt. Both men were upset—and with good reason.

Buzhardt said that he had discovered that one of the nine subpoenaed Watergate tapes had a substantial "gap" in it, one of a little more than eighteen minutes. He had run tests on the recording machine, he said, and had been unable to determine how such a gap could have occurred unintentionally. He said he understood that the gap had occurred at a time when Rose Mary Woods, the President's private secretary, was transcribing the recording.

Which recording?

One of June 20, 1972, which contained a conversation between Nixon and H. R. Haldeman.

June 20 was three days after the Watergate break-in, and the first working day. Cox had subpoenaed the tapes and attendant papers on July 23, 1973, and subsequently had filed a memorandum on August 13, which said in part: "Early on the morning of June 20, Haldeman, Ehrlichman, Mitchell, Dean and Attorney General Kleindienst met in the White House. This was their first opportunity for full discussion of how to handle the Watergate incident. . . . From there, Ehrlichman and then Haldeman went to see the President. . . ." It had seemed likely to Cox that Nixon and Haldeman would have discussed Watergate. Haldeman was under investigation, and the staff naturally was anxious to obtain any additional evidence of his knowledge of or participation in a cover-up.

Haldeman made notes of subjects discussed in presidential meetings, the staff had learned. Buzhardt said he had obtained Haldeman's notes on the June 20 meeting. Yes, Haldeman and Nixon had discussed Watergate, the notes reflected. They had talked about what impact the break-in would have on the public and what public relations steps could be taken to direct public attention from the crime. And yes, there was no discussion of Watergate on the tape; the Watergate discussion must have occurred during the vanished eighteen minutes.

Judge Sirica had to know about this new development immediately. I told Buzhardt, "We'll see the Judge as quickly as we can."

No, said Buzhardt, he wanted to conduct some additional investigation. It would take several days.

I told him it wasn't possible. The tapes had not been requested, the Judge had ordered them turned over after a legal process. It was necessary that he know about the gap today.

Running through my mind was the fear that other gaps might appear in other tapes. I put an end to the discussion and made arrangements for us to see Judge Sirica that afternoon *in camera*. "Please bring Haldeman's notes to court with you," I said to Buzhardt. He said he would.

Three weeks earlier Buzhardt had told Judge Sirica that two of the nine tapes were nonexistent, and the announcement had caused shock waves across the country. Now this new development—and only two days after President Nixon had told Republican governors meeting in Memphis that there would be no more "bombshells."

When the news of the missing tapes had been disclosed earlier Judge Sirica ordered a hearing to determine if the other tapes were being taken care of properly. White House personnel had been questioned in his court. One of them had been Rose Mary Woods.

She had testified that she had begun transcribing the tapes on September 29 at Camp David. She had continued at the White House, at Key Biscayne, and had concluded the assignment in the White House on October 23 or 24. The first tape she had worked on was that of June 20, 1972.

QUESTION: Were any precautions taken to assure you that you did not accidentally hit the "erase" button?

ANSWER: Everybody said "be careful"—which I am. I don't want this to sound like bragging, but I don't believe I am so stupid that they had to go over and over it. I was told "if you push the button, it will erase," and I do know, even on a small machine, you can dictate over something that removes it. I think I used every possible precaution not to do that.

QUESTION: What precautions specifically did you take to avoid recording over it and thereby getting rid of what was already there?

ANSWER: What precautions? I used my head. It's the only one I had to use.

31

Now it appeared that Ms. Woods may not have used her head.

Judge Sirica was a man of humor and no stranger to asperity, but in critical times he was almost impassive and he did not let his words stray from the subject at hand. With his shock of black hair and strong brown features he looked on that afternoon like an Apache chieftain. He listened, and if he was disturbed by Buzhardt's revelation it was not apparent. He said quietly, "This calls for another hearing." He said he would shortly select a panel of experts to examine the tape and the others as well.

At the first tape hearing our office had been represented by Richard Ben-Veniste, head of the Watergate Task Force, and Jill Volner, an assistant. Ben-Veniste had proved to be a good courtroom lawyer, and his examination of a witness could be devastating. Ms. Woods likely would be the principal witness at the second hearing, and it occurred to me that Ben-Veniste's strongest points might work against us. Ms. Volner had made a fine record both in school and at the Justice Department, where she had worked as a trial lawyer before joining the Special Prosecution Force. An attractive, perceptive woman of thirty, she had questioned Ms. Woods briefly at the first hearing and conducted herself ably. Since the crucial examination of Ms. Woods would be a sensitive one, I concluded that a sensitive woman should conduct it and Ms. Volner was given the task.

Rose Mary Woods began her testimony on November 26, and on that date the President sent to court the tapes and documents Cox had supoenaed for the grand jury four months and three days earlier. Later, those tapes would change my concept of the entire Watergate affair.

As for Ms. Woods, she was somewhat subdued compared with the almost testy manner in which she had responded to questions at the first hearing. Ms. Volner got her story from her with the calm tenacity of a plowman striving for a straight furrow.

Ms. Woods had gone to Camp David on the morning of September 29 with Stephen Bull, a White House aide who had temporary custody of the tapes. Bull was to mark the subpoenaed sections on each reel. Soon after their arrival, she said, as she was about to start work on a conversation between the President and John Ehrlichman, General Haig called from Washington. He told her not to transcribe the conversation between the President and H. R. Haldeman when she reached it because it had not been subpoenaed. She was still transcribing the conversation with Ehrlichman when she returned to work in Washington on November 1.

She completed the Nixon-Ehrlichman sections and discovered that the Nixon-Haldeman section followed immediately. She listened to just a bit of it, and her phone rang. She talked about five minutes—she could not recall with whom. When she hung up she saw she had pushed the "record" button on the machine instead of the "stop" button. She apparently had kept her foot on a pedal she was using to run the machine, she said. She played back the tape and heard only a hum for about five minutes.

Upset, she went to the Oval Office and told the President. He told her not to worry, she said, the section had not been subpoenaed. She returned to work. She had not thought the incident important enough to mention when questioned about her work on the June 20 tape at the first hearing.

She insisted that she did not feel responsible for the entire eighteen-minute gap on the tape. She was on the phone not more than five minutes, she had not listened to that portion of the tape before the phone rang, and as far as she knew there was no conversation on it before her mistake. Photographs were taken of Ms. Woods demonstrating how she had made her mistake. The reenactment put a slight strain on credulity, in Ms. Volner's opinion. Others had the same reaction.

But if Ms. Woods made her mistake on October 1, why was it not until November 21 that Buzhardt came to my office and then to Judge Sirica's chamber with word of the gap?

Testimony from various White House witnesses produced the following scenario: Buzhardt had not at first believed the Nixon-Haldeman conversation was a subpoenaed one. He discovered it was on November 14 and told Haig. Haig told the President the next day. Haig then looked for Haldeman's notes on the conversation. They were stored in a safe. Only Haldeman had the combination—and he was in California, where he had gone after his resignation on April 30. Haig called Haldeman. Haldeman called a former aide, Lawrence Higby, and told him how to open the safe. Buzhardt got the notes. After that he worked on the machine Ms. Woods had used and, according to Haig, couldn't find any confirmation that the device had caused the hum. During the hearing several possible causes of the gap were offered by the White House. The most interesting was advanced by Haig, who facetiously remarked that he and White House lawyers had discussed the possibility that "perhaps some sinister force had come in and applied the other energy source and taken care of the information on the tape. . . ." Reporters referred to this as Haig's "devil theory." Taking the remark at face value, Judge Sirica asked Haig if he had any idea who the sinister force was. Haig said no.

Judge Sirica's panel of experts—thoroughly checked

out and approved before appointment by our office and the White House—solved the mystery of what had happened after intensive study. The gap was not caused accidentally, the experts said. It was a deliberate erasure done in at least five, and perhaps as many as nine, separate and contiguous segments, requiring hand operation of the keyboard controls of the machine used by Ms. Woods.

Now we would have to make an investigation to learn, if possible, who had erased the conversation from the tape, and when.

The President had listed portions of the subpoenaed tapes and related documents as privileged. I asked Judge Sirica to review the material and decide what should be presented to the grand jury. And I had asked him to order the White House to turn over Ms. Wood's transcripts and summaries of the tapes.

Events had been occurring on other fronts as well. The President had been busy denying wrongdoing in his income tax payments and tax money spent on his homes at San Clemente and Key Biscayne. Egil Krogh had undergone a change of mind and heart and appeared ready to plea bargain with us; Dwight Chapin, another former White House aide, had been indicted on four counts of perjury; a surprising number of documents I had requested had found their way from the White House to my office.

And both the House and the Senate had reached the point of debating separate bills calling for a Special Prosecutor independent of the White House.

chapter three

Some Plead Guilty

THE QUESTION OF whether Egil Krogh would plea bargain with our office was answered sooner than I expected. He had worked with John Ehrlichman's law firm in Seattle, and Ehrlichman had brought him to Washington and to the White House. As the older man's top aide, Krogh had served ably as the White House's political link with the FBI and later with Treasury Department agencies concerned with the country's debilitating drug problems.

Now the young, fine-looking lawyer was in our offices saying that he no longer could use the umbrella of national security as a defense against the crimes with which he had been charged. My immediate feeling was sadness that power's corruption had tainted him and other young men of bright promise. But tainted he had been, wrongs he had done. Now he was in our hands.

In 1971 he had received a new assignment. The White House was incensed by leaks to the press and Krogh was selected to head a unit to plug them.

What had he done? He had set up the Plumbers, and the first man to join him was David Young, an assistant to Henry Kissinger on the National Security Council. Charles Colson, the President's Special Counsel, also sent over E. Howard Hunt, a former CIA agent whom Colson had hired to help him in his smear campaigns. And Krogh reached out for G. Gordon Liddy, with whom he had worked when Liddy was with the Treasury Department in narcotics enforcement. Liddy also had worked with the FBI. Both he and Hunt were lawyers.

A month earlier Daniel Ellsberg, a Pentagon bureaucrat, had been indicted for unauthorized possession of documents relating to national defense—the Pentagon Papers. Portions of the papers had been published in the New York *Times* and the Washington *Post*. Krogh was told that the FBI and the CIA suspected that a complete set of the papers had been handed to the Soviet Embassy in Washington.

Both the President and Ehrlichman impressed on Krogh the importance of his task. The President, Krogh said, instructed that further leaks would not be allowed and made Krogh feel personally responsible for carrying out this instruction. Ehrlichman gave the group authority to engage in covert activity to get information on Ellsberg. A secret headquarters was set up in the Executive Office Building and work began.

On July 28, 1971, Hunt wrote a memorandum to Colson entitled "Neutralization of Ellsberg." "I am proposing a skeletal operations plan aimed at building a file on Ellsberg that will contain all available overt, covert and derogatory information," he said. "This basic tool is essential in determining how to destroy his public image and credibility." One of the suggestions in the memo was: "Obtain Ellsberg's files from his psychiatric analyst." Dr. Lewis Fielding of Beverly Hills had been Ellsberg's psychiatrist in 1968 and 1969. On July 26, two days prior to Hunt's memo, he had refused to be interviewed by the FBI regarding Ellsberg.

Krogh and Young wrote Ehrlichman a memo on August 11 recommending that "a covert operation be undertaken to examine all the medical files still held by Ellsberg's psychoanalyst covering the two-year period in which he was undergoing analysis." Ehrlichman signed his approval on the memo and wrote, "If done under your assurance that it is not traceable."

Several days later, Hunt prepared another memo, this one about Leonard Boudin, one of Ellsberg's lawyers, describing Boudin in derogatory terms as an aggressive advocate of ultra-leftist causes. The memo went to Ehrlichman, who sent it to another White House official with a note saying, "The attached memorandum by Howard Hunt should be useful in connection with the recent request that we get something out on Ellsberg." Handwritten on the memo was, "Delivered to terHorst 8/26." TerHorst was a reporter for the Detroit *News* who later became President Gerald Ford's press secretary for a few days.

On August 25, Hunt and Liddy flew to Los Angeles to have a look at Dr. Fielding's office. They managed to get inside briefly, and took some photographs. On their return to Washington they prepared a detailed memo setting forth plans to burglarize the office. The memo contained a diagram of the office, described alternate escape routes, and set forth a budget for expenses. A few days later they showed Krogh and Young the pictures they had taken. Krogh and Young called Ehrlichman on Cape Cod, where he was vacationing, and brought him up to date. Meanwhile, Young had been circulating a memo suggesting that Colson draw up a game plan indicating how information to be obtained from Dr. Fielding's office would be used. "It is important to point out that with the recent article on Ellsberg's lawyer, Boudin, we have already started on a negative press image for Ellsberg," the memo said.

On September 1, Krogh gave Liddy $5,000 in cash for the break-in expenses. Hunt had recruited three friends from his CIA days to do the dirty work. All five flew to Los Angeles. During the Labor Day weekend, the three hirelings broke into the building where Dr. Fielding had his office, made their way to the first-floor common hallway, and climbed the stairs to Dr. Fielding's second-floor suite. They forced open the door. They broke open a wall cabinet and pried open metal file drawers. They combed through the doctor's desk. They found nothing about Ellsberg.

Back in Washington, Hunt and Liddy recommended breaking into Fielding's residence to search for material on Ellsberg. The idea was turned down, for Krogh had seen photographs of the mess the burglars had made of Fielding's office. In a written statement he made for us Krogh said, "The visibility of physical damage was somehow disturbing beyond the theoretical impression of covert activity. I recommended to Mr. Ehrlichman that no further actions of that sort be undertaken. He concurred and stated that he considered the operation to have been in excess of his authorization. . . ."

Krogh's work with the Plumbers ended shortly thereafter. He later became Undersecretary of the Department of Transportation. Liddy, after being recommended by Krogh, became counsel to CREEP, and Hunt became a White House counsel.

Hunt and Liddy were working at their new jobs when they were arrested for participating in the Watergate break-in on June 17, 1972. Krogh was not involved in that burglary, but he was questioned, under oath, by an Assistant United States Attorney who was looking into the backgrounds of Hunt and Liddy for a grand jury. Krogh had been instructed repeatedly by Ehrlichman that Nixon considered the work of the Plumbers a matter of highest national security and that under no circumstances was he to discuss it. When the government officer asked questions about travels to California by Hunt and Liddy, Krogh denied any knowledge of them.

He was secure for about a year. Then John Dean, while telling Justice Department investigators about his complicity in the Watergate break-in, revealed some of the details of the Fielding burglary. By now Ellsberg was on trial before U.S. District Judge Matthew Byrne in Los Angeles. The investigators gave Judge Byrne a memo outlining the Fielding break-in. Judge Byrne requested persons having knowledge of the affair to file affidavits with him.

Krogh asked Ehrlichman to obtain the President's permission for him to reveal his role in the affair. The permission was granted. In his affidavit, Krogh said Ehrlichman had authorized a covert operation to get information about Ellsberg, but he took full blame for its execution. A few days later he resigned from government service.

He was in my office now, at ease but far from cocky, bearing on his shoulders two counts of making false declarations to a grand jury. If convicted, each count could cost him five years, though Krogh knew that customarily the sentences would be allowed to run concurrently, resulting in a five-year maximum sentence. Judge Gerhard Gesell, who had heard Krogh's motion to dismiss the indictments and had denied it, had made some pointed comments which I was sure had shaken Krogh. Krogh's lawyer, Stephen Shulman, had argued that an official in Krogh's position had the authority and discretion to make false statements so as to protect classified national security information from unauthorized disclosure. Judge Gesell had emphatically rejected that argument as fundamentally incompatible with the very existence of our society.

Krogh was really in my office to see what kind of man I was. And I had allowed him and his lawyer inside for exactly the same reason. He had been nibbling at negotiating with the Plumbers Task Force for some time. Now it was time to deal. He knew that to get a lighter sentence he would have to give something to the prosecution. I knew that we needed his cooperation to obtain a full disclosure of the facts in the Fielding break-in. And we believed he could give us important information about Watergate.

Krogh had other things in his favor. He said he realized now that what he had done was unlawful, regardless of his motive, and the idea of discrediting Ellsberg was a repulsive national security goal. I believed him with all of my heart. I also believed that he was a good man who had been thrust down a crooked path. He said that as a matter of principle he did not want to tell us anything to incriminate others until after he was sentenced—if we made a deal. I liked that.

I liked it. But we all knew that Judge Gesell had made it clear on various occasions when he imposed sentences in cases involving plea bargaining such as this one that he was never influenced in weighing sentence by promises of a defendant's cooperation with prosecutors. We also knew, however, that Judge Gesell would lend an ear to any man he believed had honestly repented his sins.

With all of this clear between us, I told Krogh that the proper charge against him should have been and should be conspiracy to violate Dr. Fielding's civil rights, a charge that called for a ten-year maximum sentence upon conviction. It was my feeling that if Judge Gesell believed Krogh had repented and was contrite—as I did—he would be merciful regardless of the nature of the charge.

It was judgment time. I had judged Krogh and believed him decent. He judged me and apparently believed me trustworthy and considerate of his future. He did not make a decision in a flash, but shortly thereafter he stood before Judge Gesell and pleaded guilty to the conspiracy charge. We dismissed the false declaration count in the indictment. The California indictment also was dismissed.

During his plea Krogh told the court: "My coming

to this point today stems from my asking myself what ideas I wanted to stand for, what I wanted to represent to myself and to my family and to be identified with for the rest of my experience. I simply feel that what was done in the Ellsberg operation was in violation of what I perceive to be a fundamental idea in the character of this country—the paramount importance of the rights of the individual. I don't want to be associated with that violation any longer by attempting to defend it. . . ."

Judge Gesell believed him. He sentenced Krogh to a prison term of two to six years with all but six months suspended.

In THE PERIOD between Krogh's guilty plea and his sentencing, news stories quoting one of John Ehrlichman's attorneys disclosed that Ehrlichman had flown in from his home in Seattle to discuss a guilty plea with me. It was a Special Prosecution Force practice not to discuss such negotiations until they were concluded. The stories speculated that we had offered to allow Ehrlichman to plead guilty to one felony in return for his testimony in both the Fielding break-in and the Watergate cover-up. It was suggested that while Ehrlichman might be willing to plead in the Fielding break-in, he would not reveal his knowledge, if any, of the Watergate cover-up. The stories destroyed much of the confidentiality of the proceeding.

The meeting with Ehrlichman was in my office. It was not initiated by the Special Prosecution Force. With Ehrlichman were Attorneys John Wilson, Frank Strickler, and Joseph Ball. Wilson and Strickler also represented H. R. Haldeman. Ball, a California lawyer, was representing Ehrlichman on the state charges against him in Los Angeles where the Fielding break-in occurred. He was not Haldeman's lawyer. Henry Ruth also was present.

I had met Ehrlichman several years earlier when a group of American Bar Association officers had visited with President Nixon in the Oval Office. Ehrlichman apparently had been there to take notes if anyone desired them taken. He had taken none that I recall, but he had played constantly with his pencil.

On this day in my office he played with a pencil during the preliminary stage of the meeting and continued to toy with it when I got down to business. I had a list of thirteen charges which we believed could be brought against him. The charges were given in the order of their magnitude, the most serious charge, conspiracy to obstruct justice, being the first.

"Mr. Ehrlichman," I said, "here are the areas where we think you are culpable"—and I began reading from the list. His usually mobile face became stoical, but his fingers agitated the pencil. One by one I read off the possible charges, my voice the only sound in the office. The last item involved the handling of a government document under Ehrlichman's control. We had a true copy of the document, so we knew that some incriminating words and phrases had been cut out of the original, apparently with a scissors.

Ehrlichman was still impassive, still fingering the pencil, when I read, "The last possible charge is mutilation of a government document. . . ."

Ehrlichman's face twisted. He hurled the pencil to the floor forcefully, and said, *"That* I did not do!"

I fought to hold back a surprised grin. Ehrlichman's lawyers managed to hide their shock. I glanced at Ruth; he rolled his eyes drolly in disbelief.

Ehrlichman retrieved his pencil and the talk resumed. It ended with no decision. Later Strickler made some remarks to reporters from which they inferred that I had been begging Ehrlichman to accept a deal and he had refused. The implication was, of course, that Ehrlichman had refused because he was completely innocent of all wrongdoing. My own interpretation of Ehrlichman's decision was different, as I will explain later. But now I knew we were making the White House very nervous.

THEN THERE WAS the case of Dwight Chapin. He was even younger and handsomer than Krogh, even more devoted to the President, more a political animal, more the Administration soldier. When first the news media and then the Senate Watergate Committee began digging into White House and CREEP policies and practices, he drew a line with his toe and refused to budge from his position that the Administration could do no wrong.

There was never any question of Dwight Chapin's pleading guilty to the perjury charges against him. A guilty plea would have been a betrayal of his political creed and a black mark against the Administration. And he may have considered himself innocent.

Chapin had been in the Nixon camp since 1968 with H. R. Haldeman his mentor—as Ehrlichman had been guide and guardian to Egil Krogh. From tireless campaign worker he became Nixon's appointments secretary, but Haldeman was his boss. His friends were Ron Ziegler, the President's press secretary, and Gordon Strachan, another Haldeman protégé who served as liaison between Haldeman and CREEP. All were graduates of the University of Southern California. So was Donald Segretti, a young California lawyer just out of military service, whose bumbling work on the shadowy side of politics was to expose Chapin as a manipulator and bring him to a court of justice.

As appointments secretary Chapin was busy but he lusted for political intrigue as some men lust for headlines. When, in 1971, CREEP began gearing up for the 1972 presidential election, Chapin and his friend Strachan went to Haldeman with a plan to prevent the Democrats from uniting behind a single candidate. Haldeman at least tacitly approved; Chapin needed no hand-written memorandum of acceptance.

To implement their scheme, Chapin and Strachan got in touch with their old college pal in California, Donald Segretti. Segretti flew to Washington. He flew eagerly because he was anxious to hover around the seats of power occupied by his friends. He had never lost the taste for politics he acquired in campus campaigns, and he had caught a whiff of money floating over the long-distance wire. He was told in general terms what he was to do. For the money, though, he had to return to California, to Newport Beach, home base of Herbert Kalmbach, CREEP deputy finance chairman and Nixon's personal attorney. Kalmbach told him he would be paid $16,000 a year with a generous expense account.

Segretti next met Chapin at San Clemente near the Western White House. Chapin gave him a list of cities where he was to recruit helpers. Chapin would be his White House contact, he was told, but he was never to mention Chapin or the name of any other White House or CREEP official in his work. Indeed, he was never to use his own name but must operate under aliases. His job was to create suspicion and distrust among the several Democratic presidential contenders and their supporters.

Segretti may not have been aware that he was only a part of a movement being orchestrated from the White House and CREEP headquarters. Other men under assumed names were being employed to commit illegal and unethical acts of forgery, espionage, perjury, burglary, and sabotage to foment discord among the Democrats.

Segretti played his "dirty tricks" in the various cities to which Chapin had directed him. His most despicable act, which hurt three Democratic hopefuls, was to send out a letter on Senator Edmund Muskie's stationery accusing Senators Hubert Humphrey and Henry Jackson of sexual misconduct, charges that Segretti knew had no basis in fact. Along the way he occasionally found guidance in his misdeeds from the ubiquitous E. Howard Hunt and G. Gordon Liddy, at the time working under the names Ed Warren and George Leonard.

Segretti had been flushed out into the open by Reporters Carl Bernstein and Bob Woodward of the Washington *Post*. In the process they also flushed out Chapin. Segretti talked—to a grand jury and the Senate Watergate Committee. Chapin lied—to the grand jury and FBI agents. Both were indicted, Segretti on charges of distributing illegal campaign literature, Chapin on charges of perjury. Segretti pleaded guilty and was sentenced to serve six months in prison on November 5, 1973, the day I was sworn in as Special Prosecutor. Chapin was the first person indicted under my stewardship, and the first to go to trial on charges brought by the Special Prosecutor's office.

At a pretrial hearing, Chapin had sought to exclude John Dean as a government witness at his trial, claiming a lawyer-client relationship existed between them. We felt sure no such relationship existed. Chapin, we decided, knew that Dean was waiting in the wings to testify against others, including his mentor, Haldeman. If he could get Dean excluded as a government witness it might establish a precedent and keep Dean from testifying against bigger game.

Our big question was whether to allow Dean to testify as to Chapin's claim of lawyer-client relationship at the pretrial hearing. We didn't want to do it. Dean had pleaded guilty to a charge of obstructing justice but had not yet been sentenced. At this early stage, before the trial proper, we did not want to subject Dean to the

46

publicity that the questioning would bring from a hostile corner.

I had studied the case. I had been observing Richard Davis, the head of the Political Espionage Task Force, as he went about questioning Chapin. Davis, as I noted earlier, was only twenty-seven, younger even than Chapin. He had made Chapin concede point after point, skillfully undermining Chapin's position. When we broke for lunch, the issue was close. We ate, but finally Davis pushed aside his plate. "What are we going to do?" he asked. "Are we going to call Dean to testify?"

I had been thinking hard on the problem and I had made a decision—but not the one Davis was asking for. I had decided on Davis. "It's your case," I said—and I said no more.

Richard Davis, who had never been under such pressure in his brief career, chose not to call John Dean at the pretrial hearing, but he so ably disposed of Chapin's contention that Chapin's motion was dismissed. Thus Dean, in a pristine state, was available as a trial witness. His appearance would be brief but vital; he seemed to know something about everything that had occurred in the White House during his stay there.

Chapin's trial itself lasted only three days after the jurors were selected. Davis called four witnesses—Dean, Segretti, FBI Agent Angelo Lano, and Herbert Kalmbach, the moneyman who had paid Segretti's salary and expenses. Chapin was convicted of two of the four counts against him: lying when he denied that he had discussed with Segretti—or knew of—the distribution of fake campaign literature, and lying when he said that he did not recall instructing Segretti, at one point, to concentrate his "dirty tricks" efforts against Senator Muskie.

Chapin's attorney, Jacob Stein, argued that Chapin

hadn't deliberately lied to the grand jury, that he had been so busy at his job and had paid so little attention to the details of the Segretti operation that his questionable testimony was actually misstatements. And, he said, Chapin had a poor memory. Chapin admitted he hired Segretti to sow confusion among the Democratic presidential contenders. He admitted he had tried to keep the operation secret. But he said he knew little about what Segretti did. Haldeman, he said, had approved Segretti's hiring.

Stein did a good job of defending Chapin, but Davis was well prepared and he handled both government and defense witnesses like a veteran. Chapin was sentenced to prison for a term of from ten to thirty months. The jury deliberated twelve hours before returning the guilty verdict. This was the only period during which Davis appeared nervous, and I called him to congratulate him when the verdict was delivered.

Chapin's appeal was denied in the Appellate Court, and the Supreme Court refused to hear it.

THE DEBATES AND DISCUSSIONS in the House and Senate on proposals for a Special Prosecutor other than one appointed by the President weighed heavily on my mind. When committees presented both houses with separate bills for consideration it sorely taxed my spirit.

Then, in rapid order, several events occurred to change the picture. Judge Sirica and his fellow jurists indicated that they did not wish to participate in the selection of a Special Prosecutor, an action of "dubious constitutionality." And Judge Gesell ruled that Archibald Cox's firing had been and was illegal, that Cox had neither consented to his discharge nor committed an "extraordinary impropriety," the requirements essential to discharge. The suit, which had been brought to court by Ralph Nader, the consumer advocate, and three members of Congress, had not attracted much attention outside Washington and the judge's quick decision was somewhat of a surprise to me.

Judge Gesell did not order Cox's reinstatement, noting that Cox had not made a personal fight for it. And Cox, back at his Harvard post, said he didn't want it. "For me to make any legal claim under the decision would only divert attention from getting the job done," he told reporters.

The ruling obviously strengthened my position. I felt more confident when I was called to testify before the Senate Judiciary Committee. I was asked specifically about the Fielding break-in, and Senator Edward Kennedy wanted to know what assurances I had that the veil of national security wouldn't continually be drawn over the incident. I said, "One, as much as I respect the issue of national security, I'm not going to be blinded by it, and, two, there was no resistance from Haig and Buzhardt when I indicated some indictments could be brought and that I was going to pursue them."

The congressional debate continued, however, and there was nothing for me to do but continue working hard. Bork did strengthen the job charter, as he had testified he would. And Henry Ruth, called to testify, told the committee that the investigations of the Special Prosecution Force had suffered no interruption. I also had to testify again at the confirmation hearing for Attorney General Saxbe. Saxbe, for his part, promised no interference with me and all the help he could muster.

Several stories pointing to our accomplishments were published as the days went by and, on December 11, 1973, the Washington *Post* summed up what appeared to be latter-day media thinking. An editorial exploring all aspects of the situation concluded:

We think Mr. Jaworski is doing just fine. We think enactment of legislation affecting his office . . .

49

puts his continuance in office and his effectiveness at risk. And we think that very large body of congressmen and senators who have committed themselves to the creation of a court-appointed prosecutor, along with those who are committed to the passage of less drastic measures, should be seeking ways to leave these votes in abeyance for the moment. Traditionally, after all, Congress is known for a certain skill at putting off and putting over what it does not wish to bring to a final vote. Finding ways to do just that in this matter should not strain its inventiveness. . . .

Both houses, the next day, found a way. Senate Democratic Leader Mike Mansfield, saying he did not expect further interference with the Special Prosecutor's office by the White House, announced that resolutions to create an independent post would not be considered in the remainder of the Senate's session in 1973. And House leaders went along with him.

Like frosting on the cake, the media reported that Tom McBride's Campaign Contributions Task Force had obtained guilty pleas from eight corporations and corporation officers during a two-month span, from mid-October to mid-December. The firms and officers had been charged with making illegal campaign contributions.

My tread was a little lighter that evening as I walked from the office to my hotel.

But my elation was short-lived.

chapter four

The Damning
Tapes

I WAS BADLY shaken, so shaken that I didn't want anyone to notice it. I left Carl Feldbaum's office that mid-
December morning and made my way to my own. I
closed the door behind me. I needed to be alone.

My brain was acting like a ticker-tape. My thoughts
were clear, but they ran through my mind without
break, one becoming another and then quickly another.
But one thought kept coming back, hammering its way
through the others: the President of the United States
had without doubt engaged in highly improper practices, in what appeared to be criminal practices. I had
heard the evidence. I had listened to that voice I had
heard before in person and on radio and television,
so decidedly different now, as the President plotted
with his aides to defeat the ends of justice.

I had not come to Washington expecting this. I had
expected to find all sorts of wrongdoings by his aides,
conduct unbecoming and even criminal, but it had
never occurred to me that the President was in the
driver's seat.

The gravity of the situation was almost overwhelming. The *President* was involved. Even if a criminal
case was never developed against him—and he appeared to be criminally involved—the mere fact that
he had participated actively in such sordid undertak-

ings was shattering. It would come out, in some way or another, and it would jar the nation beyond anything it had experienced so far. And I could not escape the belief that in all likelihood I would be the agent of the President's unmasking. At the moment I didn't feel like even hinting what I foresaw to the closest member of my staff. For, if my premonitions were correct, the result could be more explosive than anyone in Washington might guess.

Only forty minutes earlier Feldbaum had come to my office door. He had beckoned and said, "You'd better come and listen to this." "This" was the segments of the subpoenaed presidential tapes Judge Sirica had decided dealt with Watergate. Feldbaum, who would become our "tape expert," was listening to the segments for the first time in his office.

Several members of the Watergate Task Force were in Feldbaum's office, and they made room for me. Feldbaum activated his recorder, and the President's familiar voice filled the room. Nixon, Haldeman, and Dean were worrying over money payments to the Watergate burglars with Nixon indecisive and questioning one moment, keen and demanding the next. Listening to him scheme, *knowing* he was the President of the United States, I felt as if my heart was shriveling inside of me.

Suddenly I realized that Feldbaum and the other young men were watching me intently. They were trying to determine my reaction. I couldn't afford to let them read my face, so I tried to will myself to be impassive until I had heard enough. I thanked Feldbaum, and sought solitude in my office.

Archibald Cox had subpoenaed the tapes five months earlier. It would be almost another five months before the American people would be able to read transcripts of the tapes, and then they would be transcripts drastically edited by Nixon and his helpers.

Perhaps I brooded as the days passed. Florence Campbell, my secretary, sensed I was carrying a burden and she tactfully kept me free from the minor problems of the office. She was a veteran government employee. Cox had selected her as his secretary and I had accepted her without even an interview. In this period I could feel her loyalty seep under my office door. The staff was aware that I was less communicative than usual, but no one made a point of it.

One portion of a March 21, 1973, conversation between Nixon, Dean, and Haldeman ran through my mind at intervals both day and night. It had nothing to do with payoffs and burglaries directly. No one else seemed particularly disturbed about that strip of dialogue, but I had found it the most repulsive on the tape. In that strip the President—a lawyer—coached Haldeman on how to testify untruthfully and yet not commit perjury. It amounted to subornation of perjury. For the number-one law enforcement officer of the country it was, in my opinion, as demeaning an act as could be imagined.

The three men had been seeking a way to keep Haldeman and other White House and CREEP officials from having to testify before the Senate Watergate Committee. An idea emerged of having the officials testify before a special grand jury which could be controlled through friends in the Justice Department. The President then could take credit for urging the officials to tell all.

The dialogue on the tape went like this:

PRESIDENT: The President takes the leadership of the meeting and says, "Now, in view of all this stripped land so forth, I understand this, but I think I want another grand jury proceeding and we'll have the White House appear before them." Is that right, John?

DEAN: Uh huh.

PRESIDENT: That's the point, you see. That would make the difference. *(Banging on the desk.)* I want everybody in the White House called. And that gives you a reason not to have to go up before the Committee. It puts it in an executive session in a sense.

HALDEMAN: Right.

PRESIDENT: Right.

DEAN: Uh, well . . .

HALDEMAN: And there'd be some rules of evidence. Aren't there?

DEAN: There are rules of evidence.

PRESIDENT: Both evidence, and you have lawyers.

HALDEMAN: So you are in a hell of a lot better position than you are up there [before the Committee].

DEAN: No, you can't have a lawyer before a grand jury.

PRESIDENT: Oh, no. That's right.

DEAN: You just can't have a lawyer before a grand jury.

HALDEMAN: Okay, but you do have rules of evidence. You can refuse to talk.

DEAN: You can take the Fifth Amendment.

PRESIDENT: That's right. That's right.

HALDEMAN: You can say you forgot, too, can't you?

PRESIDENT: That's right.

DEAN: But you can't . . . you're in a very high risk perjury situation.

PRESIDENT: That's right. Just be damned sure you say I don't remember. I can't recall. I can't give any honest . . . an answer that I can recall. But that's it.

The President's advice to Haldeman was damning even in the cold print of the transcripts we made, but I kept hearing his voice, its staccato urgency: *I don't remember. I can't recall.*

The public had seen and heard Dean testify before the Senate Watergate Committee, and had heard him called a liar by other White House aides who came behind him. I had read the transcript of that testimony. Dean had been interrogated intensively before the grand jury. I had read the transcript of that testimony, too. He had been questioned by my staff and I had read his answers. And I had talked with him and weighed him. Though some of the information he had offered had been substantiated, I had not been as quick to believe his story incriminating the President as had some in our office and many across the country. Now, through tapes which could not be denied, I recognized that Dean had been amazingly accurate. Without benefit of recordings or notes, he had been able to recall, almost verbatim in many instances, his conversations with Nixon and White House and CREEP aides.

Two weeks before I became Special Prosecutor, the staff had allowed Dean to plead guilty to a single felony charge of conspiracy to obstruct justice in exchange for his testimony and other help. It was a plea bargain I could have overruled, but I had decided to let it stand. Now I was glad that I had.

One of the most disputed points in Dean's testimony before the Senate Watergate Committee had concerned the paying of blackmail money to some of the Watergate burglars. Dean had testified that some blackmail money had been paid and that, at the March 21, 1973, meeting, he had told the President it would take a million dollars to satisfy the blackmailers over a two-year period. Nixon, he had testified, had said the money could be obtained, in cash, that he knew where to get it.

Haldeman, testifying after Dean, agreed that Nixon had said the money could be obtained, but Haldeman said the President had added, "but it would be wrong." For those who believed in the President it was easier to accept Haldeman's testimony than Dean's.

But now, six months after that exchange, the tape revealed that Haldeman was not even in the Oval Office when Dean and Nixon first discussed the blackmail money. The conversation went like this:

DEAN: Now, where, where are the soft spots on this? Well, first of all there's the, there's the problem of the continued blackmail . . .

PRESIDENT: Right.

DEAN: . . . which will not only go on now, it'll go on when these people are in prison, and it will compound the obstruction of justice situation. It'll cost money. It's dangerous. Nobody, nothing—people around here are not pros at this sort of thing. This is the sort of thing Mafia people can do: washing money, getting clean money, and things like that. Uh, we're . . . we just don't know about those things because we're not used to, you know, we are not criminals and not used to dealing in that business. It's uh, it's un . . .

PRESIDENT: That's right.

DEAN: It's a tough thing to know how to do.

PRESIDENT: Maybe we can't even do that.

DEAN: That's right. It's a real problem as to whether we could even do it. Plus there's a real problem in raising money. Uh, Mitchell has been working on raising some money. Uh, feeling he's got, you know, he's got one, he's one of the ones with the most to lose. Uh, but there's no denying the fact that the White House and uh, Ehrlichman, Haldeman, Dean are involved in some of the early money decisions.

PRESIDENT: How much money do you need?

DEAN: I would say these people are going to cost, uh, a million dollars over the next, uh, two years.

PRESIDENT: We could get that.

DEAN: Uh huh.

PRESIDENT: You, on the money, if you need the money, I mean, uh, you could get the money. Let's say . . .

DEAN: Well, I think that we're going . . .

PRESIDENT: What I mean is, you could, you could get a million dollars. And you could get it in cash. I, I know where it could be gotten.

DEAN: Uh huh.

PRESIDENT: I mean it's not easy, but it could be done. But, uh, the question is, who the hell would handle it?

DEAN: That's right. Uh . . .

PRESIDENT: Any ideas on that?

DEAN: Well, I would think that would be something that Mitchell ought to be charged with.

PRESIDENT: I would think so, too.

Nixon obviously felt that Dean little relished dealing with the intricacies of long-term blackmail. After Haldeman entered the Oval Office, and after a discussion of other problems, the President said, "But let's now come back to the money, a million dollars and so forth and so on. Let me say that I think you could get that in cash, and I know money is hard, but there are ways. That could be *(unintelligible)*. But the point is, uh, what you do on that. Let's look at the hard facts."

A bit later he said, "So the hard place is this. Your,

your feeling at the present time is the hell with the million dollars. In other words, you say to these fellows, 'I am sorry, it is all off'—and let them talk. Right?"

DEAN: Well . . .

PRESIDENT: That, that's the way to do it, isn't it?

DEAN: That . . .

PRESIDENT: If you want to do it clean (*unintelligible*).

HALDEMAN: See, then when you do it, it's a way you can live with. Because the problem with the blackmail—and that's the thing we kept raising with you when you said there's a money problem, when we need twenty thousand or a hundred thousand or something, was yeah, that's what you need today, but what do you need tomorrow and next year and five years from now?

Haldeman was referring to earlier payments to some of the burglars, and Dean replied, "Well, that was just to get us through November seventh [Election Day, 1972], though."

Haldeman said, "I recognize that's what we had to give to November seventh. There's no question."

There was a brief discussion about the "cover" used in handling money in the past and future, then Nixon brought the conversation back to blackmail:

PRESIDENT: Finally, though, so you let it go. So what happens is then they go out and, uh, and they'll start blowing the whistle on everybody else. Isn't that what it really gets down to?

DEAN: Uh huh.

PRESIDENT: So that, that would be the clean way, right?

DEAN: Uh . . .

PRESIDENT: Is that really your . . . you, you really go so far as to recommend that?

DEAN: That . . . no, I wouldn't. I don't think, I don't think necessarily that's the cleanest way. One of the . . . I think that's what we all need to discuss—is there some way that we can get our story before a grand jury, and so, that they can have. have really investigated the White House on this . . .

And the talk turned to other schemes. The idea of paying of blackmail was not discarded but left in abeyance. No one had said it was ethically or morally wrong to get the million dollars and pay it, as Haldeman had implied before the Senate Watergate Committee.

At the beginning of the meeting, when Nixon and Dean were alone. Dean said that E. Howard Hunt, the White House counsel who had participated in both the Fielding and Watergate break-ins, had demanded an immediate payment of $122,000, threatening to "bring John Ehrlichman down to his knees and put him in jail." Hunt also was disenchanted with his friend Charles Colson. Dean said, and could sink him also.

The President said, "Don't you, just looking at the immediate problem, don't you have to handle Hunt's financial situation damn soon?" Dean said he had talked with Mitchell about it the night before, and Nixon said. "After all, you've got to keep the cap on the bottle that much in order to have any options." Dean agreed.

The immediate payment came up again when Haldeman was present. All agreed that Hunt had them in a tight bind The President said, "That's why, for your immediate thing. you've got no choice with Hunt but the hundred and twenty or whatever it is. Would you agree that that's a buy-time thing, you better damn well get that done, but fast?"

Dean said, "I think he ought to be given some signal, anyway, to, to . . ."

Said the President: "Well, for Christ's sakes, get it in a, in a way that, uh—who's going to talk to him? Colson? He's the one who's supposed to know him . . ."

None of the three suggested that it might be unethical or immoral to pay Hunt the blackmail money. And evidence in our hands showed that money was paid Hunt the next day.

These were just two portions of the conversations that particularly stuck in my craw. There was much more, on tapes and in the documents we had received, that constituted evidence against the President and against those officials who were under investigation, but we would need even more evidence to obtain indictments of the officials. And I could not discount the possibility that we would move against the President. With that in mind, we began to assemble the evidence against him.

IT WAS SNOWING as I rode to the White House. It was December 21 and I was going home for a few days, but Haig had called. We met in the Map Room, a private place where Franklin Roosevelt had charted the course of history during World War II.

We began talking about the tapes, the March 21 tape in particular, and Haig said it was terrible beyond description. I told him it was almost unbelievable. But, Haig said, the White House lawyers had told him there was no criminal offense involved as far as the President was concerned.

I shook my head. "I can't agree, Al. Based on what I heard—and what we already knew—I'm afraid the President engaged in criminal conduct."

Haig was upset. But he said he felt I was looking at the picture from the wrong perspective, that some of the facts were different from what I thought they were.

He said he had a transcript of the tape that his people had spent long hours in obtaining. "I think it's better than yours," he said, "and I think you ought to look at it." This was an offer I wasn't about to turn down; if it were accurate, it would be better evidence than our own. He said I could have the transcript when I returned to Washington.

Haig continued to say that I was wrong, that I believed the White House lawyers. I told him, "Al, we have other evidence, but I don't have to go beyond what the recording says. It wouldn't be proper to discuss the other evidence, but it corroborates what's on the tape. The recording itself is an alarming thing, and the reason is because it shows conduct that is not only unethical and unprincipled and wrong, but I think suggests criminal culpability."

He shook his head, saying, "This is not what the lawyers say. Not at all what they say."

I say, "Al, I want to tell you something. I think you should get the finest criminal lawyer you can find—someone not connected with the White House in any way—and let him study the tapes."

We walked from the Map Room to the Diplomatic Entrance. I always entered and left this way so as not to attract attention. My car was brought to the door. The snow had blanketed the White House grounds. Haig was silent, thoughtful. "It's important, Al," I said. "Get that lawyer, the best you can find."

He was looking at the floor. Now he looked up at me and tears were glistening in his fine eyes. I left him that way, and went to my car.

I HAD BARELY ARRIVED home in Houston before Haig was on the phone from Washington. He said he had reviewed the contents of the March 21 tape again. He said he had talked with lawyers, as I had strongly urged. "We're convinced there's no criminality involved

61

because there was no overt act following the meeting," he said.

"Who were the lawyers, Al?"

He said Fred Buzhardt and Samuel Powers, who were the White House lawyers. I considered Powers an able civil lawyer.

"That's not what I suggested," I said. "I think you should get the best possible advice—from outside the White House. Someone whose forte is criminal law."

He indicated he was satisfied, and I said, "It's your problem, Al, and I hope you're right." I dismissed the subject with that, and told him I would be back in Washington on December 26. We agreed to meet on the morning of the twenty-seventh.

On my return we again met in the Map Room. Haig gave me the White House transcript of the March 21 tape as well as a statement which undertook to summarize President Nixon's view of the conversations. I told Haig that because Haldeman was a party to the conversation, and because he was under investigation, the tape would be presented to the grand jury. He reiterated that he believed the tape didn't indicate any criminality on the part of the President.

Then he told me that James St. Clair of Boston likely would be coming to the White House as Watergate counsel. He asked me what I knew of St. Clair and I told him I wasn't acquainted with him. I had anticipated a new White House Watergate lawyer. Haig had hinted several times that the President hadn't liked the way the Watergate investigation had gone. Ron Ziegler had said at a press conference that changes in the legal staff were being contemplated.

I thought I knew why Nixon was unhappy. He had been convinced that he would never have to give up any of his tapes, so he had released the other items we had requested—logs, notes, and other papers—with some degree of willingness. The logs, particularly, were invaluable to us. A special secretary had kept note of every presidential action every minute of every working day. From these logs we learned with whom the President met, with whom he talked on the phone, for almost every day of his tenure. Thus we were able to pinpoint the tapes and documents we needed or thought we needed. The President had finally realized this, and he was unhappy with his lawyers for allowing the flow of information to us.

The logs showed, for example, that Nixon held conversations with Charles Colson on January 3 and 4 of 1973. I suspected the talks dealt with Watergate and I had told Haig I wanted to listen to them. Haig had discussed my request with the President, then told me the tapes had nothing to do with Watergate, that the conversations were of a somewhat personal nature. I had insisted on listening to them. He had said he would talk with Nixon again. Now I brought up my request again and Haig said the President had agreed that I could listen to the tapes.

I told Haig I also wanted to listen to a tape of June 4, 1973, a recording of the President listening to a number of tapes he played to refresh his memory. Haig said there would be no problem. But there was a problem—with Buzhardt. He refused to let me hear the tape. He said Haig wasn't aware of a matter or two that occurred during the playing of the tapes. I told him I was going to hear that tape. I suggested he call Haig, by now in San Clemente, and clear up the situation. He finally acquiesced, and I spent the better part of two days listening to the hours-long recording.

The President had listened to the tapes made during early months of 1973. It was almost impossible to distinguish the words on the tapes, but the President's voice, as he listened and talked with Haig and other aides who came and went in his office, was quite clear.

The reason for Buzhardt's reluctance for me to listen to the recording was obvious. At one point, when the President was talking to Haig, he said, "We do have one problem—that's that damn conversation of March twenty-first."

THE PRESIDENT WAS right about the Colson-Nixon conversations of January 3 and January 4, 1973: Watergate was not discussed. But what I heard on the tapes made me sick at heart. As I listened, I recalled a time in the President's first term when the officers and board of governors of the American Bar Association met with him for an hour in the Oval Office. I was then president-elect of the ABA. President Nixon was considerate and quite eager to have the reactions of the ABA to some of the important domestic issues of the day, particularly those concerned with the administration of justice. He showed a willingness to listen, a readiness to learn. That was the public President Nixon.

What I heard now on these tapes was the private Nixon. He had crawled down on the level with Colson, his hatchet man. "Sleazy" was the first word that came to my mind as I listened. They talked of revenge against their enemies. The President's voice was full of contempt for certain Congressmen and close friends simply because they had shown a lack of enthusiasm for one policy or another. It sounded like two cheap wardheelers talking in the rear room of a neighborhood dive.

The subpoenaed tapes already had shaken my faith in Richard Nixon as President. Now the Colson tapes shook my respect for him as a man. But I couldn't reveal how I felt, even to Henry Ruth, my closest associate. Haig had quoted Nixon as saying the Colson tapes would be embarrassing to him and to others. I was bound by my honor, then, to keep silent about them because I had insisted on listening to them. And more than that, I could not let my feelings influence my actions. If I obeyed the injunction I had laid down for the staff—fairness to all—I would have to conduct myself as if I had never heard the damning conversations.

I recalled a prayer service the ministers and elders of my church in Houston held for me and my family before my journey to Washington. Now I called on the strength those prayers had given me. During the months to come, I would hear the President throw falsehood after falsehood at the American people. Only a handful in the country would know his falsehoods for what they were. It was torture to remain silent in the face of such duplicity. How I longed to cry out against him so the people would know the truth! But I swallowed my frustration each time, knowing that the rules that granted Richard Nixon his freedom to speak were the same rules that bade me hold my tongue.

As FAR BACK as July, 1973, stories about Richard Nixon's personal finances had begun appearing in the newspapers. The Washington *Post* led the way with a story about the President's donation of his vice-presidential papers to the National Archives during his first term in office. The President had taken a $482,018 income tax deduction on his gift. The *Post* said that Nixon did not sign the deed transferring the papers, that the deed was not delivered until April 1, 1970 (nine months after the effective date of a 1969 law prohibiting tax deductions for such gifts), and that the deed was never accepted by the Archives as a formal written document.

A few months later, the Providence *Journal* had reported that the President paid an income tax of $789 for 1970 and $878 for 1971. The Associated Press sent out this story on its wires in more detail shortly after

I became Special Prosecutor. On an emotional Richter Scale, this shock registered higher with many Americans than the "Saturday Night Massacre" or the eighteen-minute tape gap.

Large sums of public money had been spent at Nixon's private residences at Key Biscayne and San Clemente to provide security. There were news stories suggesting that some of the money had been spent not for security but to increase the value of the properties. And there were questions about some of his real estate dealings.

Our staff began work on these matters, cooperating with the Internal Revenue Service and, later, the Joint Committee on Internal Revenue Taxation chaired by Representative Wilbur Mills.

President Nixon made public reference to his personal finances on several occasions, and it was in this regard that he made his dramatic "I'm not a crook" declaration on national television. Speaking at the Associated Press Managing Editors Convention in Orlando, Florida, he said: "I've made mistakes, but in all my years of public life I have never profited from public service. I have earned every cent. And in all of my years of public life I have never obstructed justice. People have got to know whether or not their President is a crook. Well, I'm not a crook. I earned everything I've got."

To support the strong statement, the White House staff began to prepare a report on the President's finances that was intended to be made public. Outside counsel was called in to supervise the operation. One of these lawyers was a friendly acquaintance of mine, H. Chapman (Chappy) Rose of Cleveland, whose firm also had a Washington office.

Rose called me. "Leon," he said, "the President wants you to review the accountant's reports on his finances before a public report is made. He asked me to get together with you. Can you make yourself available?" I said I could and we agreed to meet.

I felt that Nixon's wish was really a gesture to assure me that the reports would contain no "bombshells"—that nothing was hidden. The reports, as it turned out, were extremely complicated and I could do no more than listen as Rose and another tax lawyer went over them. When the session was over, I took Rose aside for a private talk.

Haig and Buzhardt had sent me numerous documents and logs. The tapes Cox had subpoenaed were in our hands and I had listened to them. But the tapes I had requested had not been delivered though I had been promised delivery within ten days. Buzhardt always was full of excuses, some valid, perhaps. There were many jobs to do at the White House, he would say. He was short-handed. He needed more time.

I told this to Rose because Rose had the President's ear. "Now," I said, "we've reached a critical point. I'm not going to put up with this foot-dragging any longer, and I'd like for you to tell the President so, Chappy. This is Friday. If I don't get some action by early next week, I'm going to file for an order subpoenaing those tapes."

Rose heard me out. He nodded his head—his indication that he would pass the word to the President.

Immediately after the meeting I prepared a letter to Haig and Buzhardt with the same blunt promise of court action if my request was ignored. I sent it to the White House by messenger.

Haig called me late that evening. He was complaining. "I heard about it [my ultimatum] on the radio when I left the White House," he said. He was implying that I had put the White House in a bad light and that I shouldn't have done it.

I told him, "Al, I had nothing to do with your hearing it on the radio. All I can tell you is that I want some action, and I'm going to have to have it by early next week."

That was all of the conversation. Whether Rose gave Nixon my message I never learned. But early the next week some tapes arrived. They constituted only a trickle of the stream of material we needed, but they were vital, and they moved the Special Prosecution Force closer to the time when we would ask for indictments in several areas under investigation.

THE PRESIDENT'S TAX PROBLEMS were cleared up not to everyone's satisfaction when he agreed to pay some $467,000 in back taxes and interest. Both the IRS and the Joint Committee on Internal Revenue Taxation found that his $482,018 deduction for his vice-presidential papers had been taken improperly and under curious circumstances, but no fraud on his part was found. The blame fell on those who had handled the vice-presidential papers and prepared the tax returns.

Haig's complaint that he had heard a news report on the radio about my demand for the tapes was not the first complaint nor by any means the last to come from the White House about "news leaks." There was a news leak for every politician and every politician's aide in Washington and, I was quick to learn, White House aides were as adept at "planting" stories as the rest. There were leaks from the Special Prosecution Force, all of which I decried but few of which I considered damaging either to our work or those under investigation. One leak, which could have emanated from our office only, prompted me to take an affidavit from each staff member as to whether he or she had discussed the resulting story with a newsperson. I wasn't totally satisfied with the responses, but my action had a salutary effect on the staff. And I warned my colleagues by memorandum that White House aides might very well ask the FBI to interrogate us and our spouses if leaks continued.*

We were accused of leaks that were not leaks at all, and accused of others that originated elsewhere. Some strong and bitter words flowed from the White House occasionally, generally with Ron Ziegler or his deputy, Gerald Warren, the conduits. Ziegler on one occasion denounced the staff in such strong language at a news conference that at first I felt impelled to answer him publicly. I changed my mind, however, and wrote him a letter.

At the news conference, Ziegler had said at one point:

I have said before, privately and publicly, that I have personally very serious questions about the staff of the Special Prosecutor's office in political terms. Although they no doubt are attempting to work fairly, I think their political background, what they have felt, their views, their attitudes toward this Administration in the period of their adult lives, would suggest that they enter into this entire procedure with a certain amount of ingrained suspicion and visceral dislike for this President and this Administration. I am not referring to Mr. Jaworski. I am referring to the Cox group that was put together.

A reporter had said, "Mr. Jaworski speaks kindly of that staff." Ziegler had retorted, "Well, I speak unkindly of it."

---

* The memorandum stirred one staff member into unthinking anger. He said, "No FBI agent is going to interrogate my wife!" I thought then that I was blessed in that Jeannette had decided early in our marriage not to question me about a case in progress. She accepted my absorption in a case as part of her life with me. What she knew of Watergate she learned from the news media.

In the body of my letter to Ziegler I wrote:

When first I assumed this task I had been fore-
warned, based on rumor to be sure, that there
were those in the Special Prosecutor's office who
were zealots, determined to achieve their own end
regardless of truth. I am now prepared to assure
you, after close association with the staff, that
this suspicion is totally unfounded. I have worked
daily with my principal subordinates, reviewing
data that is being assembled, additional sources to
explore, recommendations to consider and action
to be taken. In my experience at the bar I have
found no group more objective, more fair-minded
and more dedicated to a search for the truth than
is this unusual group of talented lawyers. Should
I find any among them who do not meet the qualifications of fairness and objectivity, I would not
hesitate to dismiss them. . . .

In the letter I asked Ziegler for examples of unfair-
ness by staffers, and in a long, intelligent letter of reply
he listed what he considered several abuses. One of
the examples already had drawn the wrath of his
deputy, Gerald Warren. He—and Nixon, I must assume—had been incensed by a column by Rowland
Evans and Robert Novak which told of Buzhardt's
mission to my office with his story of the eighteen-
minute tape gap. Buzhardt, it will be recalled, had
asked for a delay in making the news public, saying
he wanted to make more tests to see if he could learn
what had caused the gap. The columnists had concluded that Buzhardt's request had been based on
political considerations more than scientific interest. In
any event, I had insisted that Judge Sirica be informed
about the gap immediately. Warren, at his press conference, did not say exactly why the column and its

conclusions were so terrible, but the New York *Times* drew its own inference from his remarks.

Said a *Times* editorial:

The criticism leveled by the White House against special prosecutor Leon Jaworski for allegedly leaking to the press information unfavorable to the President's cause conjures up visions of the fate that befell Archibald Cox. Viewed against the background of Mr. Cox's dismissal, the complaint by deputy Presidential press secretary Gerald L. Warren contains unmistakable suggestions of intimidation.

What, in fact, was the nature of the alleged leak? It was that Whate House lawyers had approached Mr. Jaworski . . . with the news of the obliterated eighteen minutes of taped conversation between Mr. Nixon and H. R. Haldeman and had asked the special prosecutor to agree to a delay of several days before informing the public of this latest disappearance of subpoenaed evidence. The "leak" also included the fact that Mr. Jaworski had quite properly rejected the request.

In allowing the sequence of events to become known, Mr. Jaworski's office, far from being guilty of an impropriety, merely showed that the special prosecutor refused to be a party to any cover-up, however temporary and for whatever purpose. Mr. Warren's criticism therefore seems just one more resort to the by now familiar maneuver of diverting attention from a White House impropriety by creating the impression that the offense was not in the deed itself but in the telling of it. . . .

Jeannette came to Washington soon after the New Year's holidays and set us up in a comfortable apartment in the Jefferson Hotel, a brisk walk from my office.

The apartment had two bedrooms, a small kitchen, and a sitting room. We became friends with the hotel staff and with the manager, Mrs. Edith Morgan, a wise, delightful woman who looked out on the Washington scene with amused tolerance. When she saw how much Jeannette used the kitchen, she placed a full-size refrigerator there in addition to the regular small one.

I placed a desk in one of the bedrooms and used the room for an office where I could work at night and on Sundays. The security force at the office put a strong safe in the room where I could keep the confidential material I needed to use in my work.

Jeannette and I would eat breakfast together and then I would walk to work. I usually sent out for a sandwich at lunch. In the evening Jeannette would prepare our dinner—something simple like Spaghetti Red*—or we would go out for dinner to an excellent restaurant within walking distance where we could get seafood, which I missed the most when away from Houston.

And I managed to keep up with my jogging, a custom for years. I would jog at a fast pace from bedroom to bedroom while Jeannette was preparing breakfast, zigzagging around her as she moved from the kitchen to the sitting room, where we ate. She accepted it with her usual aplomb.

The hours at the office began early and continued until late in the evening. I had a car and driver assigned me but, except for a few instances of inclement weather, I walked both to and from my office.

We went to occasional social functions, but our attendance became rarer as the pressures of work in-

---

* A mixture of lean ground beef, tomato paste, lots of chili powder, English peas, mushrooms, onion, garlic, and bell pepper spooned over spaghetti and covered with grated Parmesan cheese. The English peas give the dish a distinctive flavor. Texans insist it is not fattening.

creased. On Sunday mornings we would attend church and, on a few occasions, we spent our Sunday afternoons at performances at Kennedy Center. There was seldom a Sunday without some official calls.

We had good friends in Washington, but we did not see them as often as we wished. However, friends from Texas called us often to cheer us on, usually on Sunday mornings. And there was an abundance of messages of encouragement from around the country, with many people saying they were praying for us.

Not all the messages were friendly. Following one major decision, a message advised me: "You had a rendezvous with history and you blew it!"

A large amount of mail came from the various Polish-American communities across the country. One of our boys, the letters seemed to say, is right there in the capital and he's doing all right! I especially recall a letter from a boy with the family name of Jaworski which particularly warmed my heart. It said simply: "My name is John Jaworski. I am 15. I did not amount to anything until you came along. Now even my teachers pay some attention to me. . . ."

chapter five

The Breach in the Wall

UNTIL THE DEATH of J. Edgar Hoover on May 2, 1972, most Americans considered the FBI the paragon of law enforcement agencies. But the Watergate burglary, occurring only a few weeks after the appointment of L. Patrick Gray to succeed Hoover as Acting FBI Director, blurred the FBI image. Gray's subsequent handling of the affair and related investigations brought discredit to the bureau and, eventually, public shame to Gray himself. His exposure as an inept administrator in thrall to White House aides and other officials came in early March 1973 as he testified before the Senate Judiciary Committee. The President had nominated him as permanent FBI director; the nomination needed committee approval.

When Gray testified before Congress regarding his nomination, the Senate Watergate Hearings had not yet begun. There was no Special Prosecution Force. The stone wall erected around the White House by the President's aides had been scarred and even chinked at times, chiefly by the Washington *Post,* but it had remained standing—the cover-up was still intact. Gray, trying in his testimony to serve his President, to be honest, and to secure the directorship for himself, failed at all three. Under almost casual questioning from the committee members, he opened a breach in the stone wall.

Much of what he testified to had been reported in the newspapers but discounted as hearsay and slander in White House and CREEP statements. Some had not been made public at all. It was revealed that restraints had been placed on the FBI investigation by the Justice Department—this didn't seem to annoy him. CREEP attorneys had monitored FBI interrogations of CREEP employees. Agents had interviewed persons involved in other criminal actions allied with Watergate—men like Herbert Kalmbach—but no action had been taken against them. The investigation, as far as possible, had clearly been confined to the burglary.

In addition, Gray testified that he had been in touch with Ehrlichman and John Dean during the investigation, and had periodically sent written reports to Dean through then Attorney General Kleindienst.

John Dean? At that time Dean was an unknown. His name had appeared in print in connection with the scandal on only one occasion, when it was announced that he was conducting an investigation to see if any White House aides were involved in Watergate. Now Gray was admitting that he had supplied raw data to this man. (Later Gray would confess that he had destroyed important evidence at the behest of Dean and Ehrlichman.)

Indeed, Gray reported to Ehrlichman by phone on the progress of the hearing itself, we learned later, telling him he was "having a ball" and asking him to caution Dean against revealing the fact that he had destroyed evidence. Gray apparently thought he was making a good impression on the committee. Ehrlichman happily conveyed this opinion to Dean in a phone conversation. But Dean had been reading daily transcripts of the hearing. "It just makes me gag," he told Ehrlichman, describing Gray's testimony.

Dean added that the committee might not act on Gray's nomination until they heard testimony from

White House officials that Gray had mentioned in testimony. Meanwhile, however, the President had decided that his aides wouldn't testify; he would claim executive privilege for them. In that event, Dean said, Gray might be left hanging until the President's claim was resolved.

Ehrlichman, obviously feeling that Gray had deceived him by reporting the news from the hearing as good, told Dean, "Well, I think we ought to let him hang there. Let him twist slowly—slowly in the wind."

Gray twisted, slowly, until his nomination as FBI Director was withdrawn a month later, in April 1973.

SENATOR SAM ERVIN, who was to chair the Senate Watergate Committee, was also a member of the Senate Judiciary Committee, and Gray's testimony supplied him with numerous leads. His committee, in turn, was of inestimable help to the Special Prosecution Force. Some who appeared as witnesses before the Senate Watergate Committee told the truth. Some lied. Some told only enough to whet the curiosity of the Special Prosecution Force. But, in one way or another, we used all the information brought to light in the hearing.

Gray was succeeded as Acting FBI Director for a brief period by William Ruckelshaus, who later, as Assistant Attorney General, was fired in the "Saturday Night Massacre." Ruckelshaus began immediately to put the FBI house in order, and this work was carried on by Clarence Kelley, who was named FBI Director in July.

The performance of the FBI posed a special problem for the Special Prosecution Force, formed as it was during Ruckelshaus' brief tenure. Either the force would have to hire a staff of trained investigators, or it would have to depend on the FBI for such work. Certain members of the Force were suspicious of the FBI; on the other hand, Ruckelshaus gave every indication that he would handle FBI business in a forthright manner. And the Force had learned that agents who had worked on the Watergate and allied investigations were, for the most part, dedicated men who had chafed under restraint and had been angered by Gray's duplicity. Further, the agents knew more about Watergate and the cover-up than anyone save the participants. They were the best-trained, most experienced investigators in the country, and they were large in number. Cox decided to work with the FBI, even in matters where the Bureau itself appeared to have been implicated.

Kelley was an FBI veteran who assumed the Director's job after an outstanding career as police chief of Kansas City. We held our first meeting in my office. He was a big, well-groomed man who spoke as if he had tested each phrase elsewhere before speaking. I liked him immediately, and trusted him. We held subsequent meetings in his office, oftimes at lunch.

One of our first concerns was the 18½-minute gap in the June 20, 1972 tape. Kelley knew most of the details. I told him we wanted to know who had erased the tape. The President and Haldeman were the ones most directly concerned since it was their conversation that had been removed, but the court hearing had shown that others had access to the tapes or could have managed the erasure. FBI agents would have to go into the White House to investigate.

Kelley knew as well as I that the atmosphere could be hostile; the President and his aides would probably not welcome agents on such a mission. And Kelley, like myself, was a presidential appointee . . . but without my safeguards. I assured him he would have the full support of the Special Prosecution Force, which meant that anyone failing to cooperate with FBI interrogators would be subpoenaed before a grand jury. Kelley never hesitated. His agents interrogated, or tried to interrogate, everyone in the White House even remotely connected with the tapes except the President. The President had already told me through counsel that he would submit to questioning on Watergate-related subjects only through written interrogatories, a device I held worthless.

A number of those who resisted FBI questioning were called to testify before a grand jury, including Rose Mary Woods. Buzhardt, as usual, put off the agents with his string of excuses, but finally granted an interview. Haig did not refuse to be interviewed, but he kept agents cooling their heels through so many appointments that they finally left him to us and the grand jury.

After discussions with my staff and the FBI, there was only one conclusion to reach, in my opinion. "Gentlemen," I said, "three people could have erased the tape, but for a successful prosecution that's two too many." All hands agreed.

RETALIATION FROM THE WHITE HOUSE was petty, and it was directed not toward the FBI but toward me. James St. Clair, the President's new special counsel, called to say he wanted to meet with me. We set a time for the next morning. "What's the protocol?" St. Clair asked "Where do we meet, your place or mine?"

I told him I didn't stand on ceremony. "I'll come to your office," I said. "Will you clear my entry through the southwest gate?"

He said he would.

Ruth and Ben-Veniste were with me. It was snowing when we reached the gate and a cold wind was blowing. The guards would not let us in. After several minutes a young lawyer named Hauser came to the gate. He asked the guards why we were not admitted. I didn't hear the guards' explanation, but they told Hauser they couldn't clear us on his authority.

Minutes passed as we stood there in the wind and the snow. A man appeared through the whirling flakes.

"Do you want to see Mr. St. Clair?" he asked. My anger at the cavalier treatment we were receiving had been building slowly, and now I snapped, "Mr. St. Clair wants to see me." And I stepped past the man and started walking toward the Executive Office Building, leaving him in our wake. Finally he scuttled ahead of us, saying over his shoulder, "Follow me." He led us to St. Clair's office.

St. Clair said he had no idea why we were kept waiting. He told his secretary "find out about it." We went to discussing our business, and his secretary interrupted us shortly to explain: "The Secret Service ordered that no one from the Special Prosecutor's office could come on the grounds without being escorted." St. Clair apologized, and as he escorted us to the front door of the building he assured me again that he had known nothing of this directive.

Back at my office I called General Haig. I told him about the incident. I said I wasn't interested in finding out who gave the order to the Secret Service, but I made it clear I wouldn't go through such an exercise again. "So the question is, Al, do you want to straighten it out or do you and your people want to do the traveling to my office from now on?"

Haig said he knew nothing about the order. "I regret the incident very much, Leon," he said, "and it won't happen again."

Nothing of that nature did occur again. Though we conducted our business with the White House under ever-growing tension, nothing spiteful surfaced on either side, as far as I could ascertain.

KELLEY, AND RUCKELSHAUS BEFORE HIM, did much to restore public confidence in the FBI by their actions in a wiretapping project inspired by the White House. It will be recalled that first word of the 1971 break-in of Dr. Lewis Fielding's Los Angeles office came from

John Dean in talks with investigators in April 1973. The information was transmitted to Judge Matthew Byrne. who was presiding at the Daniel Ellsberg trial. Earlier there had been news reports that the FBI, at the direction of the White House, had conducted a number of unauthorized wiretaps on phones of government officials and newsmen. One of these taps, said the news stories, had been in connection with Ellsberg's disclosure of the Pentagon Papers. Judge Byrne ordered the FBI to produce such wiretap evidence, if it existed.

Ruckelshaus investigated. Yes, he reported to Judge Byrne. a tap had been placed on the phone of Dr. Morton Halperin. a former aide to Henry Kissinger, and at least one Ellsberg conversation had been overheard. An FBI employee remembered the incident, but no record of it could be found.

Judge Byrne, citing the Fielding break-in and the failure of Government prosecutors to produce the wiretap information. dismissed all charges against Ellsberg. A few days later Ruckelshaus held a press conference. From May 1969 to February 1971, he said, thirteen government officials and four journalists had been subjects of electronic surveillance. In July 1971 all records of the wiretap project had been removed from FBI files and delivered to John Ehrlichman at the White House, he said. Now. almost two years later, Ruckelshaus retrieved the records for the FBI files.

The Special Prosecution Force, which was already investigating the Fielding break-in, began an investigation of the wiretap project. Shortly before I became Special Prosecutor, Cox had asked that the Force be allowed to examine the FBI files. He was told to take up the matter with the Attorney General. Cox didn't want to do that at the time. He already was under considerable pressure because of his demands for the nine presidential tapes he subsequently subpoenaed. Attorney General Elliott Richardson was being hounded by the President and Haig to restrain Cox. So, while the wiretap investigation proceeded on other fronts, Cox held back on negotiating for the FBI files.

I faced no such restriction. With Kelley we worked out arrangements to review the files. We needed FBI agents to help us in several areas of the investigation, but we planned to investigate agents in the FBI Intelligence Division who had participated in the wiretap project. After we explained the matter to Kelley, he was as anxious to get the facts as we were. He arranged for us to use agents in the General Investigative Division, and though they were at times investigating brother agents, they went about their tasks with professional thoroughness.

By this time we had studied the tapes received from the White House and the documentary material from the files of White House aides. We had received information from the willing lips of John Dean, Egil Krogh, and others. Along with studying the FBI files we questioned others involved in the wiretap project, some under oath before a grand jury. This is what the total investigation revealed:

The President authorized the wiretap project in 1969. The *New York Times* began publishing the Pentagon Papers in June 1970 and before the month was out Ellsberg was indicted for releasing them. The Justice Department's Internal Security Division, which was to prosecute Ellsberg, asked the FBI if any Ellsberg telephone conversations had been overheard or recorded. The FBI said no. Accepting this, the Justice Department filed affidavits with Judge Byrne saying there had been no electronic surveillance of the defendant.

But there had been. Ellsberg had been overheard fifteen times during the twenty-one months Morton Halperin's phone was tapped. William Sullivan was then Assistant FBI Director. He was at odds with Director Hoover and expected to be discharged. He got in touch with Robert Mardian, Assistant Attorney General in charge of the Internal Security Division, and said he had custody of the wiretap files. He wanted to give them to Mardian. Hoover, he said, could use the files as a bargaining point to remain at his job as long as he wished.

Mardian talked with John Mitchell, then Attorney General, and someone at the White House. He flew to San Clemente and met with the President and Ehrlichman. The President told him to get the files. Mardian returned to Washington and delivered the files to the Oval Office. The President told Ehrlichman to put them away, and Ehrlichman put them in a filing cabinet in his office.

This all occurred in June and July of 1971. In February 1973 a White House aide learned that *Time* magazine was preparing to publish a story about wiretaps on government employees and newsmen. John Dean had heard of the FBI files from Mardian. He checked further, then called Ehrlichman. Yes, said Ehrlichman, he had the files. But he told Dean to have Press Secretary Ziegler label the *Time* story false. A White House source was quoted as denying that anyone at the White House had authorized or approved taps on newsmen or government employees. Dean reported to the President that the White House was "stonewalling totally" on the wiretap story. The President replied, "Oh, absolutely!"

Gray by now was Acting FBI Director and was before the Senate Judiciary Committee seeking the Directorship. He was asked about the *Time* story. He said there was nothing at the FBI to indicate the existence of such files and, since the White House had denied authorizing or approving such a project, he had not made an investigation.

From February 1973 until May—with the files still in the White House—the White House denied their existence. Then, when Ruckelshaus learned that Ellsberg had indeed been overheard on Halperin's phone, he sent the news to Judge Byrne and put his agents to work. Mardian was among those questioned. He said he had delivered the files to the White House. Ruckelshaus retrieved them, examined them, then made his announcement that government employees and newsmen had been subjects of electronic surveillance.

AFTER WE HAD IN HAND what appeared to be the complete story about the wiretaps, we had to consider the next step. I received a number of suggestions from the Force members closest to the case, but I had reservations about our being able to obtain indictments and convictions. I didn't voice my reservations immediately, but Phil Lacavaro, Counsel to the Special Prosecutor, was given the task of examining the various legal issues involved.

Lacavaro's memorandum on the subject concluded: "Congress has specifically provided in 18 U. S. C. Section 251 (3) that the statutory prohibition against wiretapping does not apply to measures the President believes necessary 'to protect national security information against foreign intelligence activities.' Whether any of the taps in question fit within this exception could be debated as a matter of statutory interpretation as well as a matter of actual intention, and there would also be room to contend that the duration of some of the taps showed that even an initially legitimate purpose was altered to an impermissable domestic political goal. Nevertheless, because of the numerous uncertainties in this area, I would be hesitant to recommend a criminal prosecution of any of the principles involved in initiating what appeared to be 'national security' wiretaps . . ."

Some of the wiretaps, as Lacavaro pointed out, had little or no "national security" justification but in the staff's view and mine, there simply wasn't enough evidence to bring criminal charges. We were influenced further in this regard by pure pragmatism. Some of the persons involved were under investigation in other areas where the evidence against them was strong enough to convince us that indictments and convictions were most probable.

I felt that Kelley had infused the FBI with a new spirit. Agents from fifty-eight of the Bureau's fifty-nine field offices worked with the Force in many areas of investigation, and we even received help from several FBI employees stationed abroad in FBI "legal attaché" offices.

PRESIDENTIAL TAPES and John Dean's testimony established that the White House made a determined effort to punish the Administration's enemies and reward its friends through various government agencies, particularly the Internal Revenue Service. We considered this a serious abuse of power and conducted a long, thorough investigation to see if the White House effort had accomplished anything. The investigation was conducted by the Plumbers Task Force under the direction of William Merrill.

The group was told that White House aides did obtain some confidential tax information but far less than was anticipated because of resistance in the top echelons of the IRS. Dean, for example, testified that he was turned down twice when he went to then IRS Commissioner Johnnie Walters with a list of "enemies" and Democratic campaign contributors and asked that the IRS move against them. Later on, however, when the President asked Dean if he needed "any IRS stuff," Dean told him, "We have a couple of sources over there that I can go to. I don't have to fool around with Johnnie Walters or anybody. We can get right in and get what we need."

An IRS report on an investigation of Howard Hughes's business interests contained some information about the finances of Lawrence O'Brien, Democratic National Committee Chairman. John Ehrlichman learned of this and from Roger Barth, Assistant IRS Commissioner, obtained some data on O'Brien's tax return. This was before the 1972 presidential election. Ehrlichman passed the word that O'Brien should be interviewed—and he was. It was clear that the White House hoped that news reports of the interview, coming at a politically critical time, would prove embarrassing to O'Brien and damaging to the Democrats.

In another instance, H. R. Haldeman learned that the IRS had investigated Alabama Governor George Wallace and his brother, Gerald Wallace. Through a White House aide Haldeman obtained a report of the investigation from then IRS Commissioner Randolph Thrower. Portions of the report were "leaked" to columnist Jack Anderson who wrote a story about the investigation. The account appeared while George Wallace was actively campaigning in the Alabama primary. No one in Washington believed Haldeman was trying to help the Wallace cause.

Donald Alexander was IRS Commissioner during our investigation and he aided us in many ways. I found him to be a man of probity and intelligence. We could not have conducted our investigations without his aid and that of his assistants. Alexander conducted an "in house" investigation along with ours, and made information available to us on a continuing basis.

Our chief difficulty in obtaining convictions lay in proving corrupt intent on the part of those under investigation. We realized that in almost every case it could be argued, probably successfully, that an IRS audit of an "enemy" was necessary and not outside normal IRS practices. And in no case did we find evidence of payoffs.

Our job, of course, was to obtain the kind of solid evidence on which a grand jury could base an indictment for a subsequent trial. It was a Special Prosecution Force rule that we not seek an indictment unless we believed there was a fifty percent chance of obtaining a conviction. We decided we didn't have that kind of evidence. The Senate Watergate Committee, and later the House Judiciary Committee, showed the American people the scope of the Administration's political harassment, as they should have done. Under the law, we could not.

ONE OF THE NAMES dropped by L. Patrick Gray during his confirmation hearing before the Senate Judiciary Committee was that of Herbert Kalmbach. It had surfaced earlier in the news media. While uncovering Donald Segretti and his "dirty tricks," the Washington *Post* had discovered that Segretti's paymaster was a man named Kalmbach, a California attorney and the President's personal family lawyer. The FBI had investigated Kalmbach, Gray testified, but the report he offered the committee was brief and dealt chiefly with Kalmbach's relations with Segretti.

Senator Ervin had been a member of the Judiciary Committee and, when he convened the Senate Watergate Committee shortly after Gray's hearing, Kalmbach was one of the first witnesses called to testify. Kalmbach gave Ervin's group the basic outline of his involvement in the Watergate cover-up and pointed the committee in the direction of other witnesses.

The Special Prosecution Force had reason to believe that Kalmbach was a veritable well of information but that he had so far delivered only a dipperful. As it developed over several months of questioning, this belief was well-founded. Kalmbach knew something about —or had participated in—almost every clandestine White House operation. And, to quote one of my aides,

Tom McBride, Kalmbach "adopted a posture of complete cooperation."

He was of special interest to McBride and his Campaign Contributions Task Force. Kalmbach was a super fund-raiser. McBride's group questioned him about a special money-raising scheme in what became known as the "Townhouse" investigation; about his handling of funds left over from the President's 1968 campaign and used for various purposes; about his involvement in the milk producers' campaign contributions; about his solicitation of contributions from ambassadors and would-be ambassadors.

At the same time, other Task Forces were questioning Kalmbach about the ITT affair, his payments to Segretti, and his role in the Watergate cover-up. He gave freely of his knowledge. As he did so the extent and degree of his culpability became clear.

I could not help but become philosophical about Herbert Kalmbach. He was tall and impressive. He had a California flair; it was easy to think of him sauntering into the country clubs of the Southern California coast, being welcomed cordially as much for his being the President's personal counsel as for his friendly, open manner. He was in his early fifties, but there was some of the devoted eager-beaver in him, as there was in the younger Egil Krogh. Krogh, however, confessed his guilt, repented and left court humbly but with his head unbowed. Kalmbach's happy facade crumbled totally and revealed a man broken in heart and spirit.

This view of Kalmbach was shared only by McBride and Henry Ruth. When the beaten, dejected man entered into plea bargaining with us I asked the groups most intimately concerned with his activities to give me their recommendations. The result was the first divergence of views of any consequence in the Special Prosecutor's office.

I finally decided that Kalmbach would be offered

the option of pleading to a two-year felony Corrupt Practices Act violation in connection with the "Townhouse" case, and a one-year misdemeanor violation in connection with his selling of an ambassadorship. Those investigating the milk fund cases had reservations. They felt they might get more evidence of Kalmbach's involvement, if not from him, from others. It didn't seem likely to me, and they didn't have enough evidence on hand to gain an indictment. This was also true for some members of the Watergate Task Force who were opposed to my decision. They felt that Kalmbach should be required to plead guilty to a felony in the Watergate cover-up. When pressed for the evidence needed to support an indictment, they could not satisfy what I considered to be the minimum requirements.

To clarify my stand, I wrote this memorandum:

By way of a limited amount of background, let it be noted that Kalmbach was exposed to me on several occasions. I had an opportunity to review the facts of supportable charges, both with him and his attorneys.

I came to the conclusion that (a) his title as the President's personal counsel was pure windowdressing; that it was an accolade he personally coveted, as it would be by most people but especially an easygoing, shallow-minded individual of his type; (b) he was a follower instead of a leader; did not initiate the general wrongdoing in which he participated but found himself in the chain of events because he was a good lackey to carry out the desires of others; (c) his acts were not maliciously done; (d) his acts were not venal because I am convinced that this man acted much of the time, if not all of the time, blindly and without the benefit of mental supervision (and his truthful testimony could probably convince a jury that that was the case). He was motivated more by the desire to continue to carry the title of the President's personal attorney than in engaging in a wilful criminal pursuit.

In the light of the foregoing background, my action was predicated on these, and other, considerations: This individual was exposed to Tom McBride for long periods of interviews and discussions. Tom's reactions and analyses, dispassionately and constructively made, were most helpful to me and had considerable influence on my judgment, as did those of Henry Ruth who, on at least one occasion, along with McBride, had a substantial visit with Kalmbach.

Their analyses and judgments were particularly helpful on the most fundamental issues of the provability of Kalmbach's criminal intent, his character, the strengths and weaknesses of our evidence against him in the various areas under investigation, the likelihood of conviction in future prosecutions, and the offsetting value of evidence which he could provide against others under investigation.

Kalmbach has been more and more cooperative as time goes on and has disclosed substantial information involving others. I believe he will be even more helpful in the days ahead.

The factual situation surrounding Kalmbach simply did not justify, in my judgment, the harsh, punitive consequences that I find supportable in the instances of Mitchell and Haldeman, for example.

There is considerable 'fallout' to be gained from the pleas of this individual. The pleas expose unlawful operations out of the White House, and others involved in unlawful conduct now under investigation will gain little comfort from these pleas.

I am not unmindful that there may be some criticism from those who either are not aware of the reasons I have assigned or who, although aware of them, nevertheless are satisfied with nothing less than severe treatment. Kalmbach is not in my judgment a 'master criminal' meriting such treatment. He was, rather, a not-very-smart errand runner. In the end the pleas agreed to are chargeable to me, and I am prepared to accept any criticism that is leveled.

The sentence is the responsibility of the Court. We will make no recommendation as to the sentence. It should also be noted that Kalmbach and his attorneys have been advised that he is vulnerable to being named as an unindicted co-conspirator in the Watergate cover-up and/or other indictments.

It was communicated to me that the observation had been made that the agreement with Kalmbach and his attorneys had been reached in effect before the discussion was held between the Watergate Task Force and myself. This is not true. To the contrary, in the discussions with Kalmbach and his counsel it was made clear that any tentative proposals of disposition were subject to open-minded review with the Watergate Task Force. It was not until after the comments of the Watergate Task Force were heard and weighed that another meeting was held with Kalmbach and his counsel and a decision arrived at.

May I add that I genuinely embrace the opportunities for full and constructive discussions with the staff. Objective and dispassionate observations and arguments are greatly desired and are carefully weighed before a final decision is reached. We are all going through difficult periods of decision-making and we must strive not to lose sight of the responsibilities a prosecutor bears, especially in situations where passions can so easily become inflamed. The best that can be required of the Special Prosecutor and each lawyer on the staff is that these difficult decisions be made with care, in good faith, and in reliance on proper legal, evidentiary and policy considerations. . .

My memorandum did not change all minds on the staff at once, but subsequent events bore out Tom McBride's prediction that Kalmbach would prove to be an honest, compelling witness, particularly in the trials of Dwight Chapin and those who would be indicted in the Watergate cover-up. On his guilty pleas, Kalmbach was sentenced to six to eighteen months and fined $10,000 on the felony count, and sentenced to six months on the misdemeanor count. The sentences were to run concurrently.

We dealt with Kalmbach on the clear, firm basis we used in negotiations with others who entered plea bargaining with us. Part of our agreement read:

> The United States will make no recommendation concerning Mr. Kalmbach's sentencing but will bring to the attention of the presentencing investigators information in its possession relating to Mr. Kalmbach and to the extent of his cooperation with the United States. Such cooperation will also be brought to the attention of a court or professional disciplinary body if requested.
>
> *This disposition will not bar prosecution for any false testimony given hereafter, nor to prosecution for any serious offenses committed by Mr. Kalmbach of which this office is presently unaware. . .*

* * *

THE "TOWNHOUSE" AFFAIR in which Kalmbach pleaded guilty, like so many other activities connected with the White House, was brought to public attention by the news media. It received its catchy name because it was directed with cloak and dagger secrecy from a Washington townhouse. Its purpose was to raise funds for selected Republican candidates in the 1970 Congressional elections.

Kalmbach was the money-raiser—and he arranged that $3 million be funneled into the townhouse to a former White House aide, Jack Gleason. Gleason, in turn, distributed the money to the selected candidates on instructions from members of the White House staff. His liaison man at the White House was Presidential Aide Harry Dent.

Our investigation showed that the "Townhouse" group was, in fact, a political committee that had unlawfully failed to elect officers and file financial reports. The investigation began months before Kalmbach pleaded guilty. He was of help to us, of course, both before and after his plea, but we needed the group's records to complete the case. And the records had been transferred from the townhouse to the White House files. As usual, we had to fight a long, dreary battle with the White House before the records were produced.

Even with the records we were unable to obtain sufficient evidence to move against anyone except Kalmbach, Gleason, and Dent. Both Gleason and Dent pleaded guilty to misdemeanor violations of the Corrupt Practices Act and were given probationary sentences.

Kalmbach raised vast sums of money so easily because he worked with an established group, the traditional big givers to the Republican cause. But he was also willing to go outside his normal orbit. While tapping his regular sources for the President's second-term bid, he made what appeared to be a world-wide tour of American outposts, seeking cash from American ambassadors. And, to fatten the political war chest, he apparently was ready to sell an ambassadorship for the right price. He was not the only one we suspected of such activity.

Deplorable as it is, Americans have long accepted the practice of Presidents appointing big campaign contributors to ambassadorial posts, occasionally without regard to the contributors' diplomatic qualifications. But the outright sale of an ambassadorship is illegal, and those involved in the scheme during the Nixon administration knew it. It is also illegal to purchase one, but we felt the seller, as a public servant bearing public trust, was more culpable than the buyer.

We had begun our investigation by obtaining testimony of persons we had reasons to believe were buyers. The White House, with considerable reluctance, had given us some documentary material we requested; we needed more, but it was not forthcoming.

I was in almost constant communication with Haig at this time, either meeting with him in the Map Room or talking on the telephone. He was becoming increasingly worried; I assumed he was reflecting the President's state of mind. I gathered that the President was disturbed by the progress and scope of our work, and I gathered further that he was telling Haig that somehow I must be deterred. Adding to their disquietude were the effective plea bargaining discussions we were conducting with persons near the heart of the various criminal actions under investigation. Each time we entered into an agreement permitting one of the wrongdoers to plead guilty to a felony and then accepted his testimony under penalty of perjury, there was a nervous reaction from the White House.

For example, while we were questioning Kalmbach one day, he told us he had been awakened by a phone call in his hotel room at 1:45 A.M. The caller was the

President. His voice was low-pitched and to Kalmbach Nixon seemed terribly tired. He just wanted to explain to Kalmbach that someone other than Kalmbach would be handling the Nixons' tax matters in the coming tax season, but he hastened to say that he would be getting back to using Kalmbach at a later date. He assured Kalmbach that he didn't forget his friends. Several times, in referring to Watergate, he said, "This is so much shit." And he said, "I know you only did what you were told to do by others." He added, "The truth will out." Finally he apologized for the lateness of his call and told Kalmbach to go back to bed.

It seemed to me that the phone call was a placatory gesture; the tapes showed the President had little regard for Kalmbach, and ordinarily would have dismissed him as his tax lawyer without a second thought. But he knew Kalmbach had already marred the Administration's image with his testimony before the Senate Watergate Committee. In my opinion, his phone call at 1:45 A.M. indicated that Nixon hoped to cause Kalmbach to change his mind about talking to us. The incident was one of the first disquieting intimations that the President might be absorbed in Watergate to the detriment of normal government business.

Haig could always be counted to deprecate our plea agreements. "You ought to know you can't believe him," he would say. "He's trying to get clear by laying the blame on other people."

"No," I would say, "we've got evidence that he's telling the truth."

Haig was never content to let the discussion end with my flat comment, but would continue to worry the subject. These departures from his normal suavity were more indications of White House anxiety, though the President continued unabashedly to paint himself publicly as a strong executive with nothing to hide.

When it became obvious to the White House that

neither Haig's blandishments nor his derogation of witnesses was slowing our progress, articles critical of plea bargaining began appearing in newspapers under bylines of columnists who regularly attacked any moves they construed as inimical to the Administration's political health. And Attorney General William Saxbe made some public comments on the "ills" of the practice.

Now Saxbe had been one of my strongest supporters when my job was in doubt, and had sworn, in effect, to resign if the White House curtailed my efforts in any way. He had lived by his word and had not interfered with our work previously, but I thought his comments detrimental to our progress. To save us both from possible embarrassment, I decided not to confront Saxbe directly, and it was well I did. Instead, I had Henry Ruth get in touch with Saxbe's chief deputy with the message that I considered Saxbe's actions, whether intentional or unwitting, tantamount to interference with the responsibilities of my office.

Saxbe sent word to me that he had no intention of thwarting me, that the plea bargaining remarks were being placed in his addresses by his speechwriters, and he made no further remarks about plea bargaining.

SINCE WE COULDN'T BE STOPPED one way, Haig took another tack. He took off his diplomat's top hat and put on his Army helmet. "Things are going to get bloody, Leon," he said. "You people apparently don't know how tough a lawyer St. Clair is and you're just inviting him to show you. Some of the things your assistants have done, some of the things that have been done with the grand jury, the way some of the witnesses have been handled—St. Clair won't put up with that kind of thing."

We were in the Map Room, our favorite meeting

place. "Cut out the generalities, Al," I said. "Give me some specifics."

"They don't involve you personally."

"I don't care who they involve," I said. "I want specifics."

He shook his head. He went back to talking about St. Clair, about how tough he was and how bloody things were going to get. I asked again for specific cases of wrongdoing by my staff, and again he answered by praising St. Clair and promising a blood bath.

"I don't care how tough he is," I finally said. "I've come to grips with tough lawyers many times in many places, and some of them—well, St. Clair wouldn't make a pimple on their butts!"

I always had been firm with Haig in past discussions, but this marked the first time I had come close to the boiling point. He looked at me with new eyes. He opened his mouth but didn't speak. Finally we moved to another subject and then the meeting broke up.

Perhaps my words served me well with Haig, but in truth I held St. Clair in high regard and was aware of his ability. I also was aware that he was seldom given an opportunity to demonstrate his capabilities as a lawyer because the President so obviously was calling the turns. He was not in position to make decisions. Oftimes after long discussions he would say, "I can't give you an answer now. I'll have to wait and see what the boss says about it."

As a lawyer I regretted seeing St. Clair used as a public relations man by the White House. He was put on television repeatedly and gave frequent interviews after court proceedings. He was very good in this role. He was an aggressive man with the peculiar ability of selecting exactly the right words to convey a particular meaning. He would hunch his shoulders slightly, cock his head thoughtfully and reply to questions in measured phrases, looking his questioner intently in the eye as he responded. It was most effective theatre.

St. Clair was in the midst of what the Special Prosecution Force called a "White House public relations blitz" when we decided that we would have to subpoena the material we needed for our investigation into the sales of ambassadorships. The action was taken as quietly as possible; I didn't want to give the White House an opportunity to attack us on the grounds that we were harassing the President.

I anticipated a long wait for the material at best, a court fight for it at the worst. But we received some help from a unexpected quarter. As part of the "White House public relations blitz," St. Clair was a guest on a national television program. The final question asked him by his interviewers was simple, short, and unexpected: "Are there any subpoenas outstanding?"

It was not a question St. Clair wanted to answer, but he answered in the affirmative and added, "They'll probably be responded to."

We received the material within two weeks. St. Clair's statement had been picked up by all the news media, and pressure to perform was on the White House. I could not believe, however, that public pressure alone would have made the White House responsive to the subpoena. When we received word that the material would be delivered, my first thought was that we had overestimated its value as evidence. We're getting it because the White House considers it harmless, I thought, not because of the news media pressure.

We used the material as best we could. Perhaps a dozen suspected buyers of ambassadorships, former White House officials, and fund-raisers were questioned under oath before a grand jury. Only in one case—involving Kalmbach—were we able to mount enough evidence to justify bringing charges. In such cases a crime is not proved unless the prosecution can show a prior *quid pro quo* arrangement—a prior commitment in exchange for a forthcoming contribution. And proof requires that one of the participants admit to the arrangement.

Kalmbach confessed to making a commitment to J. Fife Symington, Jr., a Maryland socialite and ambassador to Trinidad. Symington, after first withholding critical information, explained his role to the Force. Symington wanted an ambassadorship in Europe, and Kalmbach knew it. Kalmbach sold him a commitment for $100,000. Symington did not receive the appointment. Kalmbach named a person high in the White House hierarchy whom he said had "welched" on the commitment.

Some White House aides complained privately that the Special Prosecution Force had "planted" the question about outstanding subpoenas to force St. Clair into a public disclosure on the television program. Perhaps someone on my staff did "plant" the question. In any event, I knew nothing about it.

chapter six

Creating Legal Precedent

By EARLY JANUARY 1974, it became apparent that President Richard Nixon, for all his public posturing as a candid man who wanted the truth revealed, had decided in private to keep the facts buried. The first notice came from General Haig; he suggested that I had received all the material I needed from the White House. In the past, when the White House had supplied us with material at our request, Haig each time had tried to get assurance from me that I would ask for nothing more.

Each time I had told him that I could not be a party to such an agreement. "I can't determine what we will need until I have a chance to study what you've just given me," I would tell him. "And remember, we keep getting information from individuals. That gives us more reason to ask for more material."

Next, Haig cautioned me that the President was going to make all the decisions concerning our requests. "You probably won't receive any more tapes," he said.

"That would be a terrible mistake, Al. Congress won't like it and I don't believe the American people will."

"I realize that," Haig said, "but it's a calculated risk he's prepared to take."

During December a move in Congress to conduct

an inquiry into possible grounds for impeachment of the President had gained momentum. The House Judiciary Committee had assembled a staff and had appointed a chief counsel, John Doar. It seemed likely that Congress would give final authorization to the inquiry in early February. I knew this must be weighing heavily on Nixon's mind, and I mentioned this to Haig. "Well," he said, "everything he gives to you he'll have to give to the committee, won't he?"

We talked on in this vein, then I went back to a subject I had brought up before—the grand jurors' desire to have Nixon appear as a witness before them. As he had done in prior instances, Haig said the President would be willing to answer a "written interrogatory" under oath.

I told Haig that such testimony had little value because it seldom gave a full and accurate account of the facts. The answers could be prepared by lawyers and adopted by the witness. If the answers were unsatisfactory or incomplete, I could not pursue them as I could if oral testimony were given.

I had learned from several tapes that Nixon was a believer in written interrogatories. He spoke of them as a way to satisfy investigators as early as February 28, 1973, in a conversation with John Dean. On March 13, 1973, he told Haldeman and Dean: "Written interrogatories you can handle." And again on March 22, 1973, in a discussion with Haldeman, Dean, Ehrlichman, and Mitchell, he brought up written interrogatories as a means to disarm investigators.

The grand jury, early in the Watergate investigation, had accepted answers to a written interrogatory from a witness and had found the method ineffective and unsatisfactory. I explained this to Haig, and I also made my position clear to St. Clair both verbally and in writing. I even offered to have the grand jurors go to the White House in a bus, posing as tourists, and to let them assemble wherever the President wished for the giving of his testimony. I advised Haig and St. Clair—and the President through them—that possible offenses being investigated by the grand jury included obstruction of justice, conspiracy to obstruct justice, and perjury. I also advised them that evidence already presented to the grand jury indicated that the President had information that was highly relevant to the grand jury's inquiry, that the grand jury wanted to hear all relevant evidence of involvement or non-involvement of any persons under investigation. Haig and St. Clair always came back to the written interrogatory. And I continued to insist on oral testimony.

So, the President did not testify in any manner. At a news conference he told reporters he was willing to testify by way of a written interrogatory, but the subject was not pursued. When asked whether he had talked to me, he said he had not because he questioned the propriety of his talking with the Special Prosecutor. The truth was that, through Haig, he had invited me to talk with him on several occasions about tape recordings I was requesting and other matters as well. Each time I said that I wouldn't be agreeable to doing so voluntarily, that I would talk with him only if he directed me to do so. I explained that private discussions between the President and the Special Prosecutor were subject to misunderstanding by others.

Throughout January, Haig continued to tell me that I probably wouldn't get any more material from the White House. At the end of the month Nixon made it official policy. In his State of the Union speech he told Congress that "one year of Watergate is enough," and said I had received all the material I needed for the grand jury to complete its job. I would get no more.

I wrote to St. Clair on February 1. My letter said, in part:

In view of the President's comments in his State of the Union address and remarks attributed to you in a press interview at the Courthouse the following day, I seek clarification on the status of the requests I have made to the White House for tapes and documents. Some of the requests were made as far back as November and December of last year and have been renewed from time to time since then.

Specifically, will you please advise me whether it is now the position of the President that the office of the Special Prosecutor is to receive none of the items specifically requested, all of which we intend to present to the Grand Jury. If I am to receive any of them, will you please specify those to be received and when I may expect their receipt.

The President, in the address referred to, expressed the desire for prompt grand jury action on the matters under investigation. Because the items requested are necessary to the completion of the grand jurors' responsibility to "inquire with care and thoroughness before they file formal charges against anyone," we reiterate the need for compliance with our several requests. Withholding these items may well serve to delay rather than expedite the action of the grand juries. May I have your prompt response?

St. Clair's response was prompt but far from comforting. His letter was long, his approach firm. He wrote:

. . . A brief summary of the history of the matter of evidentiary materials sought from and provided by the President to your office seems appropriate by way of explanation.

In July 1972, the Special Prosecutor requested

recordings of ten Presidential conversations, which the President declined to provide on grounds of separation of powers. The Special Prosecutor then subpoenaed these recordings and the matter was heard in the District Court, which held the Court must review the recordings in order to decide whether the materials should be provided. The issue was then heard by the Court of Appeals, which affirmed the District Court decision with modifications.

As was predicted by the President and his counsel in argument to the Court, production of Presidential papers inevitably leads to demands for more documents *ad infinitum* as is now amply demonstrated. The Senate Select Committee at first sought only five tapes of Presidential conversations. This was followed by a subpoena served on the President for at least 500 such tapes and untold numbers of other Presidential documents. In this case, the original request for ten tapes, two of which never existed, and three others plus a portion of a fourth [that] were ruled irrelevant by the Court, has led to this new demand for what amounts to approximately forty tapes and an unspecified number of other documents.

As you know, the President on October 23, 1973 announced that he would voluntarily comply with the order of the Court of Appeals, in connection with a subpoena of the Grand Jury for tape recordings and other materials relating to ten specific Presidential conversations. Pursuant thereto the President did deliver to the Court the following tapes:

1. Mtg.—President & Ehrlichman 6/20/72 (55 min.)

2. Mtg.—President & Haldeman 6/20/72 (1 hr. 19 min.)

3. Mtg.—President, Haldeman & Mitchell 6/30/72 (1 hr. 15 min.)

4. Mtg.—President, Haldeman & Dean 9/15/72 (50 min.)

5. Mtg.—President & Dean 3/13/73 (1 hr. 18 min.)

6. Mtg.—President, Dean & Haldeman AM 3/21/73 (1 hr. 43 min.)

7. Mtg.—President, Dean, Haldeman & Ehrlichman PM 3/21/73 (41 min.)

8. Mtg.—President, Dean, Haldeman, Ehrlichman & Mitchell 3/22/73 (1 hr. 46 min.)

Total: 9 hr. 43 min.

In its opinion, the Court of Appeals noted that the Special Prosecutor had "made a strong showing that the subpoenaed tapes contain evidence peculiarly necessary to the carrying out of the (Grand Jury's) vital function—evidence for which no effective substitute is available. The Grand Jury seeks evidence that may well be conclusive. . . ."

Despite this "strong showing" by the Special Prosecutor, the *in camera* examinations of the materials subsequently made by the District Court led the court to uphold particularized claims of privilege with respect to three entire conversations and portions of another, thus emphasizing the narrowness of the conditions and circumstances under which the Court sustained the right of the Grand Jury to such types of material.

The President has since then voluntarily provided you and those under your supervision a large volume of additional materials, consisting of recordings of seventeen additional Presidential conversations and more than 700 documents. These materials related not only to Watergate but to a number of other matters as well, including the ITT, the milk price support and the White House Special Investigative Unit investigations. This voluntary production is unprecedented in our history. In responding to your requests, no attempt was made by the President to confine the materials provided to those which would have fallen within the narrow area specified by the Court of Appeals opinion. Indeed, as of January 8, every one of your requests for tape recordings of Presidential conversations had been met by either providing you with a copy of the recording or providing access to the recording for you or your staff. Significantly, some of the conversations for which you requested recordings turned out, as you know, to be totally unrelated to matters under investigation by the Grand Jury.

From the beginning of the investigation of the Watergate affair, there has been a conflict between two critical requirements: the need for a complete and thorough investigation; and the need to make sure that the investigation was handled in a way that the important Constitutional boundaries between the branches of government were respected and retained.

Your latest requests in my view clearly do not meet the criteria laid down by the Court of Appeals for overriding "the presumption of privilege premised on the public interest in confidentiality" where Presidential conversations are concerned. More directly to the point, if this process of escalating requests were to continue there would be no end—either to the investigation itself, or to the intrusions into the privacy of Presidential records.

It is the President's view that he has furnished sufficient evidence to determine whether probable cause exists that a crime or crimes have been committed and by whom. Continued and seemingly unending incursions into Presidential documents would ultimately so erode the executive privilege of the office of the Presidency as to render it substantially meaningless.

As early as January 1, 1974, in your year-end report and in public statements thereafter, you have stated that the Watergate Grand Juries had already received enough evidence to begin considering major indictments in January and early February of this year. If this be the fact, then certainly the new extensive requests cannot be essential to the Grand Jury's deliberations, which now have been in progress for more than 19 months.

The President firmly believes and I know that you agree that the public interest requires that these deliberations proceed with expedition. These new and extensive requests, however, will only serve unduly to prolong the Watergate and related investigations for many months. Accordingly, I have been instructed by the President to advise you that he respectfully declines to produce the additional tape recordings you requested on the ground that to do so would be inconsistent with the public interest and the constitutional integrity of the office of the Presidency.

Rather than engage in prolonged litigation over this matter, the President has authorized me to discuss with you alternative means of furnishing you such information you say you now need including, as I have suggested to you previously, furnishing answers under oath to pertinent written interrogatories together with a personal interview with the President if you so desire.

Public interest requires a prompt and just conclusion to these matters and the President desires to give you the fullest possible cooperation, as he has since you were appointed Special Prosecutor. However, he has an obligation, as I am sure you would agree, not to take any action that would be damaging, perhaps for all time, to the office of the Presidency. I hope that we can together reach mutually satisfactory solutions to the problems engendered by your new requests.

To try to reach "mutually satisfactory solutions," I had a meeting with St. Clair and wrote him a letter immediately thereafter. I ignored what I considered incorrect implications in his letter and his self-serving view of history. My letter said:

On January 9, 1974, more than four weeks ago, we requested access to some 25 particularized conversations between the President and various persons in connection with our desire to wind up the investigation of the Watergate break-in and cover-up. On January 11, 1974 you acknowledged receipt of our written request, advising us that our request would be considered and that you would reply to it in due course. *On January 22 you advised us that the matter of turning over the requested tapes was still under consideration,* but that before you could reach a decision with respect thereto you requested that we make a showing of "particularized need" for each of the conversations requested. Although we informed you that we were not obliged by the Court of Appeals decision in *Nixon* v. *Sirica* to make any such

107

showing, nevertheless, in the spirit of cooperation we responded to you on the same day setting forth particularized information in detail concerning our basis for requesting each of the 25 conversations, as well as two additional related conversations. On January 25 you responded to our letter by stating that a decision had not yet been made as to whether or not the material called for would be produced voluntarily. On February 1 we again asked in writing for your decision on compliance with our request for the enumerated tape recorded conversations. You responded on February 4 by stating that you hoped we could reach mutually satisfactory solutions in connection with our request for the 27 conversations.

In our meeting this morning you asked me whether the Special Prosecutor's office would request any further tapes in connection with the Watergate grand jury investigation in the event that the President decided to comply with our January 9 request, as amended. In view of our continuing desire to conclude this investigation, we would be willing at this time to agree not to request further tapes in connection with the Watergate grand jury investigation into the Watergate break-in and alleged cover-up if you would agree to satisfy our request promptly. (Of course, it is understood between us that this agreement would not foreclose further requests that may be occasioned by legitimate defense demands or our trial preparation needs after indictment.)

In this regard, and in view of the fact that our request has been pending for more than four weeks, we would expect that you should be able to deliver to us copies of the following tape recorded conversations and whatever transcripts or

summaries you have prepared relating thereto by
Tuesday, February 12, 1974:

1. Meeting between the President and Mr.
   Haldeman on March 22, 1973, from 9:11
   A.M. to 10:35 A.M. (No. 4 in my letter of
   January 9, 1974, with further elaboration
   of particularized need in letter of January
   22, 1974.)
2. Three meetings between the President, Mr.
   Ehrlichman, and (in the second and
   third) Mr. Haldeman on April 14, 1973
   from 8:55 A.M. to 11:31 A.M., and from
   2:24 P.M. to 3:55 P.M., and from 5:15
   P.M. to 6:45 P.M. (Nos. 8, 9, and 10 in
   my letter of January 9, 1974, with further
   elaboration of particularized need in letter
   of January 22, 1974.)
3. Meeting between the President, Mr. [John]
   Wilson and Mr. [Frank] Strickler on April
   19, 1973, from 8:26 P.M. to 9:32 P.M.
   (No. 14 in my letter of January 9, 1974,
   with further elaboration of particularized
   need in letter of January 22, 1974.)
   [Wilson and Strickler were attorneys for
   Haldeman and Ehrlichman.]

We would expect that the balance of the tape
recorded conversations could be produced no later
than Friday, February 15, 1974. . . .

The President did not accept our offer; we received
nothing. Nevertheless, we got our evidence in order
and by mid-February the grand jury was ready to return an indictment. However, we decided to delay the
return because John Mitchell and Maurice Stans were
scheduled to go on trial shortly in New York in the

Vesco affair. We had acted in an advisory capacity only in that case, but because Mitchell was among those to be indicted in Watergate we did not want to prejudice his defense in the Vesco affair. We would wait until the Mitchell-Stans jury was sequestered.

Meanwhile, on February 6, the House of Representatives authorized the House Judiciary Committee to investigate if grounds existed to impeach the President.

And I came face to face with the monumental problem of whether the President should be indicted on a charge of criminal misconduct.

REPRESENTATIVE PETER RODINO of New Jersey, chairman of the House Judiciary Committee, had stated publicly that his group would conclude its impeachment inquiry by April, but he failed to reckon with several factors regarding the assembling of evidence. For one, the White House said that it would resist any attempts by the Committee to subpoena material similar to that which the Special Prosecution Force had received. And the Special Prosecution Force could not deliver the Committee evidence it had assembled because much of it had been obtained under promises of confidentiality and through secret grand jury proceedings. It would be improper for us to reveal the information unless it was done pursuant to an appropriate order of the court.

I was eager to cooperate with the Committee, and I made this clear in an interview with the New York *Times*. But I added: "When we make a request of the White House for tapes or documents or other information in connection with our investigation, we relate that request to the grand jury procedures. We have no right of access to that information otherwise. Because of that, we are bound by the rules of secrecy attached to that information. . . ."

Further, it was obvious to me that if we boxed up all the material we had gathered and delivered it to the Committee it possibly could take months for the Committee staff to get it in presentable condition. So, within the bounds of propriety, I worked with John Doar, chief counsel, and his assistant, Albert Jenner. Although I considered it appropriate that some of the information in our possession be transmitted to the Committee through Doar, I wanted to make certain that the White House would not view this as a breach of confidentiality. Accordingly, I advised St. Clair of the requests Doar and Jenner were making, and gave him an opportunity to object to my filling them. On February 21, I wrote Doar:

In response to your request of February 12, 1974, I am writing to provide you a list of the recordings, documents and other material that the Special Prosecutor's office has received from the White House. In light of Mr. St. Clair's letter to me of February 15, 1974, I am *not* forwarding at this time a detailed list of our requests for evidence that have *not* been met, and expect to hear from you when you obtain clarification from Mr. St. Clair on the White House position on transmittal of that list.

Although much of the material we have received has been broadly identified publicly, I would ask that you keep the details of the following list confidential. I understand, of course, that you may use the list as an aid in formulating the House Judiciary Committee's request to the White House for evidence. . . .

Even with the list, Doar and his staff faced a formidable task. Rodino, apparently taking my stand lightly, had begun a news media push implying that I was under obligation to deliver evidence to his Committee. He apparently was hoping to counter media criticism that the Committee was moving about its work too slowly. It worked to some degree, because I was faced with intimations in some of the media that the blame was mine. I let this criticism develop until I finally had a fill of it. I went on the television program *Issues and Answers,* knowing this subject would be one of the first brought up by the panel. The panelists had done their homework. The interview went like this:

DAVID SCHOUMACHER: Mr. Jaworski, to move to the other side of the Hill, have you decided how you will react if confronted with a subpoena from the House Judiciary Committee in its impeachment investigation on producing information you have?

MR. JAWORSKI: That is a matter for the court. That is a matter for Judge Sirica. Obviously I don't face a dilemma. I have only one possible course that I can follow and that is to hold this evidence secret for the time being. That is all grand jury evidence.

SAM DONALDSON: Let's back up one step from the subpoena, then, that might or might not be issued on you. Are you telling us you see no way for a voluntary turning over of relevant material to the House Judiciary Committee by you?

MR. JAWORSKI: I see none at this time.

MR. DONALDSON: Is there any way that the court could order you to do so, or allow you to do so by giving an affirmative expression?

MR. JAWORSKI: Yes, sir.

MR. SCHOUMACHER: What is the position you would take if it was a subpoena directed at you and the information in your files? Not necessarily information before the grand jury although they may be one and the same? Their view is, the House, as I understand it, that this is not a judicial review process.

MR. JAWORSKI: I would meet the gentlemen at the Courthouse. I am saying what I have is before the grand jury.

MR. DONALDSON: You are saying that a subpoena, once the full House grants this Committee the subpoena power we expect it to grant this week, you think constitutionally you ought to contest, that the great power that we hear about an impeachment proceeding does not override all privileges, including the one that you are talking about?

MR. JAWORSKI: It is not a decision of my saying I think I should contest. It is my obligation to contest, because these matters are now cloaked in secrecy in the grand jury and I have no right to release them.

MR. SCHOUMACHER: Mr. Jaworksi, what would you say to those who have been obviously going to confront you with this argument: that there is no more important business under the Constitution than to determine the integrity of the Presidency? Should that not fall before all else?

MR. JAWORSKI: That doesn't give me any right to break the law. This is precisely what I would be doing. I would be breaking a responsibility, a legal responsibility. I would be breaking an absolute rule of law if I were to do it.

MR. DONALDSON: Let's back up to the point where you said of course if Judge Sirica would order you to then you would cooperate, or you would hand over, in accordance with the order. Would you entertain the idea of going to Judge Sirica along with Messrs. Doar and Jenner, the Special Counsel for the Judiciary investigation, and ask for that type of order?

MR. JAWORSKI: I would not. These gentlemen are able, distinguished lawyers who know their way to the Courthouse.

MR. DONALDSON: Would you oppose them if they went and asked for. . . . ?

MR. JAWORSKI: I will cross that bridge when I get there because of one other matter that we haven't discussed. How are they going to use this testimony? Is it going to be used in open hearings?

MR. DONALDSON: What if they pledged to you this testimony would be kept confidential, that they would guard it and they said only we, Doar and Jenner, and the Chairman, Rodino, and the ranking Republican, Hutchinson, would see it? Would that satisfy you?

MR. JAWORSKI: We are talking about whether I would oppose a motion in court. Of course, your question is completely hypothetical, but I would say it would be of considerable help to me if that sort of assurance were given.

MR. SCHOUMACHER: Have you had any exchange of ideas, let's say, with the Committee about this?

MR. JAWORSKI: Mr. Doar has come and talked to me and Congressman Rodino has talked to me over the telephone. I have written Congressman Rodino a letter explaining our position in detail. The letter was written two or three weeks ago. I must say to you that the particular matter you are inquiring about has not been discussed because they haven't apparently decided themselves on just how these hearings are to be conducted. At least they haven't advised me.

MR. DONALDSON: You have been investigating a long time. Now, Chairman Rodino made the statement the other day if he wasn't able to get your material it would take his investigators a year or more to duplicate your investigations. Do you think it would?

MR. JAWORSKI: No. One thing you haven't asked about, and it hasn't been discussed, is that this same material is also at the White House.

MR. DONALDSON: All of it?

MR. JAWORSKI: All that I think he would be interested in.

MR. DONALDSON: Then you'd rather see them go to the White House as the best source?

MR. JAWORSKI: It is not a case of what I would rather. I have no alternative, as I have explained to you, because I am bound by the rule of law not to release this. Now, the White House can take its position. I don't know what it would be, but they certainly can serve subpoenas there just as well as they could to take the matter to Judge Sirica's court.

Shortly thereafter, the Washington *Star* carried a strong editorial castigating Rodino for trying to shift the Committee's problems to my shoulders. But I had something in mind—an unprecedented action—that could go a long way toward solving the Committee's problems. At the same time, it could help the Special Prosecution Force with a major problem of its own.

I HAD BELIEVED the President to be criminally involved in the Watergate cover-up since mid-December, it will be recalled, and I had followed the only course open to me—the assembling of evidence against him. By January 7, 1974, we had prepared a document of 128 pages outlining Nixon's apparent complicity. Only

115

eight copies of the document were made; both copies and original were guarded with the greatest secrecy.

The evidence, we felt, was sufficient at that early date to indicate that the President might be chargeable with conspiracy to obstruct justice, to commit bribery, and to obstruct a criminal investigation by endeavoring through bribery to prevent communication of information relevant to criminal violations to the prosecutors. Accordingly, the President might also be chargeable with the substantive offenses of obstruction of justice, bribery, and obstruction of a criminal investigation. Moreover, the President could be charged as an accessory after the fact and misprision of felony.

I had no doubt but that the grand jury wanted to indict him. This was the original Watergate grand jury whose members had returned the indictment against the Watergate burglars. They were conscientious men and women, dedicated to getting at the truth. They had heard and studied all of the evidence. But to be valid, an indictment required the signature of the Special Prosecutor so, in the last analysis, the decision on whether to indict the President was my responsibility.

I had tried to examine the issue from every conceivable angle. I had discussed it with some of my principal assistants. I had considered their memoranda. I had attempted to assess the issue from the standpoint of what was legally sound as well as what was best in the nation's interest.

I had grave doubts that a sitting President was indictable for the offense of obstruction of justice. While legally an indictment could be returned against a sitting President for the offense of murder, say, I did not believe the U.S. Supreme Court would permit indictment of a sitting President for obstruction of justice —*especially when the House Judiciary Committee was then engaged in an inquiry into whether the President should be impeached on that very ground.* The proper constitutional process, it seemed to me, would be for the Committee to proceed first with its impeachment inquiry.

I came to the conclusion that an indictment of the President at this time would produce many months of delay in disposing of the issue of his culpability, months during which the country would be suffering from the trauma of an indicted President. Also, the President was entitled to his constitutional rights to a fair trial, whether it be an impeachment proceeding or a criminal proceeding. For both processes to be conducted at the same time could mean a denial of the right to a fair trial, and could even cause a stalemate for a long period of time.

I also concluded that the President should not be cited as an unindicted co-conspirator in the Watergate cover-up indictment, which we planned for the grand jury to return shortly. The President could contend that such action was prejudicial and denied him a fair hearing before the House Judiciary Committee. We did need to name him as an unindicted co-conspirator. However, I did not want this to be revealed so long as he was being investigated and, in effect, tried by the Committee. My goal was to be authorized by the grand jury to disclose this finding at a later date— some months away—when a bill of particulars would need to be filed in a pretrial hearing for those to be indicted. There would be no immediate publicity about his being named an unindicted co-conspirator; thus nothing would be prejudicial to the President's case before the Committee.

We needed to name the President as a co-conspirator prior to trial in order to make admissible as evidence his statements in the tape recordings at the trial of those we planned to indict in the cover-up case. Without so naming the President, some of his statements in the recordings would not be admissible as evidence.

And then there was our master plan. I wanted the grand jurors to send to court—along with the cover-up indictment—a sealed report that contained all relevant information bearing on the President's cover-up involvement. It was our view that this information could be transmitted to the House Judiciary Committee to aid its members in their impeachment proceedings.

Such action was without legal precedent, but it seemed to be legally proper—if we prepared the information properly. And it certainly would expedite the Committee's work. It was a solution to a difficult problem, in my mind, and it is a matter of public record that the grand jurors agreed.

The report—called the "road map" in our office—was not compiled without some stress and warm debate. Some of the staff members of the Watergate Task Force felt strongly that evidence they regarded as inculpatory of Nixon should be so designated. I was convinced this would be a mistake. The courts, I believed, would not permit such material to be transmitted to the Committee. The success of the plan depended on our ability to spell out simply the facts of the cover-up story as they appeared from our investigation and let the Committee members reach their own conclusions.

To achieve this, there was much writing and rewriting done by a number of staff members, but the final structuring was done by George Frampton, a brilliant young lawyer with an analytical mind and the ability to write clearly. The final product contained the information we sought to transmit, with references to particular tapes and testimony of particular witnesses, and that's all. There were no comments, no interpretations, and not a word or phrase of accusatory nature. The "road map" was simply that—a series of guideposts if the House Judiciary Committee wished to follow them.

THE MITCHELL-STANS JURY was selected and sequestered in New York on February 28, so we decided to bring in the Watergate cover-up indictment on the following day. Judge Sirica set the time at 11 A.M. I had told the judge in advance that we would be bringing him a sealed grand jury report along with the indictment; I didn't want to startle him by introducing the unexpected.

On the evening of February 28, just as I was preparing to leave my office, General Haig called. Rumors were afloat, he said, about a possible indictment and a sealed report. "Is there anything you can properly disclose to me, Leon?" he asked.

"Nothing about the indictment or the report," I said. "If the grand jury does make a report, you should expect Judge Sirica to accept it and act on it."

"Let me ask you this," he said. "Is there any indictment involving present White House aides? I'd need to make arrangements to meet the situation."

"Don't worry about arrangements," I said.

He seemed relieved. "You're a great American, Leon."

"I've just done my duty, Al, and I hope I continue to do so."

He said that he and others at the White House were expecting the grand jury evidence to be turned over to the House Judiciary Committee. "We realize it belongs there."

"It may well have serious repercussions," I said.

"I'm aware of that."

"I'm going to tell you again, Al: take a close look at the tape of that March 21 meeting and the actions that followed it. I feel that the President's counsel haven't accurately assessed the facts."

"We'll review it again," he said.

I met with Judge Sirica at 10:30 the next morning in his chambers to go over the agenda. The judge acknowledged he was a little tense. "I haven't slept since three o'clock this morning," he said. As I left the chambers, I heard him tell his marshal, "Now, don't be nervous." But when the marshal stepped up to open court proceedings he was so nervous he could hardly speak the ritual.

The reporters filling the austere courtroom were no less tense. There were few spectators. Those who were to be named in the indictment were not present. Their legal representatives were there because we had notified them that the indictment would be returned; we didn't want them to learn of it through the news media. They, too, were tense. There would be no fiery speeches this day, no legal arguments presented, no swift cross-examinations—none of the ingredients from which courtroom drama ordinarily is compounded. But the drama was there. History of a sort would be made shortly, for the indictment would name men who had been among the most powerful in the Administration, and the aura of their power still clung to them.

Judge Sirica looked at me. "Do you have anything to take up with this court?" he asked.

I rose and went to the lectern. "May it please Your Honor, the grand jury has an indictment to return. It also has a sealed report to deliver to the Court." All eyes swung to the seated grand jury. The foreman stepped forward and delivered the indictment and two locked briefcases containing the "road map." He also handed over the keys to unlock them. And a sealed letter was tendered, a brief one, that asked the judge to transmit the contents of the briefcases to the House Judiciary Committee.

"Anything else?" the judge asked me.

"Due to the length of the trial, conceivably three to

four months, it is the prosecution's view that this case should be specially assigned, Your Honor, and we so recommend." (This meant that Sirica as Chief Judge could assign the case to any of the judges, including himself; later that day he assigned himself.)

In the meeting in his chambers I had asked Judge Sirica for a gag order under Rule 1–27 restraining extra-judicial statements. And I had asked that he tell the grand jury to return in two weeks for further consideration of other matters. I had in mind the possibility of perjury indictments.

The judge so instructed the grand jury, announced the gag rule, and adjourned court. It was over that quickly.

Reporters and lawyers rushed to get their copies of the indictment (but not of the "road map"), and the courtroom emptied.

THE PRESIDENT DID NOT CONTEST the delivery of the "road map" to the House Judiciary Committee. But H. R. Haldeman and Gordon Strachan, two of those indicted, filed a writ of mandamus asking that it not be transmitted. The action of the grand jury was defended by the Special Prosecution Force; the House Judiciary Committee did not ask to become a party to the proceeding even though the report was of inestimable importance to the legislators. Judge Sirica ruled in favor of transmitting the report. The ruling was appealed. Again the Special Prosecution Force defended the grand jury's action; again the Committee did not ask to become a party to the proceeding. Chairman Rodino had concluded—for reasons I could not understand but which were predicated on some theory of separation of powers—that the Committee should not appear in court as a party to the proceeding. Rodino did write Judge Sirica a letter asking that delivery be made. But I could not help but wonder what would have been the course of the Committee's labors without the benefit of the report and the evidence it documented.

Judge Sirica's opinion on transmitting the report said:

On March 1, 1974, in open court, the June 5, 1972 Grand Jury lodged with the Court a sealed Report. The materials comprised in that Report were filed by the Court and ordered held under seal pending further disposition. The materials were accompanied by a two-page document entitled *Report and Recommendation* which is in effect a letter of transmittal describing in general terms the Grand Jury's purpose in preparing and forwarding the Report and the subject matter of its contents. The transmittal memorandum further strongly recommends that accompanying materials be submitted to the Committee on the Judiciary of the House of Representatives for its consideration. The Grand Jury states it has heard evidence that it regards as having a material bearing on matters within the primary jurisdiction of the Committee in its current inquiry, and notes further its belief that it ought now to defer to the House of Representatives for a decision on what action, if any, might be warranted in the circumstances.

After having had an opportunity to familiarize itself with the contents of the Report, the Court invited all counsel who might conceivably have an interest in the matter, without regard to standing, to state their positions concerning disposition. The President's position, through counsel, is that he has no recommendation to make, suggesting that the matter is entirely within the Court's discretion. He has requested that should the Report be released, his counsel have an opportunity to review and copy the materials. The House Judiciary Committee through its Chairman has made a formal request for delivery of the Report materials. The Special Prosecutor has urged on behalf of the Grand Jury that its Report is authorized under law and that the recommendation to forward the Report to the House be honored. Finally, attorneys for seven persons named in an indictment returned by the same June, 1972 Grand Jury on March 1, 1974, just prior to delivery of the Grand Jury Report, have generally objected to any disclosure of the Report, and in one instance recommended that the Report be expunged or returned to the Jury.

Having carefully examined the contents of the Grand Jury Report, the Court is satisfied that there can be no question regarding their materiality to the House Judiciary Committee's investigation. Beyond materiality, of course, it is the Committee's responsibility to determine the significance of the evidence, and the Court offers no opinion as to relevance. . . .

The Report here . . . deprives no one of an official forum in which to respond. It is not a substitute for indictments where indictments might properly issue. It contains no recommendations, advice or statements that infringe on the prerogatives of other branches of government. Indeed, its only recommendation is to the Court, and rather than injuring separation of powers principles, the Jury sustains them by lending its aid to the House in the exercise of that body's constitutional jurisdiction. It renders no moral or social judgments. The Report is a simple and straightforward compilation of information gathered by the Grand Jury, and no more.

Having considered the cases and historical precedents, and noting the absence of a contrary rule in this Circuit, it seems to the Court that it would be unjustified in holding that the Grand Jury was without authority to hand up this Report. The Grand Jury has obviously taken care to assure that its Report contains no objectionable features, and has throughout acted in the interests of fairness. The Grand Jury having thus respected its own limitations and the rights of others, the Court ought to respect the Jury's exercise of its prerogatives.

On appeal from Judge Sirica's order by Haldeman and Strachan, the U.S. Court of Appeals said:

This matter came on to be heard on the separate petitions for writs of prohibition or mandamus filed by Harry R. Haldeman and Gordon C. Strachan, the memorandum in opposition filed by the United States on behalf of the respondent and the grand jury, and the oral arguments of counsel.

This relief by extraordinary writ is sought to prohibit the respondent District Judge from transmitting as recommended by the grand jury, to the House Judiciary Committee a sealed report and accompanying grand jury evidence. The grand jury has characterized that material as bearing upon the inquiry currently being made by that Committee, pursuant to the authorization of the entire House, into possible grounds for impeachment of the President of the United States. The burden of the petitions is that the District Judge has abused his discretion in this instance and should be curbed by the use of our power to issue extraordinary writs. Although it was argued in the District Court that the grand jury was wholly lacking in power to make the report and recommendation in question, now it is said by petitioner Haldeman that it has never been the custom for grand juries in this circuit to issue reports, and that the question is, in any event, not one of law but of policy. Petitioner Strachan at oral argument represented that he was raising no objection to the grand jury's power to report, and that this question is unimportant to the position he asserts.

The position of both petitioners essentially is that the District Judge should not disclose to the Judiciary Committee evidence taken before the grand jury that returned the indictment against petitioners. It has been asserted, both in the District Court and here, that the discretion ordinarily reposed in a trial court to make such disclosure of grand jury proceedings as he deems in the public interest is, by the terms of Rule 6(e) of the Federal Rules of Criminal Procedure, limited to circumstances incidental to judicial proceedings and that impeachment does not fall into that category. Judge Sirica has dealt at length with this contention, as well as the question of the grand jury's power to report, in his filed opinion. We are in general agreement with his handling of these matters, and we feel no necessity to expand his discussion.

We think it of significance that the President of the United States, who is described by all parties as the focus of the report and who presumably would have the greatest interest in its disposition, has interposed no objection to the District Court's action. The interest of the petitioners is said by them to be that of persons under indictment who may be unable to receive a fair trial because of unfavorable publicity likely to result from the disclosure of grand jury evidence to the House Committee. As did the District Judge, we note that this is at best a slender interest on which to support standing to seek the relief in question, but we do not turn the petitions aside on that ground.

We note, as did also the District Judge, that, if the disclosures to the public so feared by petitioners do in fact take place and have the consequences that petitioners predict, they will be free at trial to raise these claims in the light of what has actually happened, and to seek the traditional relief ranging from continuance through change of venue to dismissal of their indictments. It appears to be premature at the least to make their speculations about future prejudice the basis for present employment of our extraordinary writ power. With respect to the substance of those speculations, we cannot be unaware of the fact that the Special Prosecutor has concluded that his interests in successful prosecutions can be reconciled with this transmittal for consideration in the impeachment process—thereby suggesting that the dangers in his estimation are not great. The District Judge who received the indictment, perused the materials accompanying the report, and expressed his general interest in the fairness of the trial over which he will preside later this year, also concluded that it is unlikely that this transmittal will interfere with a fair trial.

We are asked to employ our extraordinary powers now primarily because it is said that the District Judge, being the judge who will later try the indictment and who presently has under his control grand jury evidence which, when and if disclosed publicly, may possibly create a climate of prejudice in which a fair trial may not be possible, should take no chance in this regard and exercise his discretion in favor of the more cautious course.

This claim is, obviously, that we should intervene by prohibition or mandamus to exert our supervisory power as a barrier to a step by the District Judge which, although within the legal limits of his authority, is not sound policy. It almost goes without saying that this is not the kind of abuse of discretion or disregard of law amounting to judicial usurpation for which the extraordinary writs were conceived.

Now, therefore, it is ordered that the petitions' prohibition or mandamus are hereby denied; and it is further ordered that execution of the District Court's order is stayed until 5:00 P.M. March 25, 1974, to permit petitioners to apply to the Supreme Court for such relief as they may deem advisable.

The case was not taken to the U.S. Supreme Court, and on March 25 the "road map" was delivered to the House Judiciary Committee.

chapter seven

We Go to Court

JOHN MITCHELL ROSE to meet me. We had become acquainted when he was Attorney General and I was president of the American Bar Association. "Hello, Leon," he said. I motioned for him to sit down. "Please keep your seat, John." But he remained standing. His appearance was shocking. As Attorney General he had been tough and robust. Now he was pallid and shrunken—an old man.

"You must be very busy these days," he said.

"More so than I wish, John."

I moved on because Judge Sirica's marshal was about to call the court to order. It was a heart-rending moment; I had always liked John Mitchell.

Minutes later Mitchell and his six co-defendants stood in a group before Judge Sirica for their arraignment on the Watergate cover-up indictment: key figures in an unparalleled American tragedy. It was, in a sense, a historic moment. There stood the former chief law enforcement officer of the country, John Mitchell; the former Assistant to the President and his Chief of Staff, Harry R. Haldeman; the former Assistant for Domestic Affairs to the President, John D. Ehrlichman; the Special Counsel to the President, Charles W. Colson; an official of the Committee to Re-elect the President and a former Assistant U.S. Attorney General, Robert C. Mardian; a distinguished Washington attorney who had held many posts of honor in bar associations and who represented the Committee to Re-elect the Presi-

128

dent, Kenneth W. Parkinson*; and a young attorney once staff assistant to Haldeman at the White House and more recently general counsel to the United States Information Agency, Gordon Strachan.

All of them were charged with one count of conspiracy to obstruct justice. In addition, Mitchell was charged with obstruction of justice, perjury, and three counts of making a false declaration. Ehrlichman was charged with obstruction of justice and three counts of making a false declaration. Haldeman was charged with obstruction of justice and three counts of perjury. Strachan was charged with obstruction of justice and one count of making a false declaration.

All pleaded not guilty to all charges. Two days earlier Colson and Ehrlichman had been indicted on charges resulting from the break-in at Dr. Fielding's Los Angeles office. They were arraigned on these indictments also, and they pleaded not guilty to these charges as well.

Judge Sirica released the seven on their own recognizance, directing them to surrender their passports and not to leave the country without permission of the Court. They were to be mugged and fingerprinted at the FBI office.

Mitchell appeared broken. Haldeman and Ehrlichman appeared calm and assured, but I had the impression that their confidence was actually bravado. Colson, who had been ruthless in his dealings with others while serving the President, obviously was a frightened man.

A wry, painful thought struck me: six of the seven men were lawyers; only Haldeman was not.

Four other ranking White House and CREEP officials involved in the cover-up had pleaded guilty to various charges and thus avoided indictment: John Dean, counsel to the President; Herbert Kalmbach, Nixon's personal

---

* When brought to trial, Parkinson was found not guilty.

129

attorney and deputy finance chairman of CREEP; Jeb Stuart Magruder, deputy campaign director of CREEP; Frederick LaRue, deputy director of CREEP and aide to John Mitchell. All four had helped in our investigation. Almost oblivious to the court proceedings, I thought of the four who had pleaded guilty—and I thought of Egil Krogh, who had laid bare his soul in admitting his wrongdoing to me.

I could detect no remorse in the seven before the bar. They were once distinguished because of the high offices they held. They had owned vast power, to use or abuse, and in the end they had abused it. With that power and fame had simple honesty lost its meaning? I thought of the lines from Alexander Pope I had learned as a young man:

> Unblemished, let me live and die unknown.
> Give me an honest fame or give me none.

Now, why were these men indicted? The evidence we had gathered led us to believe this story: CREEP began gearing up for the 1972 presidential election campaign in late 1971. Jeb Magruder was in charge, but he took his orders from John Mitchell, who was still Attorney General but due shortly to take over as Nixon's campaign director.

Mitchell and John Dean, on Egil Krogh's recommendation and with John Ehrlichman's approval, hired Gordon Liddy as general counsel for CREEP. Liddy was to draw up and implement an intelligence plan. He had worked with Krogh and Ehrlichman in the Plumbers group and, with E. Howard Hunt, had organized the Fielding break-in. Liddy called in Hunt to help him at CREEP. In late January, 1972, Liddy met with Mitchell, Dean, and Magruder in Mitchell's office and laid out a plan calling for kidnaping, burglary, electronic surveillance, and the use of prostitutes. Code name: "Gemstone." Estimated cost: a million dollars.

Mitchell rejected the plan and told Liddy to cut it down. The four met again a week later. Liddy had pared the cost to half a million dollars. It was still too much for Mitchell. Finally, on March 30, 1972, Mitchell approved a budget of $250,000. The plan included the bugging of the Democratic National Committee's offices in the Watergate. Magruder kept Gordon Strachan informed about Liddy's plan. Strachan was H. R. Haldeman's White House assistant and liaison to CREEP.

On Memorial Day weekend a crew of burglars directed by Hunt and Liddy broke into DNC headquarters. They photographed documents and placed electronic devices on telephones. Some days later Magruder showed Mitchell the photographs and synopses of wiretap records. Mitchell was not satisfied with what he saw. Liddy said one of the bugs needed working on. On June 17 he and Hunt sent five men back into the DNC to repair the bug and obtain more photographs. They were caught red-handed and arrested. At police headquarters they gave false names, but would be identified as Bernard Barker, Virgilio Gonzalez, Eugenio Martinez, Frank Sturgis, and James McCord. The first four were Miamians with ties to the CIA and anti-Castro groups. Two of them, Barker and Martinez, had been involved with Liddy and Hunt in the Fielding break-in. McCord, a former CIA agent, was the chief of security for CREEP. Among them the men had $2,300 in $100 bills, most of them in sequence.

Mitchell was by now the President's campaign director, having resigned as Attorney General. He, Magruder, Robert Mardian, and Fred LaRue were in Beverly Hills, California, for a series of political meetings when Liddy called Magruder about the arrests. Mitchell told

Mardian to have Liddy get help from Richard Kleindienst, who had replaced Mitchell as Attorney General. Liddy found Kleindienst at Burning Tree Country Club in Maryland. Kleindienst offered no help. If Mitchell wanted to talk to him, he told Liddy, Mitchell should contact him directly.

The next day a statement was released in Mitchell's name in California denying that McCord had been working on CREEP's behalf or with its consent. It intimated that McCord must have been working for business clients of his private security agency. The statement was issued quickly at the suggestion of Haldeman, who was with the President at Key Biscayne.

The California group returned to Washington. Mitchell, Mardian, LaRue, Dean, and Magruder met in Mitchell's apartment. Magruder asked what he should do with the Gemstone papers. Mitchell suggested he have a fire. Magruder burned the Gemstone file in his fireplace. Liddy already had shredded his Gemstone documents. From Florida, Haldeman instructed Strachan to make certain there was nothing politically embarrassing in their White House files. Strachan reported to Dean that he had destroyed DNC wiretap reports and a note from Haldeman to Magruder instructing that CREEP intelligence efforts should be switched from Senator Muskie to Senator McGovern.

Dean met with Liddy to get the complete story. He then reported this information to Ehrlichman. Later the two met with Colson, Hunt's mentor, and Ehrlichman suggested that Hunt leave the country. Dean telephoned Liddy to get the word to Hunt, but Dean and Colson—before Hunt could act—persuaded Ehrlichman to rescind the order. Colson told Dean and Ehrlichman that Hunt's White House safe might contain embarrassing material. Ehrlichman told Dean to have the safe opened.

The safe held an attaché case full of electronic equipment, fake State Department cables which blamed the assassination of a South Vietnamese leader on the Kennedy Administration, a hand gun, and documents concerning the Plumbers' operations, including a psychological profile of Daniel Ellsberg prepared by CIA psychiatrists for Hunt. Ehrlichman told Dean to shred the documents and "deep six" the attaché case full of electronic equipment. The FBI had entered the case and too many people knew about Hunt's safe, Dean argued. He persuaded Ehrlichman that they should turn over all but the politically sensitive documents to FBI agents. To L. Patrick Gray, Acting FBI Director, they delivered the fake cables and the psychological profile of Ellsberg in a sealed envelope. They told Gray the documents were not related to Watergate but were political dynamite and should not see the light of day. Gray destroyed the documents.

Dean had been keeping a close check on Gray. Dean had learned from Mitchell that checks made out to cash and totaling $114,000 had been received by CREEP as campaign contributions from Kenneth Dahlberg, a Republican fund-raiser, and Manuel Ogarrio, a Mexican lawyer. Barker, one of the burglars, had been given the checks to cash to hide the fact that Dahlberg and Ogarrio were the contributors. Barker had deposited the checks in his Florida bank, then had withdrawn the cash and given it to Liddy. Liddy had given the cash to Hugh Sloan, CREEP treasurer and former aide to Haldeman, who placed the bills in his safe. Later, when Sloan was disbursing cash to Liddy to finance his operations, he gave Liddy some of the same bills.

FBI agents had traced the bills in the burglars' possession to Barker's bank account and had learned that Barker had cashed the Dahlberg and Ogarrio checks. That's all they knew, but Gray told Dean that agents were going to interview Dahlberg and Ogarrio. Dean knew that if Dahlberg and Ogarrio talked, the agents would learn that the two men had sent the checks to CREEP as campaign contributions and thus link the burglary to CREEP. Gray also told Dean the agents thought the money might be part of a CIA operation.

Haldeman and Ehrlichman met with Richard Helms, CIA Director, and his assistant, Vernon Walters. Haldeman told Walters to tell Gray that interviewing Ogarrio might uncover CIA operations; since five suspects already had been arrested it would be better not to push the investigation further. Helms said there was no CIA involvement and that he already had told Gray so. But Walters almost immediately followed Haldeman's instructions. Gray said he would work only around the periphery of the case. He issued orders to his agents not to interview Ogarrio.

This circumscribing of the investigation occurred on June 23, six days after the burglars were arrested. For two weeks Gray worried about what he had done. Then, on July 5, he told Walters that Dahlberg and Ogarrio would be interviewed unless the CIA ordered otherwise—in writing. Walters, the next day, gave Gray a memorandum saying there was no CIA interest in the matter. Gray issued an order that Ogarrio be interrogated.

The conspirators' attempt to keep the FBI from investigating the money connection had failed, but they had delayed the inquiry for two weeks, giving themselves time to plan and implement a cover-up story.

It was important to the conspirators that they know what the FBI was doing. Ehrlichman told Gray that Dean would conduct an investigation for the White House. Accordingly, Dean sat in on FBI interviews with White House personnel while Gray kept him informed about what agents were doing elsewhere. Dean also obtained copies of the FBI investigative files, including information on who would be interviewed and the actual interview reports. And finally Gray gave him a memorandum summarizing the state of the inquiry and projecting its direction. Dean showed this to Mitchell, Haldeman, and Ehrlichman.

He also showed the FBI reports to Mardian, CREEP's attorney. Information also was made available to Kenneth Parkinson and Paul O'Brien, attorneys Mardian had retained to handle a civil suit Lawrence O'Brien and the Democrats had filed in connection with the break-in. Dean thus made it possible for both the White House and CREEP to monitor the FBI investigation.

Though Liddy had promised to reveal nothing to investigators, the conspirators recognized that FBI agents would learn that he was the leader of the burglar crew—and that it would be necessary to explain the some $199,000 of CREEP funds he had received after Mitchell had accepted Liddy's budget. Mitchell, Mardian, Magruder, LaRue, and Dean met and decided that Liddy had acted on his own—that Magruder would say that $100,000 had been given to Liddy to finance a protection plan for surrogate speakers, officials who campaigned on behalf of the President, while the remainder was budgeted for security at the coming Republican convention. Herbert Porter, CREEP director of the surrogate speakers program, was selected to corroborate this tale.

Margruder told the cover story to FBI agents on July 20. Before his appearance before the grand jury on August 16 he was coached by Mitchell, and Dean "cross-examined" him to make sure the story would hold up. The story did hold up, but Assistant Attorney General Henry Petersen told Dean that Magruder had gotten through "by the skin of his teeth." Then the grand jury called Magruder back to ask him about entries in his diary indicating the early meetings with Mitchell, Dean, and Liddy when Liddy's intelligence plan was first discussed. Magruder, after conferring with **Mitchell** and Dean, told the grand jury that the first meeting had been cancelled and that a new election law was discussed at the second.

Bolstering the cover story, Mitchell and Ehrlichman told the FBI they knew no more about the Watergate break-in than what they had read in the newspapers. And Mitchell testified before the grand jury that he was not aware of any CREEP intelligence program aimed at the Democrats or of Liddy's political espionage activities.

Magruder, meanwhile, had asked Haldeman for a government job. The President and Haldeman concluded he shouldn't have a post requiring Senate confirmation because his perjuries might come to light under questioning. He became general counsel to the U.S. Information Service. And Mitchell had resigned as CREEP chief to return to New York, saying his wife, Martha, insisted he get out of politics.

Almost from the beginning the conspirators were pressed for money to buy the silence of the burglars. Three days after the break-in Liddy told Mardian and LaRue that those arrested would keep their mouths shut, but that commitments had been made to furnish them bail money, living expenses, and legal fees. LaRue told Liddy the commitments would be honored. The next day Liddy passed this word to Hunt. A few days later Mardian and LaRue met with Dean and Mitchell. They decided to try to pay off the burglars through the CIA.

Dean took the problem to Ehrlichman, who instructed him to see Walters, the CIA assistant director. Dean saw Walters twice and each time Walters refused to involve his agency. Dean reported this refusal to Mitchell, Haldeman, and Ehrlichman.

It was then decided to call in Herbert Kalmbach to get the money to keep the burglars "on the reservation." Kalmbach accepted the assignment and agreed to keep the project secret. A former New York City policeman, Anthony Ulasewicz, who had done investigative work for the White House, was signed on as Kalmbach's courier.

Kalmbach and Ulasewicz went to work on July 1, two weeks after the burglary. They went to comedic lengths to keep their operation secret. Kalmbach used the code name "Novack," Ulasewicz was "Rivers," Hunt was the "Writer," and Mrs. Hunt the "Writer's Wife." The burglars' demands were called the "script" and the payoff money was "laundry." The two men used pay telephones to speak to each other and Ulasewicz left the "laundry" in telephone booths and airport lockers where he could see the pickups. Ulasewicz used so much small change in making phone calls that he finally bought a bus driver's money changer to hold the coins. The payoff money went to Liddy, to Hunt, and to Hunt's wife, who distributed the money among the burglars and their lawyers.

Kalmbach got most of the money from CREEP funds, the remainder from a political contribution. He kept Dean and LaRue informed about his activities and received their approval before making a payment. And he checked Dean's authority with Ehrlichman, who told him to continue at his labors and keep them secret.

The payoffs held the cover-up together to a critical point—September 15. On that day the grand jury returned an indictment naming only Hunt, Liddy, and the five arrested burglars. None of the seven had implicated higher-ups. Dean met with Nixon and Haldeman in the Oval Office. The President congratulated Dean for the skillful way in which he had put his "fingers in the dikes." Haldeman said Watergate had "been kept away from the White House almost completely and from the President totally." No one could construe the grand jury's investigation as a whitewash because the indictment of Hunt and Liddy, former

White House aides, had taken "the edge off white-wash." Dean said that "nothing is going to come crashing down to our surprise" before the November 7 presidential election. But he added that there might be "human problems and we'll keep a close eye on that. . . ."

There were human problems aplenty. Four days after the indictment Ulasewicz delivered $53,000 to Mrs. Hunt, and Kalmbach, who wanted out, made a final accounting and burned his records in an ashtray in Dean's office. He and Ulasewicz had turned over a total of $187,000 to the defendants or their lawyers.

The payoff job then fell to LaRue. He immediately had $20,000 or $25,000 in cash delivered to Hunt's lawyer. This was enough to make a prophet of Dean: nothing came crashing down between the September 15 indictment and the November 7 election. A week after the election, however, Colson got a disturbing phone call from Hunt. Among other things, Hunt said the commitments had not been met and the "stakes are very, very high." He set a November 25 deadline for "the liquidation of everything that's outstanding." Colson recorded the conversation and gave the tape to Dean. Dean made a copy and played it for Haldeman and Ehrlichman at Camp David. Ehrlichman said Mitchell should handle the problem and Dean went to New York and played the tape for Mitchell.

Haldeman controlled a $350,000 cash fund which was in a private safe deposit box in the White House. The money had come from CREEP and, it was said, was to be used for polling. Mitchell told Dean to get Haldeman's approval to use some of the money for payoffs. Haldeman released some of the money and Strachan, his aide, delivered $50,000 to LaRue, who arranged a payment to Hunt through his lawyer. There were more demands. Haldeman released the remainder of the fund and LaRue continued to dole it out.

Hunt, meanwhile, had decided in December to plead guilty to the burglary charge. He wanted assurance from the conspirators that he would receive a minimal sentence. Ehrlichman, Dean, and Colson agreed that Colson could give Hunt a veiled assurance of clemency but no specific commitment. Colson sent a message to Hunt through Hunt's lawyer: Hunt had a good friend in the White House, his children would be cared for (his wife had died in an airplane crash), a year is a long time, and Christmas comes once a year. Hunt took this to mean that he would be pardoned the following Christmas. McCord, who was showing signs of uneasiness, was given a similar assurance.

The next month, January, 1973, Hunt and the Miamians pleaded guilty to the break-in charges. Liddy and McCord stood trial and were found guilty. No one else was incriminated. Sentencing for all was set for March 23. The cover-up was still holding.

But a week before the sentencing date Hunt passed a message to Dean through Hunt's lawyer that he wanted $72,000 for support and $50,000 for attorney's fees; he wanted his affairs in order before sentencing. If this demand were not met, Hunt threatened to review his options and perhaps disclose the "seamy" things he had done for Ehrlichman and the White House. He was referring particularly to the Fielding break-in, which was not yet publicly known.

Dean by now was weary with the intrigue, but he passed on the message to Ehrlichman and, on Ehrlichman's order, to Mitchell. The next day, March 21, he went to see the President and brought him up to date on the cover-up. Talking about Hunt's latest demand, Dean projected that the demands could reach one million dollars over the next two years. The President, it will be recalled, replied, "You could get a million dollars. And you could get it in cash. I know where it could be gotten."

During the conversation, which covered their variety of difficulties, Nixon repeatedly returned to the Hunt demand. He asked, "Don't you, just looking at the immediate problem, don't you have to handle Hunt's financial situation . . . damn soon? After all, you've got to keep the cap on the bottle that much" in the interest of "buying time."

Haldeman joined them. In discussing possible avenues of escape from their problems, Nixon said to Dean, "You had the right plan, let me say, I have no doubts about the right plan before the election. And you handled it just right. You contained it. Now, after the election, we've got to have another plan because we can't have, for four years, we can't have this thing—you're going to be eaten away. We can't do it."

But in the case of Hunt's immediate demand, the President said they had "no choice on Hunt. The Hunt problem . . . ought to be handled" in order to "buy time." The decision to pay Hunt was reaffirmed in a meeting later that day between Nixon, Dean, Haldeman, and Ehrlichman. Dean had told LaRue about the demand and LaRue had notified Mitchell. Mitchell approved payment and that night LaRue arranged to have $75,000 in cash delivered to Hunt's lawyer for Hunt's use. Tension in the White House eased. Krogh, who had been worried that Hunt might talk about the Fielding break-in, was told by Ehrlichman that Hunt now was "stable."

The next day the conspirators resumed their efforts to devise a new strategy to maintain the cover-up in the face of the Senate Watergate Hearings which were to begin in a matter of weeks. Nixon, Haldeman, Ehrlichman, Dean, and Mitchell talked about Dean's preparing a report that could be given to the press or to the Senate Watergate Committee. The report would state that no one in the White House was involved. It was a scheme to protect the President. If, as Ehrlichman said, "some corner of this thing comes unstuck," the President could say he had depended on the report. Haldeman described the plan as a "limited hang out." Ehrlichman called it a "modified limited hang out."

But "this thing" started coming "unstuck" the next day. Judge Sirica disclosed that he had received a letter from McCord which said that the burglars had been forced to remain silent, that perjury had been committed, and that others were involved in the break-in.

Dean decided to confess his part in the cover-up to the Justice Department, which had prosecuted the burglars. Magruder arrived at the same decision, and so did LaRue. The others continued the conspiracy. Mitchell was advised by Nixon to "stonewall it."

Nixon, Haldeman, and Ehrlichman worried over two major problems—Dean, and what he was telling the prosecutors, and how to explain the hush money payoffs. About the money, Nixon told Ehrlichman that everyone should "have a straight damn line: we raised money for a purpose that we thought was perfectly proper."

Dean was to be offered a carrot and a stick. The carrot was to be veiled assurances of clemency by reminding him of the President's affection for him (Mitchell and Magruder already had been told of the President's affection for them). The stick was to be a reminder, as Nixon said, that ". . . there's only one man that could restore him to the ability to practice law in the case things still go wrong."

But Dean refused to talk with Ehrlichman. Instead, he told Nixon that he was going to tell the prosecutors what he knew. The President, Haldeman, and Ehrlichman were aware that Dean already was talking to the prosecutors; Nixon had frequent conversations with Assistant Attorney General Henry Petersen, who kept him abreast of the investigation.

On April 16 Nixon, Haldeman, and Ehrlichman met to devise a "scenario" that would make Dean the villain. Dean, according to their script, had been asked to write a report on Watergate in late March. When he failed to do so, the President became suspicious and instructed Ehrlichman to make an investigation. Ehrlichman did so and discovered that Dean was deeply involved. According to Haldeman, "The scenario works out pretty well."

Dean was asked to sign a letter of resignation; the President would keep it on hand to use as he saw fit. Dean refused; he felt the letter amounted to a confession of his guilt only. He was fired on April 30. Haldeman and Ehrlichman resigned.

Haldeman and then Ehrlichman appeared as witnesses. Haldeman claimed that he had not known before March 21 that the burglars had been paid to remain silent. He also testified that the President had said on March 21 that "it would be wrong" to raise a million dollars for the burglars.

Ehrlichman claimed not to recall whether Dean had informed him in the week following the break-in of Liddy's involvement. He also claimed that he never told Kalmbach to keep his money-raising efforts secret. (He claimed that he never suggested that Kalmbach proceed with the money-raising and that he and Kalmbach had never discussed the purpose for which the money was given to the defendants.)

Later, however, Ehrlichman conceded before the Senate Watergate Committee that Dean had told him two days after the break-in about Liddy's admission that the break-in was the result of Liddy's plan.

The indictment of the seven accused was fifty pages long, but nowhere in it was the President's name mentioned. The "road map" of his involvement went to the House Judiciary Committee. Later we would learn that his involvement was substantially more than we knew when the "road map" was prepared.

THE HALDEMAN-EHRLICHMAN "scenario" to villify John Dean and thus destroy his credibility as a witness was acted out long after the two men left the White House. They played their roles before the Senate Watergate Committee, blaming Dean, as one columnist wrote, for everything done in the White House from the time Richard Nixon was elected President. The volleys at Dean increased in the weeks before the Watergate indictment was returned. Various White House "spokesmen" had unkind words to say about Dean, and White House "summaries" of the March 21, 1973, tape were released to some newsmen. The "summaries" supported the President's contention that Dean was wrong about the thrust of the conversation.

Senator Hugh Scott of Pennsylvania, the Senate Minority Leader, was called to the White House to study "summaries" of the March 21 tape and other Nixon-Dean conversations. Scott publicly announced that the summaries exonerated the President on some aspects of Watergate and provided reasons for charging Dean with perjury in his Senate Watergate Committee testimony.

But we were convinced beyond reasonable doubt that Dean had told the truth about Watergate. Indeed, in trying to obtain material from the White House, I had argued to St. Clair that if Dean were a liar—and the White House had proof of it—we needed the evidence to prevent us from wrongfully indicting Mitchell and the others. Still, the attacks on Dean's veracity continued.

Then, at Dwight Chapin's pretrial hearing, Chapin's attorney raised the question of Dean's credibility; Dean was to be a witness against Chapin. Richard Davis, the young Special Prosecution Force lawyer prosecuting

Chapin, responded that we had found nothing to discredit Dean. Three days later, on a national television show, I affirmed Davis's statement and added that I wouldn't be planning to use Dean as a witness in the anticipated Watergate trial if I considered him a liar. St. Clair countered that White House evidence supported the President, not Dean.

Judge Gerhard Gesell, who was sitting at the Chapin hearing, brought to a temporary halt what was coming to be a public debate. Jacob Stein, Chapin's lawyer, had asked that the indictment against Chapin be dismissed, the trial moved out of Washington, or Dean dismissed as a witness because of my statement. He said I had thrown the "full weight" of the Special Prosecutor's office behind Dean "in a way that utterly distorts our position in this matter. . . ."

Judge Gesell rejected Stein's motion, and said, "First, let's stop all this public debate. The court's control is over its own officers. Obviously I cannot direct the President or Senator Scott to cease doing what they are doing. The President, in a letter to me, indicated his concern about pretrial publicity. I hope every effort will be made by appropriate authorities to stop discussing matters before this court."

Then he called me before the bench. He said he hoped I realized that in the format of a talk show it was difficult not to range beyond the restrictions imposed on discussing pending cases. "I do fear that any further lapse would have very serious consequences," he said, and added, "It seems to me your good sense should keep you off talk shows."

I assured the judge that the greatest of care to obey the court's restrictions would be taken in the future. I added that the publicity made it appear that there was a concerted effort being made to destroy a government witness.

Senator Scott apparently decided he had judged

Dean on insufficient evidence. Now he was quoted in the news media as saying he had been "used" by the White House.

WITH THE WATERGATE INDICTMENT returned and the defendants arraigned, I resumed my struggle for the White House tapes. I explained my position to St. Clair in a letter dated March 12, 1974:

> Now that an indictment has been returned concerning the Watergate cover-up, it is necessary to request access to certain taped conversations and related documents that must be examined and analyzed as the Government prepares for trial. These conversations and documents, identified on the basis of the evidence now known to us, are listed in the enclosed schedule. You indicated in your letters of February 13 and February 27, 1974, that you would consider such requests on a case-by-case basis.
>
> As you know, 27 recordings previously were requested in an effort to assure that the Watergate investigation would be as thorough and as fair as possible. Although the White House did not see fit to make these recordings available for this purpose, I hope that you will understand that this present request is dictated by a different and, if anything, more important reason. Information now available to us indicates that each of the conversations shown on the enclosed schedule contains or is likely to contain evidence that will be relevant and material to the trial of the seven individuals who have been indicted, either as proof of the Government's case or possibly as exculpatory material that must be disclosed to the defense under *Brady* v. *Maryland*. (Of course, if you inform us that certain of the requested conversations

are irrelevant to the trial and you permit someone in this office, as you have in the past, to verify this by listening to them, there will be no need for you to produce those conversations, except as otherwise may be required by a court upon request of defendants.)

In a spirit of cooperation, I made available to you in my letter of January 22, 1974, the information that leads us to believe that the recordings requested in that letter are important. Similar information for a few additional recordings that were not discussed in that letter, but are now requested, is footnoted on the enclosed schedule.

Since most of the requested tapes were initially sought many weeks ago, I assume that the task of locating and examining the material now requested is largely complete. Moreover, if litigation relating to this material becomes necessary, it would be best for everyone concerned that it be initiated promptly in order to avoid any trial delay. Accordingly, I would appreciate a definitive response to this letter at your earliest convenience and, in any event, no later than March 19. Although early production of the requested materials would greatly ease the problems of trial preparation, I would deem it a sufficient response to this letter if you assure us in writing that the President will provide the materials prior to June 15, 1974. If the President wishes to withhold any of the recordings on the ground of irrelevance, I would ask that arrangements be made so that we can complete our review of those recordings prior to June 15, 1974.

The pertinent portion of St. Clair's reply followed a familiar pattern: "As I have told you, your request for production of tapes of Presidential conversations is under active consideration and I will respond thereto as soon as possible. At the moment we have under consideration a request from the House [Judiciary] Committee for much of the same material, the resolution of which will obviously bear on your request. We hope that this matter can be disposed of in the near future. . . ."

A short time later White House "spokesmen" told the news media that the President had turned over "all relevant material" I had requested. I had never publicly countered such White House claims in the past, but now I had James Doyle, our public relations chief, release a prepared statement that I assumed both the President and St. Clair would read or hear. It said in part: "Reports are incorrect in asserting that . . . all relevant materials requested from the White House have been turned over. We have made and will make requests for materials whenever we have sufficient cause to believe that they are relevant to the various investigations that fall under our mandate and which include a number of areas other than Watergate. A number of such requests are outstanding. *If there is noncompliance, subpoenas will be issued in accordance with the agreement between the President and the Special Prosecutor that such matters be submitted to the court. . . .*

There was no public response from the White House. Still, I continued privately to press for the material with both St. Clair and Haig, hoping to avoid litigation which could be damaging to the defendants and people of the country as well. St. Clair would listen, then say he would have to "talk it over with the boss." Haig would say, "Well, it's the feeling here, Leon, that you've got all you need." And, finally, hope died.

On April 11, I sent St. Clair this letter:

On March 12, 1974, I wrote to you requesting access to certain taped conversations and related documents that must be examined and analyzed as the Government prepares for trial in *United States* v. *Mitchell.* If the President declines to produce these materials, which we deem necessary for trial, I am compelled by my responsibilities to seek appropriate judicial process. As I indicated in my letter, any judicial proceedings, if they are necessary, must be initiated promptly in order to avoid unnecessary trial delays.

I have conferred with you several times during the last month about this matter. I have delayed seeking a subpoena in the hope that the President would comply with our request voluntarily. Indeed, I have sought no more at this time than an assurance that the materials would be provided sufficiently in advance of trial to allow thorough preparation. Your latest communication to this office was that we would receive any materials the President produces to the Committee on the Judiciary of the House of Representatives. As to other materials requested by my letter, you have said you would not consider our request until the President decided what to provide the House Judiciary Committee.

I have emphasized repeatedly that our request is in no way tied to the requests of the House Judiciary Committee. The requests are distinguishable both factually and legally. Nevertheless, you have refused to consider them separately, and you have been unable to tell us the criteria that will govern the President's response to our request or to assure us when we will receive a definitive response.

Under these circumstances, in accordance with my responsibilities to secure a prompt and fair trial for the Government and the defendants in *United States* v. *Mitchell,* I am obliged to seek a subpoena for those materials we deem necessary for trial. Accordingly, on Tuesday, April 16, we will apply to Judge Sirica for a trial subpoena pursuant to Rule 17(c) of the Federal Rules of Criminal Procedure.

I did not hear from St. Clair directly until April 15, one day before the deadline I had set, and that was at 6:04 P.M. A letter dated that same day was delivered to my office. It contained nothing new—and no hint of decisive voluntary compliance with our request.

The next day we went to court.

Our motion asked Judge Sirica to direct the President to turn over tape recordings and documents relating to sixty-four conversations between President Nixon and four of his former top aides—Dean, Haldeman, Ehrlichman, and Colson. We explained why the materials were needed and how long and arduously we had tried to obtain them voluntarily. We asked for a subpoena that was returnable before trial "solely for the purpose of preventing any postponement of the trial or delay during the conduct of the trial."

The White House, according to the press, had no comment. The President was vacationing at Key Biscayne. A press spokesman there said only that there would be no comment until White House lawyers had a chance to study the Special Prosecutor's requests.

The press also revived the "Saturday Night Massacre," recalling that the firing of Archibald Cox had resulted from his subpoenaing the nine Watergate tapes. Some saw my move as a similar confrontation. I had no fear of being discharged by the President. I reasoned it would be an act of utter folly on his part. My only fear was time—or rather, the lack of it. I had assumed St. Clair would attack the subpoena; he wouldn't surrender the tapes now after holding desperately to them for so long. And St. Clair was concerned with the House Judiciary Committee, which at last was moving on its impeachment proceeding. If he surrendered the tapes to my subpoena without a fight, how could he be certain their contents wouldn't wind up eventually at the Committee's office? My concern was whether I would be able to get the issue before the Supreme Court—where I expected the final decision to be made —before the Justices adjourned the present session on June 17.

WORKING WITH THE INFORMATION we had provided him in February, John Doar, chief counsel to the House Judiciary Committee, had asked the White House for materials previously supplied to the Special Prosecution Force, including nineteen tape recordings, and all recordings and papers relating to an additional forty-two conversations involving Nixon. After Judge Sirica's hearing on the grand jury "road map," St. Clair delivered to Doar all the materials the White House had produced for us but he did not fill Doar's request for the forty-two presidential conversations. A review of the materials was under way, he wrote Doar—and he made no commitment to deliver anything once the review was completed. Knowing the history of Nixon's relations with the Special Prosecution Force, the Committee, by a vote of 33 to 3, authorized issuance of a subpoena for the materials. The President was to comply by April 30.

Several days after the House and the Special Prosecution Force had made their moves, General Haig called me. "It's important we get together, Leon," he said. It was Friday, April 26, and I was on my way to Waco for the dedication of a new wing to the Baylor University Law School. I told Haig I could return to Washington on Sunday, and we agreed to meet in the

Map Room on Sunday afternoon. Haig was to return to Washington from Camp David by helicopter.

I arrived at the Map Room before Haig did. I knew that Haig believed this would be an important meeting. I also knew that the President must make some sort of response to my subpoena and to the Committee's subpoena with which he had been ordered to comply by Tuesday, April 30—only two days away. I concluded that Haig intended to inform me of the nature of the response—and to do his diplomatic best to persuade me to accept it. I thought I knew what the response would be. For several weeks the White House had been leaking "summaries" of tape recordings and, it will be recalled, had coaxed Senator Scott into examining some to gain his support in the effort to discredit John Dean. It seemed reasonable that the White House would present these "summaries" in lieu of tapes.

Haig arrived, assured as always, and began immediately to try to sell his ideas and channel mine. Both he and Nixon had great confidence in me, Haig said, and believed I was rendering a great service to the country—a flattering preamble to a list of "wrongs" committed by Archibald Cox and some members of my staff. Cox and others had mishandled witnesses, particularly John Dean. The "road map," he intimated, was drawn simply to harm the President and was not the result of credible testimony of witnesses.

"That's unacceptable, Al," I said. "The approach was totally objective."

He indicated that there had been some manipulation of the testimony of some witnesses by one of my prosecutors serving with the grand jury.

"That's rank bunk," I said flatly.

He went on. "I urge you to recheck the testimony of Fred LaRue and others, Leon, with respect to what happened the evening of March 21." He was intimating that one or more of the witnesses on which we relied had changed their story about the payoff to Hunt. He could not hide his strong dislike for Dean. "The tapes after March 21 show Dean to be a subtle but clear liar," he said. I didn't argue; the tapes completely supported Dean's testimony.

He changed stride. The President, he said, was going to take a bold stand which he hoped would turn the course of events. If it failed, he would be prepared to take the consequences; he had no alternative. The President, he said, was not going to deliver the tapes subpoenaed by me and by the Committee. Instead, a résumé of the tapes and a presentation would be delivered.

"I hope you'll study it carefully," he said, "and after you study it, let me have the benefit of any ideas you get. If you study it carefully, and believe it, it might solve some of your problems with the cover-up trial."

Obviously the résumé had been prepared to present Nixon in the best light—and I felt that it also was intended to help Haldeman and Ehrlichman . . . and perhaps even Mitchell. So I told him that my demand for the tapes was not based merely on a need to support the testimony of the prosecution. "The law requires us to obtain them for the use of the defendants. If they're not made available, it may result in a dismissal of the charges against them—and the President would be responsible for the dismissal."

"Well," said Haig, "that's what the defendants' lawyers want, of course." And he repeated, in different language, that he thought the résumé would enable me to resolve the doubts about the President's Watergate involvement and the involvement of some of the defendants. The defendants, he said, would come out "pretty good" in the résumé, particularly Ehrlichman, and the President's disclosures "may give them grounds to avoid the trials you plan." I got the impression that the résumé would not put the defendants in a good light but would try to save them from criminal responsibility. The President's new effort, Haig said, would be "bloody."

This talk of the cover-up defendants was a change of pace for Haig. In the past he had hinted on various occasions that Haldeman and Ehrlichman would plead guilty before a trial began. Apparently, this plan had been dropped because it had become obvious that neither man could plead guilty without giving us information that would implicate the President. Now the President was going to try to help clear them as he tried to clear himself.

I went back to my office with this tentative conclusion: only excerpts of the tapes would be handed over to the Committee and me, and they would discredit Dean in the eyes of the public. If the Special Prosecution Force and the Committee did not accept the résumé, litigation over the tapes would have to follow. In effect, the President was serving notice on me that he would just as soon see the matter delayed over a period of time, with appeals to the Supreme Court. This would be the President's last strong effort, I felt. If it failed, Richard Nixon's fight to hold off impeachment would fail.

THE NEXT DAY, Monday, the President appeared on national television to explain that in answer to the subpoenas he would deliver transcripts of certain recordings rather than the tapes themselves. And the day after the White House sent out to the Committee, the Special Prosecution Force, and the press edited transcripts of thirty-one of the forty-two conversations the Committee had subpoenaed, plus seven transcripts of conversations which had not been requested. The transcripts covered only twenty of the sixty-four taped conversations I had subpoenaed.

On delivery of the edited transcripts, the White House launched a strong public relations campaign whose thrust was that the transcripts did not show the President as guilty of any crimes. This was true; some of the recordings had been so edited and distorted in the transcripts as to change the meaning of important sections of them. Eight of the edited transcripts were of tapes we already had obtained. The President's transcripts of these recordings were so replete with obvious errors that we had no confidence in the remainder.

Some statements were transcribed in such a manner that the substance and tone of the actual conversation were completely misrepresented. Statements on the recordings were omitted in the transcripts. Statements not on the recordings appeared in the transcripts. Statements were attributed to one speaker when they actually were made by another. Statements were marked "unintelligible" in the transcript when they were clear on the tapes.

The President had long maintained that he first learned of the cover-up on March 21, 1973, and from that point began working to bring all the facts to light. But a section of a March 22, 1973, conversation between Nixon, Haldeman, Ehrlichman, Mitchell, and Dean demonstrated the falsity of his claim. That entire section, clear and revealing on the tape, was edited out in the transcript. The deleted material went like this:

PRESIDENT: But the one thing I don't want to do— now let me make this clear. I thought it was a very, very cruel thing as it turned out—although at the time I had to tell *(unintelligible)* what happened to Adams. I don't want it to happen with Watergate—the Watergate matter. I think he made a mistake, but he shouldn't have been sacked, he shouldn't have been. And for that reason I am perfectly willing to—I don't give a shit what happens. I want you all to stonewall it, let them plead the Fifth Amendment, cover up or anything else, if it'll save it—save the plan. That's the whole point. On the other hand, uh, I would prefer, as I said to you, that you do it the other way. And I would particularly prefer to do it that other way if it's going to come out that way anyway. And that my view, that, uh, with the number of jackass people that they've got that they can call, they're going to—the story they get out through leaks, charges, and so forth, and innuendos, will be a hell of a lot worse than the story they're going to get out by just letting it out there.

MITCHELL: Well . . .

PRESIDENT: I don't know. But that's, uh, you know, up to this point, the whole theory has been containment, as you know, John.

MITCHELL: Yeah.

PRESIDENT: And now, now we're shifting. As far as I'm concerned, actually from a personal standpoint, if you weren't making a personal sacrifice—it's unfair—Haldeman and Dean. That's what Eisenhower—that's all he cared about. He only cared about—Christ, "Be sure he was clean." Both in the fund thing and the Adams thing. But I don't look at it that way. And I just—that's the thing I am really concerned with. We're going to protect our people, if we can.

But even with all their inaccuracies, the transcripts fell far short of establishing the President's innocence in the minds of many Americans. Instead of removing suspicion they created doubt. And they created a picture of the Oval Office as a place where men met to intrigue and conspire, denying the White House's grandeur. The profanities and vulgarities on the tapes were not in the transcripts; the explanation "expletive deleted" appeared in the transcripts where the words appeared on the tape. There were so many "expletive deleted" notations that many Americans arrived at the opinion that their President was addicted to vile language and was not the model of clean speech they had thought him to be.

The House Judiciary Committee rejected the transcripts. After a vote of 20 to 18, the Committee advised Nixon he had failed to comply with its subpoena. But the members voted 32 to 5 against citing the President with contempt of Congress.

My response to the transcripts would be given in court.

chapter eight

No Room
for Compromise

In May 1974, the day after the White House issued
the tape transcripts, St. Clair went to Judge Sirica's
court and filed a motion to quash my subpoena for the
sixty-four conversations, citing the President's "executive privilege" as the principal ground of support.

We had kept secret for more than two months the
fact that the grand jury had authorized me to name
Richard Nixon as an unindicted co-conspirator in the
bill of particulars. Now I conferred with my staff on
this question: is this the time to disclose the grand
jury's action? After full discussion I concluded that
in response to St. Clair's motion it was now necessary
to do so. I felt certain that it would strengthen our
right to the tapes, perhaps make our right absolute.

But to reveal Nixon as an unindicted co-conspirator
would provoke publicity damaging to him, and just at
the time when the House Judiciary Committee members
were still smarting from his defiance of their subpoena.
It would be another "bombshell." I didn't want Nixon
and his advisors to be caught unaware when our
reply to St. Clair's motion was filed, so I called Haig,
who was out of town with the President. I told him
I had an important matter to discuss with him and
that I needed to see him Sunday afternoon (we had to
file our brief by Monday afternoon); that St. Clair

should be with him and I would have two members of my staff. I would give him no details. He agreed to the meeting and returned to Washington Saturday night.

Sunday morning he called me for information, but I told him I wouldn't discuss the matter on the telephone. I knew he was to be a guest on *Issues and Answers* that day and St. Clair was to appear on *Meet the Press*. (Both said on the programs that no more tapes would be surrendered to me or to the House Judiciary Committee.)

Haig and I met in the Map Room while St. Clair and my two assistants waited elsewhere. I told Haig about the grand jury action authorizing me, by a vote of 19 to 0, to proceed with naming the President as an unindicted co-conspirator in the bill of particulars. "I had hoped that the Judiciary Committee proceedings would be ended before this was made public," I said. "Of course, it would have to be made public eventually, at a pretrial hearing . . . unless the defendants came in and pleaded guilty."

Haig obviously had not expected this development. Usually poker-faced, he appeared shaken.

"If we can find some way of reaching an accord," I said, "we won't have to divulge the matter now . . . while the Committee is in session."

Haig agreed to talk about the matter with St. Clair and my two assistants. They were called in for a full discussion. St. Clair did not at first grasp the implications of what I was saying, and we had to explain it again. Then he reacted with surprise and concern. We offered this proposal: we would trim our demand for sixty-four conversations to eighteen and such others, if any, that the defendants could show they were entitled to under court decisions; the motion to quash our subpoena would be withdrawn and the fact that the President had been named an unindicted co-conspirator would not need to be divulged until a later date, if then.

"We should explore this with the President," St. Clair said, and Haig nodded in agreement. The meeting broke up.

The next day, Monday, Judge Sirica granted a postponement until the following Friday on the hearing of St. Clair's motion to quash the subpoena. St. Clair announced to the press that he had asked for the postponement, that he was trying to work out an accommodation with me on the delivery of some of the tapes. And Judge Sirica told newsmen: "The continuance was granted for the purpose of facilitating discussions leading to possible compliance with the subpoena. . . ."

But the following day, Tuesday, St. Clair called me in midafternoon and said the President had decided not to release the tapes. The House Judiciary Committee would get nothing else, St. Clair said. The President would announce his decision at 4 P.M.

I had wanted the President to accept my proposal, but his rejection told me something of great importance: *I believed that he had reviewed the eighteen tapes on Monday and confirmed that there was information in them somewhere that would completely destroy his position or bring further harm to Haldeman or Ehrlichman. He was willing to be named publicly as an unindicted co-conspirator rather than let that information be revealed. (I learned later that he had reviewed the tapes on that Monday.)*

Having accepted that, I also accepted that the President was probably the only person now connected with the White House who was aware of the damaging material. I did not think that Haig, for all his advocacy of the President's position, would close his eyes against

159

what he considered clearcut proof of Nixon's criminality. St. Clair on several occasions had said he never listened to the tapes. I believed him: he spoke and acted only when the President instructed him to do so.

When I commented on Nixon's seeming culpability in a Map Room meeting, Haig countered by saying, "I'm not trying to save the President, Leon. I'm trying to save the presidency." I shook my head. "You may be destroying the presidency." He just shrugged his shoulders.

More and more I was becoming convinced that Haig, not Nixon, was making the executive department of government function. The President, it appeared to me, was so enmeshed in Watergate, and spent so much time trying to get untangled from it, that he apparently had few hours left for regular business. Haig, therefore, had many jobs, not the least of which, I once mused, was to try to placate me while helping Nixon frustrate me in my efforts to move forward in the search for truth.

In any event, I called St. Clair after the President's announcement and told him I was still willing to try to keep Nixon's status as an unindicted co-conspirator secret as far as possible. The next day we met with Judge Sirica. St. Clair asked that the hearing on his motion to quash the subpoena be held *in camera* and that the defendants and their attorneys not be advised. I said that I thought the issue between the White House and the Special Prosecution Force on the subpoena could be separated from the defendants' rights under court decisions, but I believed that our answer to the motion to quash would need to be served on the defendants' counsel. Judge Sirica said he wanted to think about it. He set Friday as a date for all counsel to be present to hear the procedure that would be followed. We all met—and after the meeting someone, an attorney representing one of the defendants, or perhaps one of the defendants, leaked to the press that Nixon had been named an unindicted co-conspirator.

YET ANOTHER "bombshell' was dropped after the hearing on St. Clair's motion to quash my subpoena got under way, and this time it burst on me.

When he had filed his motion, St. Clair had asked that the subpoena be quashed on the ground that "executive privilege" gave the President the right to deny me the tapes. I was prepared to fight it out on this issue. But when the motion was argued before Judge Sirica, St. Clair introduced a new element. He took the firm position that I was without standing in the court! As a member of the executive branch I had no right to sue another member of the executive branch and, accordingly, my subpoena should be thrown out.

In view of the agreement I had with the President, through Haig, that I could take the President to court, I considered it incumbent on the President to urge the court to take jurisdiction so that any issue between the President and myself on the right to any evidence could be judicially ascertained. Instead, the President was hiding behind technical jurisdictional questions in an attempt to defeat my right to have a hearing in court.

I considered this a clear violation of our agreement. I was surprised at the move, then angered. Some members of my staff believed for a short while that the abrogation of the agreement would prompt my resignation, and there was some speculation in that regard in the media. I had no thought of resignation. Instead, we fought it out with St. Clair before Judge Sirica, and were sustained. I knew, however, that St. Clair would take the decision to the Court of Appeals. On the day of Judge Sirica's ruling, I sent a report to the Senate

Judiciary Committee, addressed to Senator James Eastland, the chairman. It said:

> When I appeared before your Committee during the hearings on the nomination of the Honorable William B. Saxbe to be Attorney General, I assured the Committee in response to a question by Senator Byrd that I would inform the Committee of any attempt by the President "to circumvent or restrict or limit" the jurisdiction or independence of the Special Prosecutor. I am constrained to advise you and the members of your Committee, consonant with this and other promises made when I testified at hearings before your Committee on the Special Prosecutor bill, that in recent days these events have occurred:
>
> Following the issuance of a subpoena for White House tapes to be used as evidence in the trial of *United States* v. *Mitchell, et al.* (which are needed for prosecution purposes and perhaps to comply with the rights of the defendant under Supreme Court rulings), the President, through his counsel, filed a Motion to Quash the Subpoena.
>
> Because of sensitive matters involved in our response to the Motion to Quash, I joined with White House counsel in urging Judge Sirica to conduct further proceedings *in camera*. After the court determined to hold further proceedings *in camera*, White House counsel for the first time urged the Court to quash the subpoena on the additional ground that the Special Prosecutor had no standing in court because the matter of his obtaining the tapes in question involved "an intra-executive dispute." As stated by counsel for the President in the argument before Judge Sirica, it is the President's contention that he has ultimate

authority to determine when to prosecute, whom to prosecute, and with what evidence to prosecute. Judge Sirica has now ruled and I am released from *in camera* secrecy.

The crucial point is that the President, through his counsel, is challenging my right to bring an action against him to obtain evidence, or differently stated, he contends that I cannot take the President to court. Acceptance of his contention would sharply limit the independence that I consider essential if I am to fulfill my responsibilities as contemplated by the charter establishing this office.

The position thus taken by the President's counsel contravenes the express agreement made with me by General Alexander Haig, after consulting with the President, that if I accepted the position of Special Prosecutor, I would have the right to press legal proceedings against the President if I concluded it was necessary to do so. I so testified in the House Judiciary Committee hearing and in the hearings conducted by your Committee. Thereafter, at the suggestion of members of your Committee, I sent a copy of my testimony on this point to counsel for the President, Mr. J. Fred Buzhardt, who acknowledged its receipt without questioning my testimony. I should add that when my appointment was announced by Acting Attorney General Bork on November 1, 1973, he stated that as a part of my agreement to serve, it was "absolutely clear" that I was "free to go to court to press for additional tapes or Presidential papers," if I deemed it necessary.

You will recall, Mr. Chairman, that when I testified at the session of your Committee on the Special Prosecutor bill, the following exchange took place between us:

THE CHAIRMAN: You are absolutely free to prosecute anyone; is that correct?

MR. JAWORSKI: That is correct. And that is my intention.

THE CHAIRMAN: And that includes the President of the United States?

MR. JAWORSKI: It includes the President of the United States.

THE CHAIRMAN: And you are proceeding that way?

MR. JAWORSKI: I am proceeding that way.

Senator McClellan put the question to me this way:

May I ask you now, do you feel that with your understanding with the White House that you do have the right, irrespective of the legal issues that may be involved—that you have an understanding with them that gives you the right to go to court if you determine that they have documents you want or materials that you feel are essential and necessary in the performance of your duties, and in conducting a thorough investigation and following up with prosecution thereon, you have the right to go to court to raise the issue against the President and against any of his staff with respect to such documents or materials and to contest the question of privilege.

MR. JAWORSKI: I have been assured that right and I intend to exercise it if necessary.

Senator Hruska also examined me on this point as is shown by the following questions and answers:

SENATOR HRUSKA: And it was agreed that there would be no restrictions or limitations, that even as to those items on the tapes, whether they were asked for or not, you would be given access to them. However, if there would occur an impasse on that point on the availability of any material, that there was expressly, without qualification, reserved to you the right to go to the courts. So that it would be at a time when General Haig, acting on behalf of the President, or in his stead, would say no to this particular paper, I don't feel that you should have it, this has high national security and other characteristics, and if you felt constrained to differ with him at that point, you could go to court, and there would be no limitation in that regard?

MR. JAWORSKI: That is a correct statement.

SENATOR HRUSKA: That is your testimony?

MR. JAWORSKI: Yes, sir.

SENATOR HRUSKA: So that by the charter and by your agreement and your discussions you are not to be denied access to the courts. . . .

When my Deputy, Henry S. Ruth, Jr., was testifying in connection with the Special Prosecutor bill, Senator Scott asked him the following question:

SENATOR SCOTT: I imagine it may be clear that he has no doubt of his right to bring action in the courts against the Executive if he so deems it to be proper?

MR. RUTH: Well, Senator, he understands his instructions are to pursue all of the evidence he needs, including to go to court if the evidence is not forthcoming.

At the time of the Saxbe nomination hearings, Senator Byrd exacted the assurance from me that I would "follow the evidence wherever it goes, and if it goes to the Oval Office and to the President himself, I would pursue it with all my vigor." And at the same time, he obtained the assurance from Mr. Saxbe that he would give me full support in matters that were within the performance of my duty even if "there are allegations involving the President."

Of course, I am sure you understand, Mr. Chairman, that I am not for a moment suggesting that the President does not have the right to raise any defenses, such as confidential communications, executive privilege, or the like. It is up to the court, after hearing, to determine whether his defense is sound. But any claim raised by White House counsel on behalf of the President that challenges my right to invoke the judicial process against the President, as I am doing in an effort to obtain these tapes for use at the trial in *U.S.* v. *Mitchell, et al.* would make a farce of the Special Prosecutor's charter and is in contravention of the understanding I had and the members of your Committee apparently had at the time of my appointment.

In a letter to me from Mr. St. Clair, counsel for the President, Mr. St. Clair undertakes to circumvent the clear and unmistakable assurance given me by the President by contending that: "The fact that the President has chosen to resolve this issue by judicial determination and not by a unilateral exercise of his constitutional powers, is evidence of the President's good faith." Of course, under

Mr. St. Clair's approach, this would make the assurance of the right to take the President to Court an idle and empty one. Counsel to the President, by asserting that ultimately I am subject to the President's direction in these matters, is attempting to undercut the independence carefully set forth in the guidelines, which were reissued upon my appointment with the express consent of the President. It is clear to me that you and the members of your Committee who were familiar with the public announcements of the President and the Acting Attorney General, did not construe them in so meaningless a manner (as is evident by the above referred to statements in questions that were propounded to me), and neither did I. To adopt Mr. St. Clair's version would give rise to this anomaly—"The President has no objection to the Special Prosecutor filing his action against him but once filed, the President will stop the Special Prosecutor from proceeding with it by having his counsel move to dismiss on the ground that the Special Prosecutor cannot sue him."

Judge Sirica, in overruling this contention of the President in an opinion made public by the Court this afternoon, pointedly said, "The Special Prosecutor's independence has been affirmed and reaffirmed by the President and his representatives, and a unique guarantee of unfettered operation accorded him: 'The jurisdiction of the Special Prosecutor will not be limited without the President's first consulting with such Members of Congress [the leaders of both Houses and the respective Committees on the Judiciary] and ascertaining that their consensus is in accord with his proposed action.' The President not having so consulted, to the Court's knowledge, his attempt to abridge the Special Prosecutor's independence with the argument that he cannot seek evidence from the President by court process is a nullity and does not defeat the Court's jurisdiction."

Because the members of your Committee exacted from me the promise at the hearings that I would report a development of this nature, I am submitting this letter.

I also expressed my views in a letter to St. Clair:

I am writing to you about the question you raised in litigation before Judge Sirica concerning my authority to seek judicial review of claims of executive privilege made as the basis for withholding evidence that in my judgment is important to the conduct of criminal cases under the jurisdiction that has been assigned me.

In recent days I have had occasion to review my own clear recollections of the several assurances I received on the availability of White House evidence. These assurances were given by General Haig and Acting Attorney General Bork and were re-stated in the presence of J. Fred Buzhardt, Leonard Garment, and Attorney General nominee Saxbe, before I agreed to the urgings of General Haig, speaking for the President, to accept the position of Special Prosecutor. In addition, I have now reviewed the testimony of Mr. Bork and Mr. Saxbe at Senate hearings, and the questions and answers on this issue seem to me to confirm my conviction of the understanding I had. Nothing to the contrary was ever indicated until you filed the *in camera* motion in Judge Sirica's Court. On the contrary, all of the assurances given to me, to the Senate Judiciary Committee, and to the American people were that I would have full access to White House evidence but that in the unlikely event that the President elected to claim executive privilege, I would have the "right and power" to resort to the judicial process to have the courts make the final judgment on the claim of privilege.

Although I am aware that questions of jurisdiction cannot be waived or stipulated by the parties, what is involved here, in my view, is a clear and firm understanding that the President, and his counsel, would, at the very least, not affirmatively contend that an independent special prosecutor is a constitutional impossibility and that he cannot have the authority which the President and the other gentlemen mentioned above publicly stated I was to have when I agreed to accept this appointment.

There is to be further litigation over the trial subpoena in the Watergate criminal case, it is now clear. Should the Court of Appeals or the Supreme Court direct the parties to present arguments on the jurisdictional question you raised in the district court, I fully recognize that we must both present our best judgments on the legal issues. However, if you take the initiative in pressing arguments that I am not entitled to go to court to have these claims of privilege adjudicated, I have no choice but to consider that a second and more profoundly serious breach of the solemn commitments that were made at the time of my appointment.

St. Clair replied:

I note that you do not now base your claim on the terms of the Special Prosecutor's Charter but rather on assurances given you by General Haig and others that you would have the "right and power" to resort to Court for a determination of the issue in the event the President elected to assert executive privilege, as he has done with respect to the subpoena which is the subject of the pending litigation. My inquiries indicate that you were assured that you would be free to litigate disputes with the President and that you would not be given any orders limiting you in any way in presenting arguments in support of your position. These assurances are still in effect.

In all frankness, when I made this argument it never occurred to me, nor apparently did it occur to Mr. Lacovara when he made his reply, that the argument was somehow a violation of commitments made at the time of your appointment. I doubt very much if anyone really focused on this problem at the time of your discussions.

However, as you suggest, the question of jurisdiction of the Court is not something that can be waived or stipulated by the parties. I am sure you would also agree that counsel are under a duty to call the Court's attention to the possible lack of jurisdiction where a question thereof exists. Of course the President may not prevail in this argument and you are perfectly free to contest the issue, as indeed you have done, so far at least, successfully.

Accordingly I cannot see that I have any alternative but to raise the question of the Court's jurisdiction in the forthcoming proceedings. I should also add that of course this is not the only basis on which we believe we should prevail in this litigation.

St. Clair's letter to me was a completely unsatisfactory response to the issue I raised in my letter. I wrote to him:

You take a detached stance on this grave issue by choosing to speak in terms of "in my view," as you did repeatedly in your White House press conference on this subject . . . and by using the qualification "as a lawyer" as you have done in your letter. With due deference, the crucial question is not what "your view" may be but rather what is the President's view. Before we get to the legal stratagems you seek to invoke, we must face the threshold issue of what the President promised the Special Prosecutor on November, 1973, and the good faith reliance of the Special Prosecutor on that promise. "As a lawyer" you have every right to invoke whatever legal concepts are honorably and ethically available to you, but you must know that "as a lawyer" you do not have the right to repudiate the agreement of your client. My agreement was with the President speaking through his Chief of Staff, after the latter had reviewed the terms of the understanding with the President.

Your "view" ignores the disquieting setting that prevailed on November 1. It ignores the White House appeals that were made to me and the repeated assurances and promises, each of which is entirely consistent with the Special Prosecutor's charter. It is not necessary at this point to review all that was said and promised, inasmuch as the substance of these solemn assurances has been recorded in Congressional hearings. Let me simply add that at a time when the nature and extent of the promises to the new Special Prosecutor were fresh on the minds of those who were participants, Acting Attorney General Bork, on November 5, 1973, testified before the House Committee considering a bill for the appointment of an independent Special Prosecutor, as follows: "Although it is anticipated that Mr. Jaworski will receive co-operation from the White House in getting any evidence he feels he needs to conduct investigations and prosecutions, it is clear and understood on all sides that he has the power to use judicial processes to pursue evidence if a disagreement should develop."

Would you please interpret that testimony for me if it does not mean that the Special Prosecutor is entitled to have his contentions passed on by a court. Does it or does it not mean that the Special Prosecutor has a right to be heard on the merits of his subpoena without being foreclosed by a motion that denies him a hearing?

To insist, as you do, that there is nothing to keep me from taking the President to court is rank sophistry if it is to mean no more than what you "as a lawyer" say it means, namely, that upon taking the President to court, his counsel is entitled to urge a motion which under your contention denies the Special Prosecutor access to the courts on the ground that as a member of the Executive Branch he cannot sue the President, also a member of the Executive Branch. Let us take the acknowledgment in your letter in which you state that I "would be free to litigate disputes with the President." This is a meaningless statement if I cannot have the court adjudicate the dispute that exists, as you are contending by your pleadings in court. If your Motion to Quash the Subpoena for the tapes is good, as you contend, on the ground that I cannot proceed against the President, I am deprived of an opportunity to have a judicial ruling on the dispute that exists and, thus, it is evident that I have not been free to litigate with the President.

The inescapable truth is that your contention not

only violates the letter and spirit of my agreement with the President, it also contravenes the charter under which the Special Prosecutor is appointed and serves. The charter plainly provides that the Special Prosecutor "shall have full authority with respect to determining whether or not to contest the assertion of executive privilege or any other testimonial privilege." There is no way for the Special Prosecutor to test the claim of executive privilege asserted by the President if he is to be denied a standing in court to be heard on that subject.

I am not concerned about the contention that jurisdiction cannot be waived or stipulated. Neither am I concerned about our legal position in court. Judge Sirica has upheld our contention, and I know of no reason why the Supreme Court should not also do so. I *am* concerned about the moral and ethical aspect of the point you raise on behalf of the President, to wit, that he is not subject to process I institute against him for evidence needed at trial. Such a contention violates both the charter and the unmistakable understanding I had with General Haig acting for the President and which, according to General Haig, was approved by the President.

As the matter now stands, a principle is involved—not a legal issue. Therefore, I respectfully request that the contents of this letter be made known to the President and that I receive a response from the President, through you, advising me of his personal position.

I felt certain that Nixon was telling St. Clair to pull out all stops to keep the tapes from me. I had hoped that my immediate response might cause St. Clair to reconsider. The Senate Judiciary Committee could not order the President or St. Clair to drop the new element from the lawsuit, of course, but the Committee did vote a resolution, 14 to 1, that I was acting within the scope of my authority in seeking evidence from the President. (Senator Kennedy voted against the resolution, saying it did not go far enough in supporting me.) The resolution was a political and public relations blow at the President, but it had no practical legal effect. Some of the Senators, however, feared that Nixon was entertaining the idea of discharging me, and they felt the resolution could discourage such an attempt.

In a letter both signed, Saxbe and Bork (who was now Solicitor General) asked me to try to find grounds on which to compromise with St. Clair. A similar letter was sent to St. Clair. I wrote back that a "highly significant principle is involved, as I see it—one that involves not only the integrity of others but mine as well —and accordingly there is no room for compromise. . . ." I assumed that their placatory suggestion was the result of being pressured on the one side from the President and on the other by the Senate Judiciary Committee.

As usual, Haig was the man on the tightrope. Nixon depended on him and Haig felt that he had to support the President's position. But he also was fearful I would resign. He called and said, "You've got us all punchy, Leon. You've got Bork uptight."

"He should be uptight in view of the position the White House is taking," I said, "and you should be reading his sworn testimony before the Senate Judiciary Committee—and Saxbe's at the time of his nomination hearing."

"Well," Haig said, "Sirica ruled with you."

He was acting as if he failed to see the principle involved, so I proceeded to explain it.

174

"Leon," he said, "it hurts me that you think I've broken the agreement we made."

"I don't know who broke it, but I know what St. Clair has done and maybe he broke it for you." And I reminded him of the last words he spoke when I agreed to accept the job of Special Prosecutor: "When you make your statements to the news media remember that the key words are that you can take the President to court."

Haig called me again after he had been on a Potomac cruise with the President, and I met with him in the Map Room. He said, "You need to know where we're going and we need to know where you're going." Nothing came of the meeting; he emphasized how much he wanted me to believe that no agreement was broken by him. I gave him little solace.

St. Clair filed his brief with the United States Court of Appeals, asking the court to overrule Judge Sirica. Time was running out for me. Trial of the Watergate defendants had been set for September 9. The Supreme Court was scheduled to recess on June 17. If we didn't get a ruling on the subpoena in short order from the Supreme Court, I could see the Watergate trial being postponed time after time with the government's case deteriorating and, perhaps, never coming to trial at all.

I conferred with my staff about the possibility of bypassing the Court of Appeals and going directly to the Supreme Court. Under a Supreme Court rule, a case can bypass the appeals court and go directly to the Justices if it is of such "imperative public importance as to require immediate settlement." Only twice since World War II had the Supreme Court taken a case under the rule. One case involved a 1947 United Mine Workers strike, the other concerned President Harry S. Truman's seizure of the country's steel mills during the Korean War.

Would the Supreme Court consider our case of such

"imperative public importance as to require immediate settlement"? There was only one way to find out: file a pleading with the Justices asking them to permit us to bypass the Court of Appeals. It would be a drastic step and, if the stratagem failed, our case would be set back seriously. I decided the move had to be made. The pleading to bypass the Court of Appeals was filed.

In the meantime, the Fielding break-in trial was ready to begin, and three members of my staff resigned over what the news media called "The Kleindienst Affair."

chapter nine

Ordinary Fairness

THE CASE OF Richard Kleindienst caused me great concern, consumed much of my time, and drew sharp criticism from some of the news media where the complexities of the case were not fully understood.

Kleindienst had been an Assistant Attorney General in early 1971 when the Justice Department was conducting an antitrust suit against ITT (International Telephone and Telegraph Corporation). John Mitchell was the Attorney General. The Justice Department had lost a round in the suit, which sought to compel ITT to divest itself of three acquisitions—the Grinnel Corporation, the Hartford Fire Insurance Company, and the Canteen Corporation. Kleindienst wanted to appeal the case to a higher court. So did Richard McLaren, chief of the antitrust division of the Department of Justice, and so did Ervin Griswold, the Solicitor General. It was up to Kleindienst to make the decision: he decided to appeal.

On April 19, 1971, the day before the appeal was to be filed, Kleindienst received a telephone call from John Ehrlichman. Ehrlichman said the President had ordered that Kleindienst not appeal the case. Kleindienst was unwilling to take the direction from Ehrlichman. Then the President called Kleindienst.

I know what was said on that April day in 1971, because I listened to the tape recording of the conversation more than two years later. Nixon's voice was angry and his words abusive. It was a tirade in which he threatened to fire McLaren. He directed Kleindienst not to appeal the case. Several times Kleindienst tried to interrupt, but the President wouldn't let him. Nixon concluded his denunciation by expressly directing Kleindienst not to file an appeal and adding, "This is an order!"

Kleindienst took the abuse, but he didn't let the matter rest. He asked the court for a thirty-day extension of time in which to file the appeal. He went to John Mitchell and told him he was going to resign unless the President retracted the order.

Mitchell called on Nixon and told him of Kleindienst's threat to resign. He said that Griswold likely would resign and that McLaren might possibly resign also. A short time later the President withdrew his order and the appeal was filed. In due course the case was settled in the government's favor.

A year later, after Kleindienst had been nominated for Attorney General, there were published reports that the case had been settled because ITT had promised to provide $400,000 for the 1972 Republican National Convention. In his nomination hearing before the Senate Judiciary Committee, Kleindienst refused and failed to answer accurately and fully. He denied that he had ever discussed the ITT cases with the White House staff or advisors to the President. He claimed that he could not recall any conversation about the cases with anyone at the White House.

There was no evidence to the contrary, and Kleindienst became Attorney General. He resigned a year later. The Special Prosecution Force a short time later undertook an investigation of the White House's relations with ITT, focusing particularly on the reported $400,000 payoff. The ITT Task Force was headed from its beginning by a young lawyer, Joseph Connolly, who was inexperienced in criminal law.

While Archibald Cox was still Special Prosecutor,

he had received a call from a prominent Washington attorney, William G. Hundley. Hundley and Kleindienst were friends. Hundley told Cox that Kleindienst had important information about the President and ITT. Cox was eager to receive the information. Kleindienst was invited to the Special Prosecutor's office, where he told Cox about Ehrlichman's call, the President's call, and the subsequent events.

Cox, in a private meeting, told Senators Edward Kennedy and Philip Hart about Kleindienst's revelations. A short time later the New York *Times* published a story about Kleindienst's talks with the President, quoting Cox as the source. Cox candidly admitted to his conversation with the Senators, but said he believed the newspaper obtained its information from sources other than the Senators. Shortly thereafter Kleindienst was called to testify before the grand jury.

Cox's invitation to Kleindienst to come forward, and Kleindienst's response—under the rules of the Special Prosecutor's office—entitled Kleindienst to some consideration in regard to any possible charges that could be brought against him.

The ITT Task Force, and particularly Connolly, was determined to prosecute Kleindienst to the fullest extent possible under the law without regard to his voluntary statement or the unfortunate story in the New York *Times* quoting Cox as its source. I could not ignore those factors, nor could I ignore the fact that Kleindienst, at the time he testified, was subordinate to the President. Had he revealed the pressures which had been brought to bear on him, it would have caused great embarrassment to the President and produced domestic repercussions and possibly international ones. This did not justify Kleindienst's failure to tell the truth, but I could not discard it as being without extenuating value.

I sent the following memorandum to the staff:

179

Discussions have in the past few days convinced me that the matter of the disposition of contemplated charges against Richard Kleindienst cannot be viewed in the light of the ordinary situation. Normally, to be consistent with office policy invoked in other instances, and in the absence of any special considerations, we would be willing to let Kleindienst plead to a one-count felony, either perjury or obstructing the Senate. But there *are* special considerations.

I have reviewed these considerations with you and I am convinced that fair dealing on our part requires that we recognize them. We may differ as to the *degree* of special considerations to be given, but reasonable minds should not differ on the proposition that two separate factual situations giving rise to bases for special consideration do in fact exist.

Both of these exist by virtue of action of my predecessor, wholly unintended by him to create any problem. I could as well have committed both. The fact remains, however, that each must be analyzed and weighed—not with the design of avoiding or circumventing any adverse prosecutorial effect but in light of plain, ordinary fairness.

I am attaching a summary of my notes on my review with Archibald Cox of the first of these situations—over the telephone just yesterday.

The other situation—less grave—is the publicity traced to Cox's remark which Kleindienst and his lawyer insist was the reason that induced Kleindienst's appearance before the grand jury and which appearance, you advised me, worsened his defense. Can we completely write off this consequence and not be concerned as to how it squares with the standards of fairness that permeate our endeavors? Suppose he does go to trial and faces a "worsened situation" because of his grand jury testimony?

This brings me to the conviction that a solution short of a felony plea should be the answer. If the misdemeanor, calling for a mandatory jail sentence, is not the answer because of inapplicability, then let us find another solution. The answer does not lie in the Section 1505 felony charge because both you and I would have given this arrangement to him without the existence of the special considerations alluded to above.

I see no immediate rush in disposing of this matter. I would like for you to address yourselves to the suggestion embodied in the next preceding paragraph. . . .

My notes on the telephone conversation with Archibald Cox went like this:

In conversation with Archibald Cox I asked him to outline to me his contacts with Bill Hundley that brought Kleindienst into the office, and also asked whether anything was held out to Kleindienst or to Hundley. I stated further that I would like to have his thoughts on what consideration if any Kleindienst was entitled to because of his coming in and giving information.

Cox said the matter presented a "terrible problem" and that he was glad that he did not have to pass on it; that it was one of the matters that he was greatly relieved to leave behind.

He stated that although a memorandum had been written by him, it probably did not indicate what was in his mind, and he then described that what was in his mind was that "if Kleindienst came in voluntarily, he certainly was entitled to some consideration." He said that while he may have indicated to Kleindienst or to Hundley that Kleindienst would be given some consideration, he never did say just what it would be.

He also referred to the fact that "unhappily, people who testify on the Hill regard it more as a public relations matter" and that they do not think of its being under oath as in a court. He thought that this should be taken into account in passing judgment on Kleindienst's situation. On the other side of the ledger, he said that he had some feeling that Kleindienst did not act properly when he failed to come forward with information on Liddy's approach to Kleindienst at Burning Tree.

Finally, he said that had he remained as Special Prosecutor he would have regarded Kleindienst's coming forward as being "in his favor"; that he was "on the fence" on the matter when he left— that he had a "sinking feeling" that he might have to come forward with something against Kleindienst but he did not know "just what."

Joseph Connolly had said he would resign if I allowed Kleindienst to plead guilty to anything less than a felony. A misdemeanor plea, he contended, would have an adverse effect on the ITT investigation. I could understand his frustration, but I could not allow it to blur my judgment. He felt frustrated because the ITT investigation had produced only information and suspicion; no evidence had been uncovered that ITT paid or promised to pay money in exchange for a settlement of the antitrust litigation. Moreover, it did not seem likely to me that Kleindienst, who had resisted the order of the President to drop the ITT appeal, would then permit a disposition of the case through bribery. Kleindienst's failure to tell the truth to the Senate Judiciary Committee was all Connolly had to show for his efforts, and he wanted to make the most of it. I sent him a memorandum containing this paragraph:

The premise on which I stand and from which the Kleindienst matter must be judged, in my view, requires an independent assessment of his situation regardless of the "adverse effect of a misdemeanor plea on the ITT investigation" you predict will follow. If fairness to Kleindienst requires that under the peculiar circumstances of his situation a misdemeanor plea is appropriate, he is entitled to it no matter how inimical it may be to the ITT investigation. Conversely, if his factual situation requires a felony plea and the ITT investigation is aided by it, we are entitled to that fall-out without our fairness to Kleindienst being subject to question. Incidentally, I am not as doleful about the effect of a misdemeanor disposition as you are, for reasons I will state should it be concluded that this is the appropriate disposition.

I had asked Philip Lacovara, my counsel, to research the appropriateness of a Kleindienst plea under Section 192 of 2 U.S.C.—a Contempt of Congress Information. He wrote me a memorandum which said in part:

It has been suggested that outstanding criminal charges against Richard Kleindienst be resolved by his pleading to the misdemeanor of contempt of Congress . . . arising out of his appearance before the Senate Judiciary Committee. The basis for such charge would be Kleindienst's false and evasive answers to questions posed by the Committee and his refusal to produce certain papers which had been requested by the Committee. It is a close question whether a charge based on false or evasive answers would be proper under this statute, but I concluded it could be attempted. . . .

It seems to me that the facts with which we must work could arguably be stretched to fit within the "refusal to answer" clause of the contempt statute. Kleindienst's evasiveness, which concerned a highly material matter, pervaded his entire appearance before the Committee, covering several days of testimony. Moreover, as his attorney now admits, Kleindienst participated in the Senate Judiciary Committee hearings with the specific intent not to divulge these relevant facts. We could fairly take the position that this deliberate pervasive evasiveness, designed to obstruct the Senate inquiry, is a "refusal to answer" within section 192. . . .

I recommend that, since a plea under this section is being actively pressed by Kleindienst's counsel, we request a memorandum of law from counsel putting "on the record" (with us) his arguments about the pertinence of section 192 to the facts Kleindienst will acknowledge. . . .

I concluded to charge Kleindienst under that statute, and did so. Connolly resigned, as did two other members of the ITT Task Force. The resignations were well covered in the news media, and some editorialists were quick to criticize my action, not understanding that the charge against Kleindienst was by no means a light misdemeanor but a rather severe one. A New York *Times* editorial contained this misleading paragraph: "By pleading guilty to a misdemeanor, Mr. Kleindienst has bargained his way out of a possible perjury conviction that would have cost him a prison term and certain disbarment. As it is, he is subject to no more than thirty days' imprisonment, and even that penalty may be suspended."

The facts are that even if a person pleads guilty to a felony, the penalty may be suspended and the accused spend no time in prison nor pay any fine. The editorialist should have read the penalty provisions of Section 192 of Title 2:

Every person who having been summoned as a witness by the authority of either House of Congress to give testimony or to produce papers upon any matter under inquiry or concurrent resolution of the two Houses of Congress, or any committee of either House of Congress, willfully makes default, or who, having appeared, refuses to answer any question under inquiry, shall be deemed guilty of a misdemeanor, punishable by a fine of not more than $1,000 nor less than $100 *and imprisonment in a common jail for not less than one month nor more than twelve months.* [Italics added.]

Kleindienst pleaded guilty to the charge before Judge George L. Hart, Jr. He concluded his statement to the court with these words:

I was less than candid [in testimony before the Committee] because I viewed the President's order as ill-conceived, quickly retracted, in my opinion privileged and in any event not the focus of the Committee's inquiry, which dealt with the reasons why the three ITT cases were settled during the summer of 1971.

I was wrong in not having been more candid with the Committee and I sincerely regret it. It is my earnest prayer that in due time history will record that in ITT the Department of Justice fulfilled its charge fairly and fully to enforce the laws of the United States without fear, interference or favor. So far as I know, this is the truth.

In making my guilty plea . . . I do so out of respect for the criminal justice system of the United States and the indisputable fact that the system must have equal application to all. This same respect for the criminal justice system required that I voluntarily and fully cooperate with the Watergate Special Prosecution Force, and I am morally certain that I have done so.

On sentencing Kleindienst, Judge Hart said:

Had the defendant answered accurately and fully the question put to him in this case, it would have reflected great credit on this defendant, but would have reflected discredit upon another individual.

While this was technically a violation of law, it is not the type of violation that reflects a mind bent on deception; rather, it reflects a heart that is too loyal and considerate of the feelings of others.

The presentence report, the Special Prosecutor's report, and the many letters written to the probation office from people in all walks of life, reflect a defendant of the highest integrity throughout his personal and official life; a defendant who has served his country well in war and in peace; a defendant whose family life is above reproach; a defendant who has been and still is universally respected and admired.

It is the judgment of this Court that in Criminal No. 74-256 you be sentenced to one month in the custody of the Attorney General, or his authorized representative, and that you be fined $100. The sentence both as to imprisonment and fine is suspended, and you will be put on one month's unsupervised probation.

Judge Hart was criticized roundly in many quarters, both for the sentence imposed and the remarks he made at the time of sentencing. Some of the criticism spilled over on me, though my office had nothing to do with the sentencing. Judge Hart did not ask us for a recommendation—and I knew well that he would not have permitted us to volunteer one. He had made that clear.

He told me that he received more than four hundred letters of criticism within a few days after the sentencing. "I'm not surprised at receiving critical letters," he said, "but I am surprised that so many are so vicious." I told him I had received several myself.

Despite public criticism and office problems, I believed I had made the right judgment in the Kleindienst case. I was convinced that the prosecutor's function —any prosecutor—is one of taking into consideration all factors having a material bearing on the disposition to be made, not just a few of them.

CHARLES COLSON APPEARED to be an amiable, charming man, but I had learned through our investigations that he had been devious and utterly ruthless with President Nixon's so-called enemies. Although his title had been Special Counsel to the President, he was called the White House "hatchet man," and specialized as a smear artist.

He had appeared so loyal to Nixon that it came as a shock to many when he came to us to plea bargain. He was under indictment in both the Fielding break-in and the Watergate cover-up. His attorneys wanted me to agree to Colson's pleading to a misdemeanor. I told them that under no circumstances would a misdemeanor plea suffice. Colson finally pleaded guilty to a felony: obstruction of justice, in that he devised and implemented "a scheme to defame and destroy the public image and credibility of Daniel Ellsberg and those engaged in the legal defense of Ellsberg." Judge Gesell sentenced him to serve one to three years in prison and fined him $5,000. The remaining charges against him in the two cases were dismissed.

It will be recalled that Colson released a scurrilous and libelous memorandum about an Ellsberg lawyer to some of his favorites in the news media. And, had the Fielding break-in borne fruit, Colson's game plan was to use any material about Ellsberg in the same manner. Colson was further involved in the case in that it was he who obtained the $5,000 that was given to Liddy to finance the crime.

Because of the guilty plea, William Merrill, head of our Plumbers Task Force, was able to use Colson as a witness in the Fielding break-in trial. Merrill also was able to use as a witness Egil Krogh, who had pleaded guilty in the case much earlier than Colson. I was positive that Krogh was truly remorseful for his crime. Colson professed to have embraced Christianity and said he wanted to atone for his sins. Noble as this appeared to be, there was at the time no way of testing his sincerity. I found him difficult to understand and, in my discussions with him, even more difficult to accept as fully truthful. However, he testified openly and competently at the Fielding break-in trial.

Those on trial before Judge Gesell were Ehrlichman, who had approved the break-in; Liddy, who, with Hunt, "masterminded" it; and Bernard Barker and Eugenio Martinez, who had committed the act. Hunt had been immunized by the Justice Department soon after his conviction in the Watergate break-in. David Young, Krogh's co-chairman of the Plumbers, also had been immunized by the Justice Department, and Felipe De Diego, the third burglar, had been granted immunity by the district attorney in Dade County, Florida. Hunt and Young testified for the government.

Merrill built his case as solidly and as painstakingly as a beaver builds a dam. The already threadbare cloak of "national security" was in tatters by the time he completed his arguments. (The tapes showed that "national security" and "executive privilege" were not used in their true meaning at the White House but were cynical devices to hide the facts.) The White House group had long contended that the burglars had exceeded their authorization by breaking into Dr. Fielding's office, implying that the White House group had authorized nothing illegal. But Merrill demolished that public relations ploy. He conceded that the burglars had exceeded their authorization by breaking into the office and by breaking open file cabinets. Their authorization was to conduct a covert operation, he pointed out, which meant a surreptitious entry and a surreptitious search so that Dr. Fielding would not be aware immediately of the crime. But a surreptitious entry and search would have been a violation of Dr. Fielding's civil rights as much as the violent entry and search. Ehrlichman, Merrill established to the jury's satisfaction, had committed perjury to minimize his part in the conspiracy.

All were found guilty on the conspiracy charge, and Ehrlichman was found guilty on three of the four perjury charges. He was sentenced to concurrent prison terms of twenty months to five years. Liddy was sentenced to a prison term of one to three years, with the sentence to run concurrently with the sentence he received in the Watergate break-in. Barker and Martinez received suspended sentences and three years' probation.

My plea bargaining with Colson brought on another spate of criticism of the practice. I issued a brief statement in an interview: "Permitting an accused to plead to charges that the Special Prosecutor concludes, after full consideration of all relevant factors, are commensurate with the gravity of the offense will continue to be the policy of the office. This has been the practice from the time the office was established."

I believed I was standing on solid ground. The American Bar Association, with a membership at the time of 200,000 lawyers, had released a volume combining its approved Standards of Criminal Justice. This monumental work, begun in 1965, was completed in 1973 when approval was given to the final set of standards. The committee in charge of this project was composed of eminent jurists and outstanding members of the bar, including defense counsel and prosecutors. An Advisory Committee on Criminal Trials addressed itself to the practice of plea bargaining. At one point the Committee's report said:

Trials, however, by no means represent the major activity of a prosecutor in the administration of criminal justice in the United States. The vast majority of criminal cases are disposed of without trial as the result of guilty pleas and, if the system as a whole is working properly, *this is as it should be*. The process of plea discussion serves important social interests and is one of the *most important social functions of both prosecution and defense counsel*.

Properly conducted, plea discussion may well produce a result approximating closely, but informally and more swiftly, the result which ought to ensue from a trial, while avoiding most of the undesirable aspects of that ordeal. Disposition without trial of course provides a substantial cost saving to the accused and to the public in terms of the time of lawyers and all other participants. *Although the cost saving alone would not be an appropriate justification for abridging the legal process if it were achieved at the expense of fairness or equal justice, from the standpoint of the objectives of the criminal law, a fair and just disposition of a case without trial is obviously preferable to its disposition by trial, as is true in civil litigation. The speed and certainty of a disposition by plea promotes deterrence, a basic goal of criminal justice.*

I saw nothing unfair in plea bargaining, either to society or to the individual. What was important to me was this: men with whom we had plea bargained were paying their debt to society by serving time in prisons, and were working their way to freedom and rehabilitation. There were some who were brought to the halls of justice because of appropriate plea bargaining. Otherwise they would have escaped the processes of the law. The public had demanded that the story of White House wrongdoing be known, and through the process of justice under law the story was being told. And I knew beyond doubt that were we not practicing fair and just plea bargaining, the full account would never be unfolded.

Most important, successful plea bargaining was bringing us to a point where I could ask the United States Supreme Court to bypass the Court of Appeals and rule on our right to the President's tapes.

chapter ten

Subject to the Law

WE PETITIONED THE Supreme Court for certiorari before judgment and a bypassing of the Court of Appeals on May 24 under the Court's rule of "imperative public importance." We pointed out in our petition that if Judge Sirica's decision were to proceed through normal appellate processes, it was likely that there would be no final decision in the Court of Appeals before the Supreme Court adjourned on June 17. If the Supreme Court did not convene a special term to hear the case, the case could not be heard and judged until late in the year—and the cover-up trial could not be held until the spring of 1975, particularly if Sirica's decision were upheld and the tapes studied and transcribed.

We contended that immediate consideration by the Justices "would not sacrifice any benefits of intermediate appellate review" because the Court of Appeals had ruled on the principal constitutional issues when it ordered the President to deliver to Cox the first nine tapes subpoenaed.

Anticipating St. Clair, we pointed out that Judge Sirica, in ruling for the Special Prosecutor, had "emphasized the 'unique guarantee of unfettered operation' given to the Special Prosecutor, and noted that under these regulations . . . the Special Prosecutor's jurisdiction, which includes express authority to contest claims of executive privilege, cannot be limited without the President's first consulting with the leaders of both houses of Congress and the respective committees on the judiciary and securing their consensus. . . ."

We asked the Court to decide the following: whether the President was subject to a judicial order directing him to comply with a subpoena for evidence in his sole personal control relating to obstruction of justice charges; whether a federal court was bound by the President's claim of executive privilege to withhold such evidence needed for a trial of his own White House aides and party leaders simply because he said release of the evidence was contrary to the public interest; whether a claim of confidentiality as grounds for withholding evidence was valid for discussions that occurred in the course of the criminal conspiracy charged in the cover-up indictment; whether the President had waived any executive privilege he might have had by permitting his aides to testify and by releasing publicly the 1,254 pages of edited transcripts of his Watergate tapes; whether Judge Sirica had ruled properly when he ruled that the subpoenaed tapes were relevant and admissible as evidence.

Four days passed while we waited for a signal from the Court. Then, on May 28, it invited the President to express an opinion on whether the Court should intervene—actually a notice to St. Clair that he could file an opposing brief if he desired. Two days later, on May 30, St. Clair submitted a brief that warned the Court against a "rush to judgment" and asked the Justices to let the Court of Appeals hear the case before they considered it.

To help St. Clair, the President had summoned Professor Charles Alan Wright of the University of Texas Law School. Wright had worked for the President during Cox's suit for the nine tapes, and reportedly had sat in the councils where the decision was made to fire Cox. Now he was back.

"When a case raises the most fundamental issues

of the allocation of power among the three branches of the federal government," their brief said, "it is more important that it be decided wisely than that it be decided hurriedly." On that same point, the brief noted, "Attempts in the past by the Court to make a hurried disposition of an important case have not been among the proudest chapters in the history of the Court."

St. Clair agreed with us on the importance of the tape issue, but argued that it lacked the overwhelming significance needed to justify a departure from the normal appellate processes. "The trial of persons charged with crimes cannot be equated with the magnitude" of the last case that was allowed to bypass the Court of Appeals: President Truman's seizure of the steel mills during the Korean War.

The brief remarked that the Justices already were under grueling pressure with dozens of difficult cases to be decided before the June 17 adjournment; adding to the schedule would not give the Court "the opportunity for careful reflection and deliberation that wise decisions require."

The brief also disputed our contention that the Court of Appeals could shed no further light on the question of executive privilege since it had covered the issue thoroughly in Cox's suit for the nine tapes. "It can only be of value to this Court to have the advantage of a decision by the Court of Appeals applying the rules it announced in the earlier case to the very different facts of the present case," the brief said.

Both sides had their say. I expected a quick decision. I thought the Court would agree to hear the case, but I knew that hope was father of the thought. And the decision was quick. It came the next day, May 31— and it was in our favor!

The order, signed by Chief Justice Warren Burger, said: "The petition for a writ of certiorari to the United

States Court of Appeals for the District of Columbia Circuit and the motion for an expedited schedule are granted. The parties shall exchange and file briefs by 1:00 P.M. on June 21 and any responsive briefs shall be filed by July 1, 1974. Oral argument is set for July 8, 1974, at 10:00 A.M. Each party is allowed one hour for argument." There was a sentence at the bottom of the order, like a postscript. It said: "Mr. Justice Rehnquist took no part in the consideration or decision of this petition." This meant only eight of the nine Justices would decide this historic case.

As customary in decisions to accept a case for argument and ruling, there was no announcement on the vote. The decision must have surprised quite a few lawyers and politicians in Washington because some who were supposed to have inside "political savvy" had been predicting that the Court would turn its head away from us. As for Justice Rehnquist, I assumed he had disqualified himself because he had served in the Justice Department when John Mitchell was Attorney General. With him not participating, the voting on a final decision could come out even—a 4 to 4 tie. In that event, Judge Sirica's decision would stand, and the President would be bound to turn over the tapes.

But would he do it? In the earlier suit with Cox, the President had said publicly that if the case reached the Supreme Court, he would abide by a "definitive" decision. Some of his aides had intimated the same thing, but neither Nixon nor his aides had defined a "definitive" decision. I had reason to believe now that if the vote against him was close he would go on television and tell the people that the presidency should not be impaired by a divided Court. Agony would be piled upon agony.

If he were to win—if the Court should reverse Judge Sirica and support the President's claim to withhold the tapes—it most certainly would strengthen him in

Congress. The House Judiciary Committee could still vote a bill of impeachment, but a victorious President could very well muster support to defeat it on the House floor. Failing that, he could still win in the Senate, where an impeachment trial would be held. At this stage of affairs, his supporters were in the majority in the Senate. Haig, I knew, was optimistic, or appeared to be. "We're not worried about the House and we're not worried about the Senate," he told me. "We've got the votes."

Strong in my mind was the thought that if the President were to win, our chance of obtaining the eighteen taped conversations we deemed most important as evidence would be considerably diminished, perhaps wrecked completely. Without those eighteen tapes, I felt certain that the complete story of the cover-up would never be known.

The Court's decision to accept the case prompted media "think pieces," some of which attributed to me a cunning I did not possess. My argument why the Court should hear the case was not persuasive enough in itself, the reasoning went, but I had calculated that a "Nixon-dominated" Court could not afford to ignore me and run off on vacation without creating public belief that the Justices were callously aiding the President—and neglecting the country's major business. Four of the nine Justices, including Chief Justice Burger, it was pointed out time after time, were Nixon appointees. So the Justices, it was concluded, had made a political rather than a legal decision.

The media also quoted at length various legal scholars who were fascinated by what would be the first Supreme Court test of "executive privilege," as well as St. Clair's contention that my suit against the President was "intra-executive" and the Court had no jurisdiction over such suits. There were even arguments among the scholars as to where and when the term "executive privilege" was first used and by whom. Certainly it was not written into the Constitution. Most agreed it was first used during the Eisenhower Administration in the wake of Senator Joe McCarthy's numerous demands for information from the executive branch. Then Deputy Attorney General William P. Rogers concluded that the President had "uncontrolled discretion" to withhold information from Congress. But a Deputy Attorney General was not the Supreme Court.

St. Clair also introduced a new issue into the case. He asked the Court to supplement the record of the case with the evidence which led the grand jury to name the President a co-conspirator by a 19–0 vote. Without the secret material, he said, the President was being denied potentially favorable evidence, faced a trial without a chance to obtain it, and had fewer rights for pretrial recovery than an ordinary criminal defendant. He said the grand jury material delivered to the House Judiciary Committee did not contain evidence to support the co-conspirator charge. What evidence there was, he said, established that Nixon did not authorize the payment of Howard Hunt's attorney fees. (The grand jury indictment said the $75,000 payment to Hunt was hush money, and the tapes showed that Nixon authorized it.)

We countered that the courts considered grand jury action conclusive as to whether probable cause existed for an indictment. The policy against going behind a grand jury action was even stronger, we said, when the challenge was from an unindicted co-conspirator who was not the focus or target of the indictment and who suffered no direct legal burden because of it. We added that "the opinion of any lawyer that the evidence against his client is not persuasive cannot be accepted as a sufficient reason for granting unrestricted access to grand jury proceedings and exhibits." And we said the House Judiciary Committee did not have all of the grand jury evidence against the President in any event.

I did not believe the Court would concern itself with any issue outside "executive privilege" and the question of jurisdiction. It was obvious to me that we must prove our right to sue the President before the "executive privilege" issue would be considered by the Court. With that in mind, I decided to devote much of my opening statement to the Court in establishing jurisdiction.

Excerpts from St. Clair's major brief reflected White House thinking and showed us how he intended to proceed:

In a very real sense, every case that comes before this Court is unique; but few in the nation's history have cut so close to the heart of the basic constitutional system in which our liberties are rooted.

Thus the stakes are enormously high, from a constitutional standpoint. At the same time, and making the Court's judgment more difficult, the case comes wrapped in the passions of a dramatic conflict which has dominated more than a year. This is a conflict which now has involved all three branches of the Government, and pits their constitutional rights and responsibilities one against another.

Just as the first allegiance of this Court is to the Constitution, the first responsibility of this Court must now be to decide the case before it in a way which preserves the balances that are central to the Constitution.

At its core, this is a case that turns on the separation of powers.

All other considerations are secondary because preserving the integrity of the separation of powers is vital to the preservation of our Constitution as a living body of fundamental law. If the arguments of the Special Prosecutor were to prevail, the constitutional balance would be altered in ways that no one alive today could predict or measure.

The questions presented reach beyond the exigencies of the moment; beyond the interests of any particular criminal prosecution; beyond the needs of any particular Administration.

The extraordinary nature of this case stems partly from the issues directly presented, and partly from the coloration placed on those issues by the surrounding circumstances.

It would do justice neither to the parties nor to the issues if this were treated as just another case, or simply as an appeal from a discovery procedure in a criminal action against private individuals. It is, in fact, an extraordinary proceedings intrinsically related to the move now pending in the Congress to impeach the President of the United States.

In effect, court process is being used as a discovery tool for the impeachment proceedings—proceedings which the Constitution clearly assigns to the Congress, not to the courts. This is so because of the particular relationship which has evolved among the Special Prosecutor, the District Court and the House Judiciary Committee, and because of the impact which any Presidential action with regard to the subpoenas issued would inevitably have on the impeachment proceedings.

As a result of the history of the so-called Watergate cases in the District Court, the Special Prosecutor is well aware that the District Court feels obligated to turn over to the Judiciary Committee any information that might bear on the pending Congressional action.

Thus the effect, whatever the intent, of the discovery procedures being passed by the Special Prosecutor would be to produce evidence for the Congress that the Congress could not obtain by its own procedures.

As a result, there has been a fusion of two entirely different proceedings: one, the criminal proceeding involving various individual defendants, and the other the impeachment proceedings involving the President. The first lies in the courts; the second lies in the Congress.

The Special Prosecutor strengthens this fusion by utilizing the unsubstantiated, unprecedented and clearly unconstitutional device of naming the President as an unindicted co-conspirator in the criminal cases, with the apparent purpose of strengthening his claim to recordings of Presidential conversations as potential evidence in the criminal cases.

The processes—each with an entirely different history, function and structure—have become intertwined, and the resulting confusion, both conceptual and procedural, is manifestly unfair to the President as an individual and harmful to the relationship between his office and the legislative branch.

To place the present events in perspective, it is useful to reflect on how this case would have been viewed in normal times. If there were no impeachment pending, and if the Special Prosecutor used the device of naming the President as an unindicted co-conspirator in order to obtain recordings of private Presidential conversations, on which the President had interposed a claim of executive privilege, the Special Prosecutor's request would be given short shrift.

If this procedure were allowed to go forward,

inevitably affecting the impeachment inquiry, it would represent an expansion of the Court's jurisdiction into the impeachment process that the Constitution assigns solely to the House of Representatives.

Whatever the combination of circumstances producing it, the result would be clear: an expansion of the Court's jurisdiction into a realm that the Constitution clearly prohibits. It follows necessarily that the courts may not be used, either deliberately or inadvertently, as a back-door route to circumvent the constitutional procedures of an impeachment inquiry, and thus be intruded into the political thicket in this most solemn of political processes.

Anyone who has practiced before this Court is familiar with the observation of Justice Holmes that "great cases, like hard cases, make bad law." This is true if the pressures of the moment allow the courts to be swayed from their rigid adherence to great principles; if remedies for the perceived passing needs of the moment are allowed at the expense of those enduring constitutional doctrines that have preserved our system of ordered liberty through the ages.

Of these doctrines, none is more fundamental to our governmental structure itself than the separation of powers—with all of its inherent tensions, with all of its necessary inability to satisfy all people or all institutions all of the time, and yet with the relentless and saving force that it generates toward essential compromise and accommodation over the longer term even if not always in the shorter term.

Often a price has to be paid in the short term in order to preserve the principle of separation of powers, and thereby to preserve the basic constitutional balances in the longer term. The preservation of this principle, the maintenance of these balances, are at stake in the case now before this Court.

The District Court order of May 20, 1974, is an appealable order under 28 U.S.C. 1291, for unless review is granted now the President's claimed right will be irremediably lost. This Court also has jurisdiction to entertain and decide the petition for mandamus transmitted by the Court of Appeals under 28 U.S.C. 1651 because the lower court's decision exceeded that court's jurisdiction.

Under the doctrine of separation of powers, the judiciary is without jurisdiction to intervene in the intra-branch dispute between the President and the Special Prosecutor. The duty to determine whether disclosure of confidential Presidential communications is in the public interest has not been, and cannot be, delegated to the Special Prosecutor.

Under the standards set forth in *Baker* v. *Carr*, 369 U.S. 166 (1962), this intra-branch dispute raises a political question which the Federal courts lack jurisdiction to decide. The District Court does not have the power to substitute its judgment for that of the President on matters exclusively within the President's discretion.

Inherent in the executive power vested in the President under Article II of the Constitution is executive privilege, generally recognized as a derivative of the separation of powers doctrine. The powers traditionally asserted by the other branches support the validity of the claim of confidentiality invoked by the President.

Even if the Court were to determine that a Presidential privilege is subject to judicial supervision, the lower court erred in refusing to quash the subpoena since the Special Prosecutor failed to demonstrate the "unique and compelling need" required by *Nixon* v. *Sirica* . . . to overcome the presumptively valid claim of Presidential privilege. However, even before a determination can be made as to whether the President's assertion of executive privilege is overcome, the Special Prosecutor has the burden of proving that his subpoena meets the requirements of Rule 17(c), Federal Rules of Criminal Procedure.

An analysis of the showing made by the Special Prosecutor in the court below demonstrates that he failed to meet the case law criteria developed to prevent abuse of Rule 17(c). For this reason alone the District Court erred in refusing to squash the subpoena.

The President is not subject to the criminal process whether that process is invoked directly or indirectly. The only constitutional recourse against the President is by impeachment and through the electoral process. The naming of the President as an unindicted co-conspirator by an official body is a nullity which both prejudices the ongoing impeachment proceeding and denies due process to the President. The grand jury's action does not constitute a *prima facie* showing of criminality and is without legal effect to overcome a Presidential claim of executive privilege. . . .

Our brief outlined our contentions. Excerpts show how we intended to proceed.

The narrow issue presented to this Court is whether the President, in a pending prosecution against his former aides and associates being conducted in the name of the United States by a Special Prosecutor not subject to Presidential directions, may withhold material evidence from

203

the Court merely on his assertion that the evidence involves confidential government deliberations.

The Court clearly has jurisdiction to decide this issue. The pending criminal prosecution in which the subpoena *duces tecum* was issued constitutes a "case or controversy," and the Federal courts naturally have the duty and, therefore, the power to determine what evidence is admissible in that prosecution and to require that evidence be produced.

This is only a specific application of the general but fundamental principle of our constitutional system of government that the courts, as the "neutral" branch of government, have been allocated the responsibility to resolve all issues in a controversy properly before them, even though this requires them to determine authoritatively the powers and responsibilities of the other branches.

Any notion that this controversy, arising as it does from the issuance of a subpoena *duces tecum* to the President at the request of the Special Prosecutor, is not justiciable is wholly illusory.

In the context of the most concrete and vital kind of case—the Federal criminal prosecution of former White House officials—the Special Prosecutor, as the attorney for the United States, has resorted to a traditional mechanism to procure evidence for the Government's case at trial. In objecting to the enforcement of the subpoena, the President has raised a classic question of law—a claim of privilege—and the United States, through its counsel and in its sovereign capacity, is opposing that claim. Thus, viewed in practical terms, it would be hard to imagine a controversy more appropriate for judicial resolution.

The fact that this concrete controversy is presented in the context of a dispute between the

President and the Special Prosecutor does not deprive this Court of jurisdiction. Congress has vested in the Attorney General, as the head of the Department of Justice, the exclusive authority to conduct the Government's civil and criminal litigation, including the exclusive authority for securing evidence.

The Attorney General, with the explicit concurrence of the President, has vested that authority with respect to Watergate matters in the Special Prosecutor. These regulations have the force and effect of law, and establish the functional independence of the Special Prosecutor. Accordingly, the Special Prosecutor, representing the sovereign authority of the United States, and the President appear before the Court as adverse parties in the truest sense.

The President himself has ceded any power that he might have had to control the course of the pending prosecution, and it would stand the Constitution on its head to say that this arrangement, if respected and given effect by the courts, violates the "separation of powers."

Throughout our constitutional history the courts, in cases or controversies before them, consistently have exercised final authority to determine when even the highest executive officials are acting in accordance with the Constitution. In fulfilling this basic constitutional function, they have issued appropriate decrees to implement those judicial decisions. The courts have not abjured this responsibility even when the most pressing needs of the nation were at issue.

In applying the fundamental principle, the courts have determined for themselves not only what evidence is admissible in a pending case, but also what evidence must be produced, including whether particular materials are appropriately subject to a claim of executive privilege. Indeed, this Court has squarely rejected the claim that the executive has absolute, unreviewable discretion to withhold documents from the courts.

This case highlights the inherent conflict of interest that is presented when the executive is called upon to produce evidence in a case which calls into question the executive's own action. The President cannot be a proper judge of whether the greater public interest lies in disclosing evidence subpoenaed for trial, when that evidence may have a material bearing on whether he is impeached and will bear heavily on the guilt or innocence of close aides and trusted advisers.

In the framework of this case, where the privilege holder is effectively a third party, the interests of justice as well as the interests of the parties to the pending prosecution require that the courts enter a decree requiring that relevant and unprivileged evidence be produced.

The "produce or dismiss" option that is sometimes allowed to the executive when a claim of executive privilege is overruled merely reflects a remedial accommodation of the requirements of substantive justice and thus has never been available to the executive where the option could not satisfy these requirements.

This is particularly true where the option would make a travesty out of the independent institution of the Special Prosecutor by allowing the President to accomplish indirectly what he cannot do directly—secure the abandonment of the Watergate prosecution.

There is nothing in the status of the President that deprives the courts of their constitutional power to resolve this dispute. The power to issue and enforce a subpoena *duces tecum* against the President was first recognized by Chief Justice Marshall in the Burr case in 1807, in accordance with two fundamental principles of our constitutional system: first, the President, like all executive officials as well as the humblest private citizens, is subject to the rule of law. Indeed, this follows inexorably from his constitutional duty to "take care that the laws be faithfully executed." Second, in the full and impartial administration of justice, the public has a right to every man's evidence.

The persistent refusal of the courts to afford the President an absolute immunity from judicial process is fully supported by the deliberate decision of the Framers to deny him such a privilege.

Although it would be improper for the courts to control the exercise of the President's constitutional discretion, there can be no doubt that the President is subject to a judicial order requiring compliance with a clearly defined legal duty. The crucial jurisdictional factor is not the President's office, or the physical power to secure compliance with judicial orders, but the Court's ability to resolve authoritatively, within the context of a justiciable controversy, the conflicting claims of legal rights and obligations.

The Court is called upon here to adjudicate the obligation of the President, as a citizen of the United States, to cooperate with a criminal prosecution by performing the solely ministerial task of producing specified, unprivileged evidence that he has taken within his sole personal custody.

The qualified executive privilege for confidential intragovernmental deliberations, designed to promote the candid interchange between officials and their aides, exists only to protect the legitimate functioning of government. Thus, the privilege must give way where, as here, it has been abused.

There has been a *prima facie* showing that each of the participants in the subpoenaed conversations, including the President, was a member of a conspiracy to defraud the United States and to obstruct justice as charged in the indictment in the present case, and a further showing that each of the conversations occurred in the course of and in furtherance of the conspiracy. The public purpose underlying the executive privilege for governmental deliberations precludes its application to shield alleged criminality.

But even if a presumptive privilege were to be recognized in this case, the privilege cannot be sustained in the face of the compelling public interest in disclosure. The responsibility of the courts in passing on a claim of executive privilege is, in the first instance, to determine whether the party demanding the evidence has made a *prima facie* showing of a sufficient need to offset the presumptive validity of the executive's claim. The cases have held that the balance should be struck in favor of disclosure only if the showing of need is strong and clear, leaving the courts with a firm conviction that the public interest requires disclosure.

It is difficult to imagine any case where the balance could be clearer than it is on the special facts of this proceeding. The recordings sought are specifically identified, and the relevance of each conversation to the needs of the trial has been established at length.

The conversations are demonstrably important to defining the extent of the conspiracy in terms of time, membership and objectives. On the other hand, since the President has authorized each participant to discuss what he and others have said, and since he repeatedly has summarized his views of the conversations while releasing partial transcripts of a number of them, the public interest in continued confidentiality is vastly diminished.

The District Court's ruling is exceedingly narrow and, thus, almost no incremental damage will be done to the valid interests in assuring future Presidential aides that legitimate advice on matters of policy will be kept secret.

The unusual circumstances of this case—where high government officials are under indictment for conspiracy to defraud the United States and obstruct justice—at once makes it imperative that the trial be conducted on the basis of all relevant evidence and at the same time make it highly unlikely that there will soon be a similar occasion to intrude on the confidentiality of the Executive Branch.

Even if the subpoenaed conversations might once have been covered by a privilege, the privilege has been waived by the President's decision to authorize voluminous testimony and other statements concerning Watergate-related discussions and his recent release of 1,216 pages of transcript, 43 from Presidential conversations dealing with Watergate.

A privilege holder may not make extensive disclosures concerning a subject and then selectively withhold portions that are essential to a complete and impartial record. Here, the President repeatedly has referred to the conversations in support of his own position and even allowed defendant Haldeman access to the recordings after he left public office to aid him in preparing his public testimony.

In the unique circumstances of this case, where

there is no longer any substantial confidentiality on the subject of Watergate because the President has made far-reaching but expurgated disclosures, the Court may use its process to acquire all relevant evidence to lay before a jury.

The District Court, correctly applying the standards established by this Court, found that the Government's showing satisfied the requirements of Rule 17(c) of the Federal Rules of Criminal Procedure that items subpoenaed for use at trial be relevant and evidentiary.

The enforcement of a trial subpoena *duces tecum* is a question for the trial court and is committed to the Court's sound discretion. Absent a showing that the finding by the Court is arbitrary and had no support in the record, the finding must not be disturbed by an appellate court. Here, the Special Prosecutor's analysis of each of the 64 conversations, submitted to the District Court, amply supports that Court's finding. . . .

The Special Prosecution Force staff members had continued working in the other areas of investigation as my top aides and I were preparing for the Supreme Court showdown. The White House legal team also had other fish to fry. While a group prepared the briefs for the Court, St. Clair had been allowed by the House Judiciary Committee to conduct a defense of the President before the Committee members.

The Committee originally had planned to be finished with its inquiry in April. Later it was decided that Committee voting on a bill of impeachment would come no later than July 23. Now, with the Supreme Court accepting our suit against the President, there was a great deal of debate among the members on whether they should wait until after the Court rendered a decision. Some, anticipating that the Court would order the President to relinquish the tapes, wanted to wait until they were available.

I didn't voice my thoughts, but I felt that the Committee had enough evidence to vote an impeachment resolution if the members never heard another tape. It will be recalled that on January 7—only two months after I became Special Prosecutor—the staff at my direction had compiled a secret document outlining President Nixon's involvement in the cover-up. From time to time we had updated and added to that document. Committee investigators, guided by the materials supplied by the grand jury, had gathered almost as much information as we possessed.

St. Clair, while proclaiming the President innocent of any wrongdoing to the Committee, so far as I could ascertain, had not made as much as a dent in the hard evidence. Indeed, by presenting the Committee with edited material and arguing from edited material which the Committee members could not help but know was edited, St. Clair was reflecting the President's apparent contempt for that body. But the hard evidence in the Committee's hands was of the kind that reasonable men had acted upon from the beginning of our legal system.

chapter eleven

The Case Against the President

IN CRIMINAL LAW the rule is well recognized that one who learns of an ongoing criminal conspiracy and casts his lot with the conspirators becomes a member of the conspiracy. Once the existence of a conspiracy is shown, slight evidence may be sufficient to connect a defendant with it. But one does not become a member of a conspiracy simply because of receiving information regarding its nature and scope; he must have what the courts describe as a "stake in the success of the venture." He "must in some sense promote the venture himself, make it his own, have a stake in its outcome. . . ." Although one member of the conspiracy *must* commit an overt act, it is not necessary that every conspirator do so.

The indictment returned in the Watergate cover-up case charged that the defendants conspired to defraud the United States, to obstruct justice, and to make false statements and declarations, all in violation of 18 U.S.C. 371. The indictment charged that the conspiracy continued up until March 1, 1974, the day the indictment was returned. And the grand jury also charged that President Nixon conspired with those indicted.

Furthermore, the available evidence reasonably indicated that the President participated in a conspiracy to violate certain other statutes in addition to those specifically charged in the indictment, and that he fairly could be held culpable, both as a principal and on a theory of vicarious liability, for additional substantive offenses.

There was evidence that the President conspired with others to violate 18 U.S.C. 1503—obstruction of justice—via the means set out in the cover-up indictment. This included paying of funds and offers of clemency and other benefits in order to influence the testimony of witnesses, making and facilitating the making of false statements and declarations, obtaining information about the ongoing investigation from the Justice Department for the purpose of diverting or thwarting the investigation.

There was evidence that the President conspired with others to violate 18 U.S.C. 1623—perjury—which included the President's direct and personal efforts to encourage and facilitate the giving of misleading and false testimony by aides.

There was evidence that the President conspired with others to violate 18 U.S.C. 201(d)—bribery—by directly and indirectly suggesting and impliedly offering something of value—money and clemency in the case of Howard Hunt, clemency and/or a pardon in the case of some aides—with the intent to influence their testimony before grand juries, courts, and congressional committees.

There was evidence that the President conspired with others to violate 18 U.S.C. 1505—obstruction of a congressional committee—by corruptly endeavoring to influence testimony of various persons before the Senate Watergate Committee.

And there was evidence that the President conspired with others to violate 18 U.S.C. 1510—obstruction of a criminal investigation.

At the very least, evidence establishing that President Nixon was a member of a conspiracy that had as its means or objects violations of these statutes would also establish violations by Nixon of the particular statutes themselves on the theory of vicarious liability. In addition, 18 U.S.C. 2 provides that one who "counsels, induces or procures" the commission of an offense such as bribery, obstruction of justice or of a criminal investigation, or perjury by another is "punishable as a principal."

Available evidence was sufficient to make out at least a *prima facie* case that the President participated directly and personally in each of the four most important phases of the conspiracy. Also, he was a major actor in seeking to conceal the existence and later the scope of and participants in the conspiracy, which efforts themselves may be shown to have been part of the original cover-up conspiracy or, possibly, a second illegal conspiracy.

These events appeared to support the charge of the President's direct, affirmative participation in the "hush money" phase of the conspiracy:

1. In his meeting on the morning of March 21, 1973, with Dean and Haldeman, the President learned—if he did not already know—most of the material facts tending to show the involvement of his highest White House and CREEP aides in a cover-up effort that had begun soon after June 17, 1972. He was told that covert cash payments had been made to the defendants and why those payments were made. The President also learned of Howard Hunt's new demand for $120,000 and of the dangers that might be posed for some of the conspirators if Hunt told what he knew about the Fielding or Watergate break-ins or both.

2. The President demonstrated familiarity with the fact that payments had been made, volunteering his own belief that this had been done through a "Cuban Committee;" suggested they might have to be continued; told both Dean and Haldeman that what had already been done could be "handled" in the future, even

though he apparently recognized in suggesting that the "cover" of the "Cuban Committee" be retained for future payments that such payments probably amounted to criminal activity.

3. The President agreed with Dean that some "new strategy" was needed for dealing with the Watergate problem and repeatedly urged that John Mitchell be called to Washington on an urgent basis to sit down with Dean, Haldeman, and Ehrlichman and develop such a new approach. A number of possible strategies were discussed.

4. During the March 21 morning meeting there was considerable discussion about the desirability and feasibility of continuing to make cash payments to the Watergate defendants indefinitely, in terms of the cash cost of such a course, political ramifications, and possible course of grand jury and Congressional inquiries into Watergate. On several occasions Nixon reiterated that it would be possible to get a million dollars for this purpose, he knew where it could be obtained. But there was also discussion about the difficulties of paying the money and the likely futility of such a course.

5. The President and Dean agreed that if a course of paying the defendants indefinitely were followed, Mitchell should probably be the one to arrange for the mechanics of delivering the cash.

6. With respect to Hunt's current demand, the President on at least ten separate occasions during the meeting specifically urged and encouraged that Hunt's "financial problem" be "handled" and "damn soon" in order to "buy time."

7. Following the March 21 morning meeting, Haldeman telephoned Mitchell in New York City. Thereafter, it appeared that Mitchell had a telephone conversation with Fred LaRue. That evening, LaRue caused $75,000 to be delivered to Hunt's attorney.

8. In the late afternoon of March 21, Nixon met with

Dean, Haldeman, and Ehrlichman. Early on in this meeting, the President again raised the question of what should be done about Hunt's demand. Either Haldeman or Ehrlichman told Nixon that Mitchell and LaRue were "aware of it so they know *(inaudible)* feeling is." There was more discussion about whether anything would be done or about the fact that something would be done; inaudibility of the tape made it impossible to determine the precise import of this conversation.

9. The next morning, Haldeman and Ehrlichman learned from Mitchell that Hunt's "problem" had been "taken care of." Ehrlichman apprised Krogh that the possibility of Hunt's talking had been alleviated.

10. Within a short time and well before mid-April, Haldeman informed Nixon that funds had been paid to Hunt.

11. On April 16, in a conversation with Dean, the President acknowledged that because the payment to Hunt was discussed with him and then paid shortly thereafter, that "assumes culpability on that" as to the President himself. This statement followed a discussion initiated by Nixon in which he suggested to Dean that Dean had *not* told him about Hunt's threat on March 21 but only about a need by Hunt for money; Dean corrected Nixon and reminded him of the true chain of events, including Dean's belief that Mitchell had had the money paid. The President expressed approval that the money had been paid "on the Mitchell level."

12. Thereafter, the President did not disclose and, indeed, apparently tried to conceal from Henry Petersen, Chief of the Criminal Division of the Department of Justice, the fact that a specific threat by Hunt was discussed with him on March 21, and that he had learned shortly thereafter that money had in fact been paid in response to this demand.

13. At about the same time, the President had a number of conversations with Haldeman and Ehrlich-

man in which he urged them to get a story together about *their* understanding of the purpose for which cash payments to the defendants had been made. On one occasion the President stated that they did not raise money "to obstruct justice," even though, in fact, the President had previously been informed that those who participated directly in making and authorizing payments did it for that purpose, and that Haldeman and Ehrlichman had well understood that themselves.

14. On June 4, 1973, after the President had listened to a number of his own tape recordings, he stated on several occasions that the biggest problem would be the March 21 meeting, but that Haldeman had been present at that meeting and could "handle" it in his testimony before the Senate Watergate Committee.

15. During and after April, 1973, President Nixon repeatedly made incorrect and misleading public statements about his role and that of others in making cash payments to Watergate defendants. For instance, on May 22, 1973, Nixon claimed that he did not know until March 21 of any efforts to provide the defendants with funds; and on August 15, 1973, he stated that he was not told on March 21 that money had been paid to procure the defendants' silence.

The President himself, while claiming that he did not instruct that Hunt be paid during the March 21 morning meeting, did acknowledge with considerable understatement that the tape recording of that meeting permitted "differing interpretations." The preponderance of the evidence showed at the very least that Nixon repeatedly *urged* that Hunt be paid, expressed the opinion that Hunt should be paid, and possibly instructed that Hunt be paid, in order that the conspirators could "buy time" to work out a new approach to the entire Watergate dilemma. During the meeting the President over and over returned to the subject of Hunt's demand. Not once did the President instruct that this *particular* demand for money by Hunt, made urgent by Hunt's impending sentencing, not be paid. Thus, at the least, the tape showed the President consistently in favor of paying Hunt. Moreover, the tape showed that his views were expressed throughout the conversation, including the final time the subject arose in the meeting.

Even if Hunt had never been paid on March 21, the undisputed facts still showed that the President learned on March 21 of past payments of cash for silence and understood that this was illegal; that he knew that at the least Dean, Haldeman, Ehrlichman, Mitchell, La-Rue, and Kalmbach were involved; that Nixon never took steps to inform prosecutorial authorities about these facts but instead suggested to Dean and others (and pursued) a course of "handling" those payments through a "cover" story; that Nixon had numerous discussions with Haldeman and Ehrlichman in which he urged them to get together a consistent innocent story about their role in making cash payments, and urged them to be sure others would also "stick to their line" of an innocent purpose; that after he learned that La-Rue had confessed, Nixon instructed that Kalmbach be informed so that Kalmbach could meet LaRue's testimony; and that Nixon subsequently made false exculpatory statements concerning his own knowledge of hush money payments and the timing of such knowledge.

In an ordinary case, the President's actions would probably be sufficient to permit a jury to conclude beyond a reasonable doubt that he joined the conspiracy. Moreover, the President's role as Haldeman's and Ehrlichman's superior must also be considered. For instance, in a case in which Haldeman and Ehrlichman were corporate vice-presidents and the President was their chief executive officer, the President's role in "ratifying" past action and assisting his subordinates in concealing it or minimizing their criminal liability for it

218

takes on special importance because he would be playing a "part" in the conspiracy that only he could play. That is, when the chief executive officer learns of the conspiracy he is in a position to end it immediately, but by permitting it to continue and encouraging it to continue he is, in effect, joining up with the conspiracy, and lending his status and resources to it. At the least, that is what occurred in the case of Richard Nixon.

The following events appeared to support the charge of the President's direct, affirmative participation in the "clemency" phase of the conspiracy.

1. In January, 1973, probably on the afternoon of January 4, the President had a conversation with Charles Colson in which, according to Nixon, he told Colson that of course clemency could be considered for Howard Hunt on the basis of his family situation. On January 3 and January 4, Colson had two meetings with Hunt's attorney. Prior to these meetings Colson discussed with Dean and Ehrlichman their desire to have Colson reassure Hunt concerning the length of time Hunt would have to spend in jail, without making any overt assurances.

2. Prior to March 21 the President had a conversation with Dean in which he asked if the defendants were keeping quiet because they expected or anticipated clemency; Dean replied in the affirmative. Nixon asked Dean what he would advise on that; Dean said the situation would have to be watched closely.

3. At the March 21 meeting Nixon learned from Dean that Colson had conveyed assurances to Hunt via his lawyer that Hunt would get out of jail within a year—or at least that Hunt so understood it. Nixon took no issue with this information; indeed, later in the meeting he told Haldeman that, "as you know," Colson had "gone around" on the "clemency thing" with Hunt *and the others."*

4. During the March 21 morning meeting, the Presi-

dent at no point repudiated or rejected the propriety of the offer of clemency about which he had heard. He did agree with Dean's assessment that clemency was "impossible" prior to the 1974 elections, as a political matter, and questioned Dean about Dean's view that it would never be possible because of the political climate.

5. On March 27 Haldeman mentioned to Nixon that a "super-panel" idea had merit because it would drag out the Watergate matter and, since Nixon could pardon everyone anyway after the 1974 elections, no one involved would be subject to more than a two-year prison liability.

6. On April 14 Nixon, Haldeman, and Ehrlichman determined that the latter should meet separately with John Mitchell and Jeb Magruder. Nixon urged Ehrlichman to convey the President's "personal affection" for Magruder in meeting with him, since "that's the way the so-called clemency thing's got to be handled. . . ." Later that day, after meeting with Mitchell, Ehrlichman reported back to the President that he had delivered the message of good feelings to Mitchell (as the tape of their conversation shows he did), to which the President responded, "He got that, huh?" Then, as Ehrlichman was leaving to meet with Magruder, Nixon reiterated, "Be sure you convey my warm sentiments." Later Ehrlichman reported back that he had done exactly that.

7. On the evening of April 14 Nixon had an extensive conversation with Ehrlichman about how Ehrlichman might "move" John Dean around from a position of putting the blame on Haldeman and Ehrlichman. The President stated that the only thing that was likely to be effective in such an effort was Dean's realization that if things went wrong "down the road" only the President could pardon Dean and restore Dean's license to practice law.

8. On April 15 the President told Dean that he, the President, had been "foolish" to talk to Colson about clemency for Hunt.

9. Throughout his conversations with Henry Petersen, the President failed to communicate his knowledge that Colson (whether on Nixon's instructions or in excess of them) had in effect promised clemency to Hunt, and failed to tell Petersen that Nixon himself had urged Ehrlichman to make veiled offers of clemency to others.

10. After April, 1973, the President repeatedly made incorrect and misleading public statements concerning his knowledge of this aspect of the conspiracy. For instance, on May 22, 1973, he said: "At no time did I . . . know about any offer of executive clemency for the Watergate defendants." On August 15 he again stated that he had consistently maintained a position that "under no circumstances could executive clemency be considered for those who participated in the Watergate break-in." And on November 17, 1973, he claimed that although clemency was raised with him by his aides, he "turned it down whenever it was suggested."

To prove the President's complicity in this phase of the conspiracy it would be unnecessary to show that he personally made or authorized explicit "offers" of executive clemency to anyone in exchange for their continued silence. It would be sufficient to show that with knowledge that such attempts had been made or might be made as a part of the effort to conceal the truth from coming out in Congressional hearings or before a grand jury the President took affirmative action to assist these attempts and to conceal that they were being taken by others. But, as indicated in the ten points, the proof appeared to be much stronger.

The following events appeared probative of the President's involvement in that phase of the conspiracy that comprehended the counseling, facilitating, assisting, and giving of false statements and testimony:

1. In a public press conference on August 29, 1972, the President falsely stated that Dean had conducted an investigation for the White House into Watergate and had found that no one there was involved.

2. Prior to March 21, 1973, the President learned from Dean that Gordon Strachan had "stonewalled" investigators in a number of interviews and would continue to do so.

3. On March 21 the President learned from Dean precise details of how Egil Krogh and Jeb Magruder had committed perjury. He then conversed with Dean about the question of whether Krogh's perjury could be detected and/or proved.

4. On the morning of March 21, in a discussion of the possibility of White House aides going to the grand jury and of the risk of perjury in case that route were pursued, the President told Haldeman: "If you're asked, you just say: 'I don't remember, I can't recall, I can't give an answer to that, that I can recall.' "

5. On March 27 Haldeman suggested to the President that Magruder might be convinced to admit that he'd perjured himself on his "own motive" and not as a part of a conspiracy.

6. In the period April 14–17, Nixon urged Haldeman and Ehrlichman to get their story together about what their position would be on the payment of hush money since they would have to acknowledge, at the least, that they knew money was being paid. On another occasion, Nixon stressed that the important thing was for all those involved in raising money to "stick to their line" that money was not paid to obstruct justice; this was after Haldeman and Ehrlichman had told the President that those directly involved *had* done it for that purpose, and that Haldeman and Ehrlichman had

also known that. On more than one occasion, Nixon actually *urged* that such a story be put forth.

7. In the period April 14–17, Nixon had a number of conversations with Haldeman and Ehrlichman about what Strachan would testify to; among other things, the President urged that Strachan be given full information about Magruder's testimony in order to be prepared to "meet those points."

8. On the evening of April 17, in a conversation with Haldeman and Ehrlichman, Nixon learned that Dean had in fact told Kalmbach the purpose of the raising of cash funds for the Watergate defendants, and that Dean had admitted this to Ehrlichman. The President replied: "You can say that he told you on such and such a date that he did *not* tell Herb Kalmbach what the money was for."

9. On the morning of April 16 Nixon led Dean through his "recollections" of a number of important events. Nixon's "recollections" did not coincide with the facts. In some (but not all) instances Dean corrected the President. For example, the President suggested that he had called Dean in for a "report" in late March, but Dean corrected him as to the timing and circumstances of that meeting. The President claimed Dean had told him only "fragmentary" information on March 21 and had not told him about Hunt's explicit threat to "bring Ehrlichman to his knees." The President repeatedly told Dean to be sure to testify that he had asked Dean for an investigation and that Dean had reported back that no one was involved. The President several times mentioned that the problem with clemency seemed to be "solely Mitchell," to which Dean replied that it was primarily Ehrlichman and Colson.

10. The President made a variety of false and misleading public statements beginning on April 17 and

continuing into November, 1973, concerning his own knowledge and involvement in Watergate-related events.

11. On June 4, 1973, the President had a number of conversations with Ron Ziegler and Alexander Haig in which he stated that Haldeman could "handle" the March 21 meeting in testimony. Subsequently, Haldeman testified before the Senate Watergate Committee in line with the President's assurances and suggestions.

12. Throughout his conversations in late April with Henry Petersen, Nixon made a number of false or misleading statements concerning what had happened on March 21, and what he was or was not doing with the information Petersen was giving him about testimony being obtained by the United States Attorney.

Based on the above events, it could reasonably be said that President Nixon participated in the "perjury" phase of the conspiracy in a variety of different ways, each of which was designed to further the aims of the conspiracy: to "cut losses" at as low a level as possible, to conceal the scope of and participants in the conspiracy, and to minimize the liability of Nixon's own closest White House aides.

First, Nixon learned in intimate detail that a number of persons had committed perjury and that at least two had suborned perjury, and he failed at any time to bring this to the attention of prosecutive authorities.

Second, a jury could certainly conclude beyond a reasonable doubt that the President himself urged various individuals to commit perjury: his "perjury lesson" to Haldeman and Dean on March 21, his April 16 meeting with Dean in which it could be concluded that he coached Dean about what to say regarding Dean's contacts with him, and his encouragement of Haldeman and Ehrlichman to develop an exculpatory version of money payments.

Third, President Nixon was instrumental in developing a "cover story" respecting the collapse of the conspiracy in late March and April, 1973, which he himself put out in several public statements, beginning on April 17. The cover story implied that the President had broken the case after an investigation by Dean and Ehrlichman and then had "gotten in" the Justice Department and given them his information. It was demonstrably false.

Fourth, the President made false exculpatory statements about his knowledge of hush money and clemency and his attempts to get the truth out.

Fifth, Nixon directly made false and misleading statements to Henry Petersen. These statements could constitute an offense under 18 U.S.C. 1001 and current caselaw interpreting it. On and after April 15, the President began a series of almost daily meetings with Petersen in which he repeatedly sought information from Petersen about the process of the investigation and, especially, about the evidence being accumulated against Haldeman and Ehrlichman. On one occasion, according to Petersen's testimony, the President pressed for a written summary of the evidence against his top aides, but Petersen refused to provide it. Nixon justified his desire for this detailed information on the ground that he needed it to make policy and to decide what should be done about Haldeman and Ehrlichman. In truth, Nixon was passing on information to Haldeman and Ehrlichman in order to protect their interests and those of his other aides, and himself.

In addition to giving information to Haldeman and Ehrlichman to help them protect themselves, Nixon had them pass along information to three others for the protection of those other persons—all of whom in fact were eventually charged with conspiracy or alleged to be co-conspirators in the cover-up indictment.

Nixon instructed Haldeman and Ehrlichman to notify Kalmbach that LaRue had made a full confession to the prosecutors. This was before Kalmbach's grand jury appearance in April, 1973. Ehrlichman did in fact have a telephone conversation with Kalmbach and inform him of this fact.

Nixon discussed on the evening of April 14 the need to give Colson a "touch up" on events that were rapidly unfolding in order to permit Colson not to perjure himself unnecessarily.

It was obvious from the White House transcripts that Nixon, on April 14-16, was extraordinarily concerned with the testimony that Gordon Strachan would provide with respect to allegations by Jeb Magruder that wiretap material from the Democratic National Headquarters had been sent to Strachan for transmission to Haldeman. On the 14th Haldeman reported to Nixon that Magruder was cooperating with the prosecution, that Magruder had implicated Strachan in connection with the transmission of wiretap materials to the White House, and that, according to Magruder, Fred LaRue was also about to confess. Repeatedly over the next several days Nixon, Haldeman, and Ehrlichman discussed how to handle this situation. The President urged that Ehrlichman meet with Magruder "particularly" to learn "what the hell he is going to say about Strachan," agreed that what Strachan "has to do is prove the defense that . . . meets these points," and advised that Ehrlichman "should put Strachan through a little wringer there" in preparing him for interrogation by the prosecutors.

It seemed reasonable that all of the following actions by the President would be admissible evidence of his participation in a conspiracy to obstruct justice and to obstruct a criminal investigation.

1. Between March 21 and April 15, 1973, the President made no attempt to bring to the attention of legitimate prosecutorial authorities the knowledge he had acquired that was highly incriminating of many of his top aides and associates. In fact, Nixon on two

occasions authorized public statements in his name of his continued confidence in Dean, who had admitted to Nixon that he was involved in obstruction of justice.

2. On March 21 and 22, 1973, the President and his aides decided upon development of a new strategy to continue the Watergate cover-up. It included preparation of a written report focusing on pre-June 17 events that was plainly calculated both to conceal highly incriminating evidence of post-June 17 activities and to influence the Senate Watergate Committee and grand jury investigations by narrowing their likely ground of inquiry, thus preserving White House officials including Haldeman, Ehrlichman, Dean, Strachan, and Colson from criminal liability.

3. After McCord's letter of March 23, Dean's reluctance to produce a written report, and the beginning of the collapse of the cover-up, the President was a central figure in developing a different, "limited hang out" strategy to accord with the developing situation. This included sacrificing Mitchell and Magruder and developing a cover story that Nixon himself had broken the case by ordering an investigation by Dean and then Ehrlichman—the results of which, the President would claim, he then made available to the Justice Department. Even after Dean began cooperating with the prosecution, this false scenario, rehearsed over and over again in the presidential transcripts, was put into effect in Nixon's April 17 public statement and adhered to thereafter.

4. After it became clear that Dean was talking to the prosecutors, Nixon had numerous conversations with Henry Petersen during which he obtained information from Petersen that he then related to Haldeman and Ehrlichman in order that they could be prepared to meet the testimony of those who were cooperating. Nixon misled Petersen during these conversations. He also attempted to prevent Petersen from giving Dean

immunity for fear that Dean could then testify fully against Haldeman, Ehrlichman, and possibly Nixon himself.

We had subpoenaed the sixty-four conversations because we needed them to round out the evidence in the cover-up case before it went to trial—and to provide the defendants with any exculpatory information they might find in them.

Strong in my mind was the President's refusal to supply us with the eighteen conversations I considered most vital to our case after he had reviewed them—electing instead to be exposed as an unindicted co-conspirator in the bill of particulars. Somewhere in those conversations, I was sure, was evidence even more damaging than that we had compiled, but it would never be made public if we lost our case before the Supreme Court.

chapter twelve

"We Affirm
the Order..."

I HAD EXPECTED the entrance to the Supreme Court building would be crowded—that we would be inundated by newspersons and photographers—but the scene was more frantic than I anticipated. As I got out of my car we were swamped. Along with the reporters was a crowd of several hundred young people, many of whom were shouting encouragement.

"Go, Leon!" someone shouted. Another yelled: "Go, America." Then, louder than all the others: "Shut up! That's partisan."

Ahead of me, I saw that St. Clair and his group were making slow progress to the building and they were being applauded. But with the commanding words about partisanship the clapping also faded away.

Most of the young people I saw had sleeping bags. An aide told me that they had been sleeping on the lawn since Saturday night—this was Monday morning, July 8—to be sure they got a chance at seats inside. One large young man pushed through the crowd and thrust an autograph book at me. I smiled him away. "I'll see you later," I said. I was nervous. "Fractious" is the Texas word for it—an itching eagerness for the action to begin. I am always that way before a court case, and have been since my first trial. The hard part of my mind was on the suit and the impending debate, but on another level of consciousness I was absorbing sights and sounds around me.

"Ninety degrees already, and it's not ten o'clock," someone said. Fragments of other conversations came to me. "Fifty lawyers won seats in a lottery." "Justice Rehnquist conducted the lottery." "Reporters from everywhere." "Twenty seats for Congress." "These people? They'll herd 'em in a couple of dozen at a time and a group gets to stay five minutes." I was thinking that the Court, in a most unusual move, had directed that both sides would have ninety minutes for argument. I had never heard of the Court allowing so much time for oral arguments. And then we were inside the building and the Courtroom, blessing the welcoming coolness. An aide whispered excitedly, "Look who's sitting next to Mrs. Jaworski!" Seated next to Jeannette was H. R. Haldeman, his hair much longer than he had worn it before his resignation. Our son Joseph, a trial lawyer in his own right, was seated on the other side of Jeannette.

I was to take the laboring oar and open our argument for an hour. St. Clair then was to argue some seventy-five minutes. My counsel, Philip Lacovara, was to have thirty minutes to close, then St. Clair would have fifteen minutes more. Lacovara and I seated ourselves at the counsel table facing the bench. Nine empty chairs behind the bench awaited the Justices. I looked around me. There are larger rooms than this, I thought, but it seems as massive as a great cathedral. Even the dark rows of seats emitted strength, as if they had been carved from an imperishable wood. I had argued several cases before this Court and I was struck as always by the vast dignity this room imposed on one. It seemed that every face around me reflected the sudden knowledge that this was a *special* place where the honor of the Republic reposed. The double row of pillars on each side of the room appeared capable of holding up every good intention every Administration had entertained.

"Oyez! Oyez! Oyez!" The marshal was calling the Court into session—and my nervousness disappeared. Behind the bench, from behind heavy burgundy drapes, emerged the eight black-robed Justices who would hear the case. All of these months, I thought suddenly, it has been like walking on a tightrope, hoping I wouldn't slip, hoping someone else wouldn't make me slip, knowing always that a slip would be pounced on, knowing that a slip could cost it all. The timing had been everything, I thought. An unseen hand had arranged the timetable so that even the grinding frustrations had played their part in delaying or hastening the action so that all of us, at this precise moment in time, had reached this rendezvous with history.

The preliminaries were over and I was on my feet facing the Justices. To my far left was Justice Powell. Then Justice Marshall. Justice Stewart. Justice Douglas. Chief Justice Burger in the center. Then Justice Brennan, Justice White, Justice Blackmun. Justices Rehnquist's chair was empty.

From the beginning it was obvious the Justices were not in the frame of mind for oratory. They wanted facts and the truths on which they rested. In my allotted hour I was interrupted 115 times. There was no opportunity for a sustained, orderly presentation. Despite the lack of continuity in my argument, I was grateful for the interruptions; they enabled me to explain more fully salient points, and they allowed the Justices to get a better grasp on the ramifications of the issues.

I began by referring to the cover-up indictment, the grand jury's vote that the President should be named as an unindicted co-conspirator, our subpoena for the tapes, St. Clair's motion to quash it, and the subsequent revelation of the President's unindicted co-conspirator status.

A Justice broke in. "I don't see the relevancy of the fact that the grand jury indicted the President as a co-conspirator to the legal issue as to the duty to deliver pursuant to the subpoena that you are asking for."

While I was explaining the relevancy, Justice Stewart broke in, and he was followed by Justices White, Brennan, and Powell. We thrashed out the question, and I made my point that the President's status made evidence admissible for trial that otherwise would not be, that his being named a co-conspirator made absolute our right to the tapes. In the process I also was striking a blow at executive privilege since in this instance it was a shield for wrongdoing in the White House, and not a safeguard for military or diplomatic secrets.

I made my way through the questions to bear down on what I considered to be the heart of our argument:

Now enmeshed in almost 500 pages of briefs, when boiled down, this case really presents one fundamental issue—who is to be the arbiter of what the Constitution says? Basically this is not a novel question—although the factual situation involved is, of course, unprecedented.

There are corollary questions, to be sure. But in the end, after the rounds have been made, we return to face these glaring facts that I want to review briefly for a final answer.

In refusing to produce the evidence sought by a subpoena *duces tecum* in the criminal trial of the seven defendants—among them former chief aides and devotees—the President invokes the provisions of the Constitution. His counsel's brief is replete with references to the Constitution as justifying his position. And in his public statements, as we all know, the President has embraced the Constitution as offering him support for his refusal to supply the subpoenaed tapes.

Now, the President may be right in how he reads the Constitution. But he may also be wrong. And if he is wrong, who is there to tell him so? And if there is no one, then the President, of course, is free to pursue his course of erroneous interpretations. What then becomes of our constitutional form of government?

So when counsel for the President in his brief states that this case goes to the heart of our basic constitutional system, we agree. Because in our view, this nation's constitutional form of government is in serious jeopardy if the President, any President, is to say that the Constitution means what he says it does, and that there is no one, not even the Supreme Court, to tell him otherwise. . . .

St. Clair argued that the Court had no right to rule on the case because, he said, it was a political procedure from which the Court was excluded. The House Judiciary Committee's impeachment inquiry was political, he said, and because the Special Prosecutor would give the tapes to the Committee, the entire process was political.

Justice Marshall said, "The only thing before us is as to whether or not the subpoena should issue. That's not political . . . you are still saying the absolute privilege to decide what shall be released and what shall not be released is vested in one person and nobody can question it. . . ."

St. Clair replied, "Insofar as it relates to the presidential conversations, that is correct, sir. . . ."

In his rebuttal argument, Lacovara said, "This is a criminal proceeding, a federal criminal case against six defendants. A subpoena has been issued to obtain evidence for use at the trial. . . .

"The Court cannot escape the fact that this is a trial of tremendous national importance, but a trial that was brought to a head without regard to the impeachment inquiry. . . ."

St. Clair wound up by saying that the Court should stay its hand until after the impeachment hearing had run its course. "Because those are political decisions being made, they should not bear the burden, either way, of a judicial decision."

Said Justice Douglas: "Well, under that theory, all the criminal trials that are going on should stop, then."

Said St. Clair: "That would not be the first time, Mr. Justice Douglas, that a criminal trial was delayed. And in balancing the importance to this nation, I would suggest that this is clearly indicated."

Time was up. As I made my way out of the Court I recalled a pointed statement by Justice Douglas. I had been emphasizing that St. Clair's briefs time and time again insisted that only the President was the proper one to interpret the Constitution on executive privilege.

Justice Douglas had leaned forward and said, "Well, we start with a Constitution that does not contain the words 'executive privilege'—is that right?"

"That is right, sir," I had said.

And Justice Douglas had said, "So why don't we go on from there. . . ."

As I neared the sunlight I didn't feel exhilarated, but I did feel that we would prevail, and by a one-sided margin. I was preoccupied with my thoughts, and some of the reporters who greeted me outside later said that I appeared unhappy. St. Clair, some wrote, appeared triumphant. I may have been a bit brusque when the press questioned me.

Suddenly a crowd was around me at the top of the

steps. The applause was loud, and someone shouted, "Way to go, Leon!" I had to push my way through, and then the crowd followed me. A few people were knocked down in the crush, and one man tumbled into a flowerbed. Finally I made it to my car. "Law students," said one of the staff. "Ninety percent of those people are law students."

PETER KRIENDLER, my executive assistant, had labored long and hard during the preparation of the Supreme Court briefs, and he had been a tower of strength to me. So, of course, had Henry Ruth and Lacovara. But there was another whom I leaned on heavily— James Neal, a brilliant trial lawyer in his early forties whom I had induced to rejoin the Special Prosecution Force. He was a country boy from Tennessee who had attended the University of Wyoming on a football scholarship, then had taken his law degrees from Vanderbilt and Georgetown. He was practicing law in Washington when Robert Kennedy, then Attorney General, lured him into the Department of Justice. Neal prosecuted big cases around the country, including the government's case against James Hoffa, the labor leader. He was a United States District Attorney in Nashville for a couple of years, then resigned in 1966 to practice law and teach at Vanderbilt.

During his years with the Department of Justice he had become acquainted with Archibald Cox. When Cox became Special Prosecutor in May, 1973, Neal was among the first assistants he hired. He agreed to work for two weeks; he stayed, heading up the Watergate Task Force until he resigned the day before the "Saturday Night Massacre." He had accomplished much. Under his direction the Watergate Task Force had dealt with Dean, Magruder, and LaRue, thoroughly vacuum-cleaning them of facts about Watergate and the cover-up. At his leave-taking from the Force, Neal had told Cox he would consider returning to try a major case.

I had talked with him about his heading the staff of the cover-up case. He was interested. "But I'm going to be chief counsel," he said. "You make the policy, of course, but I'm going to make the courtroom decisions."

"You wouldn't be worth your salt if you didn't want it that way," I said.

Still he was hesitant. "It could be delicate," he said. "There might be some resentment."

Ben-Veniste had commanded the Watergate Task Force since Neal's departure, and both he and Jill Volner had worked hard and well. Both expected to have key prosecuting roles in the cover-up trial. Neal had been gone while they had labored through many a hearing, had pieced together many a pattern of evidence. Good lawyers that they were, they wanted to have a say in how the trial would be conducted. I understood that—and I appreciated all of their efforts. But the lawyer in charge of the cover-up trial had to be one experienced both as a prosecutor and a defender, and Neal was the man.

But the resentment, as he had suggested, was there. And Neal said he wouldn't return without the goodwill of the staff. I didn't want the situation to simmer into a boil, so finally I made the decision. To the Force I explained that either Neal was going to head the staff in the cover-up trial or I was; if Neal didn't accept the assignment, nobody on the Watergate Task Force would get it.

Ruth then came to my aid and helped persuade Neal to come aboard. And Neal, as charming and thoughtful as he was brilliant, in short order won total support, assigning Ben-Veniste and Volner to important jobs in the fray that we anticipated.

Now he was counseling me during the agonizing period of waiting for the Supreme Court decision. If the Court decided against us, Neal's wait to try the cover-up case could last as long as a year.

AT THE HOUSE JUDICIARY COMMITTEE, Doar and Jenner had done an excellent job of gluing together the thousands of lines of testimony into a tapestry of evidence. And Rodino, the chairman, had so skillfully guided the Committee over the investigatory shoals that he had won the respect of all who were aware of his problems.

The question of timing had been resolved; the Committee would hold public hearings, beginning on July 24, and the nation would witness the debate via television. The Committee, then, was prepared to vote on a resolution or resolutions of impeachment without benefit of additional information. Doar, I felt sure, was as certain as I that the strongest evidence against Nixon and some of his top aides rested somewhere in the eighteen tapes I had designated as the most important of the sixty-four subpoenaed. But the pressures to begin the hearings had been tremendous, and Doar obviously had felt that he had evidence enough.

Then, on July 23—the day before the Committee's public hearings were to start—the Special Prosecution Force was notified that the Supreme Court would render its decision at 9:30 A.M. the next day. However desperately they tried to remain unmoved by the Court's announcement, the Committee members, in my opinion, would be affected to some degree by the decision.

OUTSIDE THE SUPREME COURT, the crowd had seemed larger than when we had tried the case—and louder. Inside the packed hall the tension was palpable. Neal and Lacovara were with me at our table. St. Clair was

237

not at his table; others were there to take the decision. St. Clair was with Haig and other presidential aides in San Clemente. The President, I had strong reason to believe, was waiting confidently for news of victory, though I had no idea of what St. Clair had been telling him. Further, I had reason to believe that Nixon, from the time he first concluded not to surrender the tapes, was confident that his assertion of executive privilege would prevail. We would soon know.

The marshal cried out his ancient command. The drapes parted and the eight Justices took their seats. At that moment my body relaxed. I felt relieved of a burden. All will be well, I thought. I waited for Chief Justice Burger to read the Court's opinion, which he had written.

But he spoke first in memory of former Chief Justice Earl Warren, who had just died in California. It was fitting, I thought, that he should speak of Warren on this day, in this Court. Warren had been both praised and demeaned because he stretched and broadened the power of the Court. Today Chief Justice Burger and his associates would plow virgin land.

He began reading the opinion in a clear and expressive manner, speaking with an assurance, it appeared, that the holding he was revealing was sound and just. The case, he said, had satisfied all the legal requirements to be properly before the Court; and then he launched into the Court's opinion on the question of the Special Prosecutor's right to sue the President.

In the District Court [he said] the President's counsel argued that the court lacked jurisdiction to issue the subpoena because the matter was an intra-branch dispute between a subordinate and superior officer of the Executive Branch and hence not subject to judicial resolution. That argument has been renewed in this Court. . . .

The President's counsel argues that the federal courts should not intrude into areas committed to the other branches of Government. He views the present dispute as essentially a "jurisdictional" dispute between two congressional committees. Since the Executive Branch has exclusive authority and absolute discretion to decide whether to prosecute a case, it is contended that a President's decision is final in determining what evidence is to be used in a given criminal case. . . .

The mere assertion of a claim of an "intra-branch dispute," without more, has never operated to defeat federal jurisdiction; justiciability does not depend on such a surface inquiry . . . the Court has observed, "courts must look behind names that symbolize the parties to determine whether a justiciable case or controversy is presented. . . ."

Congress has vested in the Attorney General the power to conduct the criminal litigation of the United States Government. It has also vested in him the power to appoint subordinate officers to assist him in the discharge of his duties . . . the Attorney General had delegated the authority to represent the United States in these particular matters to a Special Prosecutor with unique authority and tenure. The regulation gives the Special Prosecutor explicit power to contest the invocation of executive privilege in the process of seeking evidence deemed relevant to the performance of these specially delegated duties. So long as this regulation is extant it has the force of law. . . .

Here . . . it is theoretically possible for the Attorney General to amend or revoke the regulation defining the Special Prosecutor's authority. But he has not done so. So long as this regulation remains in force the Executive Branch is bound by it, and indeed the United States as the sovereign composed of the three branches is bound by it. . . .

In light of the uniqueness of the setting in which the conflict arises, the fact that both parties are officers of the Executive Branch cannot be viewed as a barrier to justiciability. It would be inconsistent with the applicable law and regulation, and the unique facts of this case to conclude other than that the Special Prosecutor has standing to bring this action and that a justiciable controversy is presented for decision. . . .

We had the right and the power to sue the President! St. Clair had challenged our subpoena on the ground that the Special Prosecutor had failed to satisfy the requirements of Rule 17(c), which governs the issuance of subpoenas in federal criminal cases. Chief Justice Burger said:

If we sustained this challenge, there would be no occasion to reach the claim of privilege asserted with respect to the subpoenaed material. . . .

In order to require production prior to trial, the moving party must show that the documents are evidentiary and relevant; that they are not otherwise procurable reasonably in advance of trial by exercise of due diligence; that the party cannot properly prepare for trial without such production and inspection in advance of trial and that the failure to obtain such inspection may tend unreasonably to delay the trial; that the application is made in good faith and is not intended as a general "fishing expedition." . . .

The Special Prosecutor, in order to carry his burden, must clear three hurdles: relevancy, admissibility, specificity . . . and we are unwilling to conclude that the District Court erred in the evaluation of the Special Prosecutor's showing under Rule 17(c).

With respect to many of the tapes, the Special Prosecutor offered the sworn testimony or statements of one or more of the participants in the conversations as to what was said at the time. As for the remainder of the tapes, the identity of the participants and the time and place of the conversations, taken in their total context, permit a rational inference that at least part of the conversations relate to the offenses charged in the indictment. . . .

We also conclude there was a sufficient preliminary showing that each of the subpoenaed tapes contains evidence admissible with respect to the offenses charged in the indictment. The most cogent objection to the admissibility of the taped conversations here at issue is that they are a collection of out-of-court statements by declarants who will not be subjected to cross-examination and that the statements are therefore inadmissible hearsay. Here, however, most of the tapes apparently contain conversations to which one or more of the defendants named in the indictment were party . . . accordingly, we cannot say that the District Court erred in authorizing the issuance of the subpoena *duces tecum*. . . .

From our examination of the materials submitted by the Special Prosecutor to the District Court in support of his motion for the subpoena, we are persuaded that the District Court's denial of the President's motion to quash the subpoena was consistent with Rule 17(c). . . .

We also conclude that the Special Prosecutor has made a sufficient showing to justify a subpoena for production *before* trial. The subpoenaed materials are not available from any other source, and

their examination and processing should not await
trial in the circumstances shown. . . .

Our subpoena was justified!

While the Chief Justsice had been reading smoothly,
placing emphasis where emphasis was needed, it seemed
to me that now he took a longer pause than usual, as
if he were preparing to explain the heart of the matter.

We turn to the claim that the subpoena should
be quashed because it demands "confidential conversations between a President and his close advisors that it would be inconsistent with the public
interest to produce." The first contention is a
broad claim that the separation of powers doctrine
precludes judicial review of a President's claim
of privilege. The second contention is that if he
does not prevail on the claim of absolute privilege,
the court should hold as a matter of constitutional
law that the privilege prevails over the subpoena
duces tecum.

In the performance of assigned constitutional
duties each branch of the Government must initially interpret the Constitution, and the interpretation of its powers by any branch is due great
respect from the others. The President's counsel,
as we have noted, reads the Constitution as providing an absolute privilege of confidentiality for
all presidential communications. Many decisions of
this Court, however, have unequivocally reaffirmed
the holding of *Marbury* v. *Madison* . . . that "it is
emphatically the province and duty of the judicial
department to say what the law is."

No holding of the Court has defined the scope
of judicial power specifically relating to the enforcement of a subpoena for confidential presidential communications for use in a criminal prosecu-

tion, but other exercises of powers by the Executive Branch and the Legislative Branch have been found invalid as in conflict with the Constitution. . . .

Since this Court has consistently exercised the power to construe and delineate claims arising under express powers, it must follow that the Court has authority to interpret claims with respect to powers alleged to derive from enumerated powers. . . .

Notwithstanding the deference each branch must accord the others, the "judicial power of the United States" vested in the federal courts . . . by the Constitution can no more be shared with the Executive Branch than the Chief Executive, for example, can share with the Judiciary the veto power, or the Congress share with the Judiciary the power to override a presidential veto. Any other conclusion would be contrary to the basic concept of separation of powers and the checks and balances that flow from the scheme of a tripartite government. . . .

We therefore reaffirm that it is "emphatically the province and the duty" of this Court "to say what the law is" with respect to the claim of privilege presented in this case. . . .

I had said, "Now the President may be right in how he reads the Constitution. But he may also be wrong. And if he is wrong, who is there to tell him so?" The Chief Justice had just answered that question—the Court would tell him so.

Chief Justice Burger read on. His voice, reaching every corner of the hall, was the only sound to be heard. His listeners were rapt. What was the law with respect to the claim of privilege presented in this case?

We conclude that when the ground for asserting privilege as to subpoenaed materials sought for use in a criminal trial is based only on the generalized interest in confidentiality, it cannot prevail over the fundamental demands of due process of law in the fair administration of criminal justice. The generalized assertion of privilege must yield to the demonstrated, specific need for evidence in a pending criminal trial. . . .

On the basis of our examination of the record we are unable to conclude that the District Court erred . . . accordingly we affirm the order of the District Court that subpoenaed materials be transmitted to that court. . . .

We had won.

Chief Justice Burger continued, explaining the District Court's heavy responsibility in seeing that presidential conversations which were not relevant to the case were "accorded that high degree of respect due the President of the United States." He concluded: "Since this matter came before the Court during the pendency of a criminal prosecution, and on representation that time is of the essence, the mandate shall issue forthwith. . . ."

We had won. And then came the information I had so much wanted to hear: the holding of the Court was unanimous!

Court was adjourned; the Justices disappeared behind the heavy drapes. And I was mobbed by my colleagues and other lawyers who had come to hear the decision. Shouts of congratulations came from every corner, from old friends and from people I had never seen before. Neal, the former blocking back, helped me make my way toward the exit. Young people and older people shook my hand. I used one of the pillars as a backstop as I signed as many autograph books as possible with a red felt pen that someone handed me.

The press reported the scene outside as "near pandemonium." It was a forest of cameras—television cameras, still cameras, home-movie cameras, pocket cameras. Newsmen were tugging at me, shouting questions at me. I tried to express my sentiments for the television people as best I could, but the full impact of the Court's decision had not yet penetrated through the warm glow of the moment.

As we worked our way to the car I was stopped time and time again by questioning newspersons. Yes, I hoped the cover-up trial could proceed on schedule, starting September 9. No, the requirement that the President yield the tapes for trial use was not related in any way to whether they must be given to the House Judiciary Committee. No, I didn't have to have all the tapes at once, but I wanted some quickly.

And finally we reached the car. As I fell back in the seat I thought of the President in San Clemente. The unanimous decision had completely disarmed him of whatever plans he had to disobey and circumvent the Court. The unanimous holding, I was convinced, had saved the country from an even more terrible trauma than it was experiencing.

THE WORD FROM WASHINGTON reached the President's San Clemente quarters by news service ticker. Immediately the question arose: who would tell the President? There were no volunteers. Then General Haig took the ticker copy and went with it to the President. Nixon read it and burst into a tantrum. He reportedly reviled the Justices, particularly Chief Justice Burger. Haig calmed him.

That afternoon in California St. Clair announced that the President would comply with the Court's decision. Shortly thereafter, in Washington, Rodino and his Committee began debate on Article I of an impeachment resolution which accused the President of obstruction of justice.

St. Clair had said Nixon would release the tapes, but he hadn't said when. We needed them quickly if they were to be processed and studied in time for the cover-up trial. And remembering the "missing tapes" and the "gaps" in others, I decided to minimize a recurrence. I went before Judge Sirica the next morning with a motion asking that the President turn over the sixty-four conversations, in installments, within ten days.

We asked for twenty conversations within two days, twenty-one more within six days, and the remaining twenty-three within ten days. The first twenty conversations were those for which the White House had released the edited, misleading transcriptions. The conversations we wanted most were in the second group, particularly those involving Nixon, Haldeman, Ehrlichman, and Colson and beginning on June 20, 1972, three days after the Watergate break-in.

St. Clair flew in from California and we argued on the motion the next day. St. Clair told Judge Sirica it would take "some time" to process the tapes. I said if they were not turned over quickly the cover-up trial would be delayed. Judge Sirica said he wanted the trial to start as scheduled. "I'm calling a recess," he said. "I want you two to get together and work out a timetable. If you can't, I'll do it myself."

It took us an hour and fifteen minutes to work out the timetable. St. Clair knew that this was the one time he could not stall and delay as he had in the past. On my part, I relaxed my requested schedule, but not much. Under the agreement the Judge approved, St. Clair was to deliver the first twenty conversations within five days and as many of the remaining forty-four as soon as possible—with priority on ones I designated—within three days thereafter.

St. Clair did not dally. As soon as duplicates could be made of the tapes they were delivered. The first ones to begin arriving were, of course, the ones from which the President had made the edited transcripts. We were eagerly awaiting the second batch.

Meanwhile, the House Judiciary Committee, with the American people looking on via television, voted 27 to 11 on Article I of an impeachment resolution charging the President with obstruction of justice. Two days later the Committee adopted Article II of the resolution charging the President with misuse of powers and violation of his oath of office. And the next day Article III was adopted, charging the President with failure to comply with a House subpoena.

This was a severe blow, but Nixon was expected to fight back with every weapon at his command. But the finishing blow was soon to come; the tapes would do him in.

GENERAL HAIG CALLED ME at home on the morning of August 5; St. Clair, he said, also was on the line. Haig obviously was under a strain. There had been a development of considerable importance, he said, and the President would be making a statement about it at four o'clock in the afternoon. "I wanted you to be aware of it before the fact, Leon."

"What is it, Al?"

"Well, we were reviewing the tape recordings we are going to send you and we found one that's significantly different from the others."

"In what way?"

"It's some conversations between the President and Haldeman on June 23, six days after the Watergate break-in. They talk about getting the FBI out of the

247

investigation by using the CIA—having the CIA say it was a national security matter. . . ."

All three of us on the line knew that Haldeman and Ehrlichman *had* tried to use the CIA to halt the investigation.

"We didn't know it, Leon," Haig said. "He didn't tell us about it. He didn't tell anyone. St. Clair and I have been pushing him to come out with a statement saying he was the only one who knew about it. That he didn't tell any of his attorneys and that's why St. Clair made misleading statements to the Judiciary Committee."

St. Clair broke in. "I told him he was going to have to reveal this publicly or I was going to resign. The advice I've been giving him didn't take any of this into account, Leon. And the positions I took before the Committee didn't either."

I told St. Clair I could readily understand his concern, on a professional and on an ethical basis. "You have a problem if he doesn't disclose it right away."

St. Clair said the conversations appeared to constitute a violation of the law since they pertained to a contemplated misuse of a government agency as well as obstruction of justice. "The explanation the President gives will lessen the damage to some degree," he said, "but I have no idea of what the full effect will be."

Haig still wanted to hold an umbrella over the President. "I believe the President didn't focus on the matter," he said.

I interrupted. "But the President reviewed those conversations on Monday, May 6—after I offered to drop my subpoena if you would deliver just eighteen of the tapes. Isn't that true?"

"That's correct," Haig said.

"It's true," said St. Clair. "He listened to them from four o'clock in the afternoon until nine o'clock that night."

"He knew what was in the conversations," I said.

"Do you want him to go into your offer when he makes his statement this afternoon?" St. Clair asked.

"It's not important to me, Jim. All that's important is for him to let the facts be known and remove the false impressions he's left . . . and clear the record for you and the others."

St. Clair said he was seeing to it that all the tapes were being delivered to Judge Sirica and that the Judge would have them all within two days. "The documentary matter will be right behind them," he said.

Haig said, "I'm particularly anxious that you believe me, Leon. I didn't know what was in those conversations."

"I remember, Al, that you told me you couldn't see why I wanted those tapes because there wasn't anything of value in them."

"That's right! And that's what I believed!"

St. Clair said he didn't want this new development to adversely affect the cover-up trial date. I told him there was no way he could avoid releasing the conversations immediately, regardless of the consequences.

We broke off the conversation and I called my office. Ruth was on vacation, so I talked with Neal, Lacovara, and James Vorenberg, a Harvard Law School professor who had joined the Special Prosecution Force as a consultant at its inception and had served intermittently since. I had high regard for him and valued his advice. I told them of my conversation with Haig and St. Clair and gave instructions that no comments of any kind about the matter be issued from our office.

chapter thirteen

End of a Nightmare

THAT AFTERNOON, WHEN the President released his statement, I recalled it was exactly one week since John Dean had been sentenced to prison to serve from one to four years. The President also released transcripts of the three conversations he had held on June 23, 1972, with Haldeman in the Oval Office. Portions of the transcripts, he said, were "at variance with certain of my previous statements." Indeed they were. For one, they proved false his oft-repeated statement that he first learned of the cover-up from Dean on March 21, 1973. The Special Prosecution Force had long believed that he was given the details of the Watergate break-in and informed of the incipient cover-up on June 20, 1972, just three days after the break-in, but the proof was lost forever in the eighteen-minute gap in the tape of that day's conversations. Now his own transcripts showed that he knew of the cover-up—and participated in it—six days after the break-in.

For me the revelation was the end of a nightmare. The galling frustration I had experienced for long months as Nixon had continued to mislead the public was over. The conclusions I had reached about his culpability were now confirmed absolutely and clarified. Whatever rationalizations or explanations had been offered to minimize his conduct in the past were no longer valid. I had walked the streets of Washington knowing that he continually twisted the facts while I, who knew the truth, had had to remain silent. The relief I felt is impossible to describe.

In the past, because of the defection of several of his aides and testimony before various bodies, the President had been forced to acknowledge that he was aware that Haldeman and Ehrlichman had involved the CIA in the break-in investigation. In the past he had said: "Within a few days [of the break-in] however, I was advised that there was a possibility of CIA involvement in some way. It did seem to me to be possible that, because of the involvement of former CIA personnel, and because of some of their apparent associations, the investigation could lead to the uncovering of covert CIA operations totally unrelated to the Watergate break-in." He had instructed his top aides, he said, "to insure that the investigation of the break-in not expose either an unrelated covert operation of the CIA or activities of the White House investigations unit [Plumbers]." He had added: "It was certainly not my intent, nor my wish, that the investigation of the Watergate break-in or of related acts be impeded in any way. . . ."

But his latest statement now said that his previous comments were "based on my recollection at the time—some 11 months later—plus documentary materials and relevant public testimony of those involved." Listening to the June 23 tapes had cleared his memory. "The June 23 tapes clearly show that at the time I gave those instructions I also discussed the political aspects of the situation, and that I was aware of the advantages this course of action would have with respect to limiting possible public exposure of involvement by persons connected with the reelection committee."

How did the June 23 tapes fit into the cover-up picture? It will be recalled that in Chapter Eleven I detailed the evidence which prompted us to ask for the cover-up indictment. On June 20 Dean learned from John Mitchell that checks made out to cash and totaling $114,000 had been received by CREEP as campaign contributions from Kenneth Dahlberg, a Republican fund-raiser, and Manuel Ogarrio, a Mexican lawyer. Bernard Barker, one of the Watergate burglars, had been given the checks to cash to hide the fact that Dahlberg and Ogarrio were the contributors. Barker had deposited the checks in his Florida bank, then had withdrawn the cash and given it to Gordon Liddy, the break-in mastermind. Liddy had given the cash to Hugh Sloan, CREEP treasurer and former aide to Haldeman, who placed the bills in his safe. Later, when Sloan was disbursing cash to Liddy to finance his operations, he gave Liddy some of the same bills. Liddy had used the bills to pay the burglars, and they were found in their possession.

On June 21, Dean went to see L. Patrick Gray, FBI Acting Director, to see how he was handling the break-in investigation. Gray told Dean that FBI agents had traced the bills found on the burglars to Barker's Florida bank account and had learned that Barker had cashed the Dahlberg and Ogarrio checks. That's all they knew so far, Gray said, but agents were going to interview Dahlberg and Ogarrio. This upset Dean. He knew that if Dahlberg and Ogarrio talked, the agents would learn that the two men had sent the checks to CREEP as campaign contributions and thus link the burglary to CREEP. Gray also told Dean the agents thought the money might be part of a CIA operation.

On June 22, Dean told Mitchell about the impending FBI interviews with Dahlberg and Ogarrio and that the agents suspected they were investigating a CIA covert operation. He also gave this information to Haldeman.

In our chain of evidence, we next had Haldeman and Ehrlichman meeting with CIA Director Richard Helms and his assistant, Vernon Walters, on June 23. But the

June 23 tapes revealed that before that meeting Haldeman met with Nixon—and the President told him what to say to Helms and Walters.

Portions of the conversations were excised because they did not deal with Watergate. The first conversation was from 10:04 A.M. to 11:39 A.M.

HALDEMAN: Now, on the investigation, you know, the Democratic break-in thing. We're back in the problem area because the FBI is not under control. Because Gray doesn't exactly know how to control them. And they have, their investigation is now leading into some productive areas because they've been able to trace the money, not through the money itself but through the bank. You know, sources—the banker himself. And it goes in some directions we don't want it to go. Also there have been some things like an informant who came in off the street to the FBI in Miami, who was a photographer or has a friend who is a photographer who developed some films through this guy Barker, and the films had pictures of Democratic National Committee letterhead documents and things. So I guess, so it's things like that are gonna, that are filtering in. Mitchell came up with yesterday, and John Dean analyzed very carefully last night and concludes, concurs now with Mitchell's recommendation that the only way to solve this . . . the way to handle this now is for us to have Walters call Pat Gray and just say, "Stay the hell out of this business here. We don't want you to go any further on it." That's not an unusual development, and that would take care of it.

PRESIDENT: What about Gray? You mean he doesn't want to?

HALDEMAN: Pat wants to. He doesn't know how to, and he doesn't have, he doesn't have any basis for doing it. Given this, he will then have the basis. He'll call Mark Felt [Assistant FBI Director] in, and the two of them . . . and Mark Felt wants to cooperate because he's ambitious. And he'll call him in and say, "We've got the signal from across the river to put the hold on this." And that will fit rather well because the FBI agents who are working the case at this point feel that's what it is. This is CIA.

PRESIDENT: But they've traced the money to 'em.

HALDEMAN: Well, they've traced to a name, but they haven't gotten to the guy yet.

PRESIDENT: Would it be somebody here?

HALDEMAN: Ken Dahlberg.

PRESIDENT: Who the hell is Ken Dahlberg?

HALDEMAN: He's ah, he gave $25,000 in Minnesota and the check went directly in to this guy Barker.

PRESIDENT: He didn't get this from the committee though. From Stans.

HALDEMAN: Yeah. It is. It is. It's directly traceable and there's some more through some Texas people that went to the Mexican bank which they can also trace to the Mexican bank. They'll get their names today.

PRESIDENT: Well, I mean, ah, there's no way . . . I'm just thinking if they don't cooperate, what do they say? They were approached by the Cubans? That's what Dahlberg has to say, the Texans too. Is that the idea?

HALDEMAN: Well, if they will. But then we're relying on more and more people all the time. That's the problem. And they'll [the FBI] stop if we could, if we take this other step.

PRESIDENT: All right. Fine.

HALDEMAN: And you feel the thing to do is to get them to stop?

PRESIDENT: Right. Fine.

HALDEMAN: They [Mitchell and Dean] say the only way to do that is from White House instructions. And it's got to be to Helms and, ah, what's his name? Walters?

PRESIDENT: Walters.

HALDEMAN: And the proposal would be that Ehrlichman and I call them in.

PRESIDENT: All right. Fine.

HALDEMAN: And say . . .

PRESIDENT: How do you call him in? I mean you just, well, we protected Helms from one hell of a lot of things.

HALDEMAN: That's what Ehrlichman says.

PRESIDENT: Of course this is a Hunt [Howard Hunt], you will—that will uncover a lot of things. You open that scab, there's a hell of a lot of things and that we just feel that it would be very detrimental to have this thing go any further. This involves these Cubans, Hunt and a lot of hanky-panky that we have nothing to do with ourselves. Well, what the hell. Did Mitchell know about this thing to any much of a degree?

HALDEMAN: I think so. I don't think he knew the details, but I think he knew.

PRESIDENT: He didn't know how it was going to be handled though, with Dahlberg and the Texans and so forth? Well, who was the asshole that did? Is it Liddy? Is that the fellow? He must be a little nuts.

HALDEMAN: He is.

PRESIDENT: I mean, he just isn't well screwed on, is he? Isn't that the problem?

HALDEMAN: No, but he was under pressure, apparently to get more information, and as he got more pressure he pushed the people harder to move harder on. . . .

PRESIDENT: Pressure from Mitchell?

HALDEMAN: All right. Fine. I understand it all. We won't second-guess Mitchell and the rest. Thank God it wasn't Colson.

HALDEMAN: The FBI interviewed Colson yesterday. They determined that would be a good thing to do. Ah, to have him take a, an interrogation, which he did. And that, the FBI guys working the case had concluded that there were one or two possibilities—one, that this was a White House, they don't think that there is anything at the Election Committee. They think it was either a White House operation and they had some obscure reasons for it, non-political, or it was a . . .

PRESIDENT: Cuban thing—

HALDEMAN: Cubans and the CIA. And after their interrogation of, of . . .

PRESIDENT: Colson.

HALDEMAN: Colson, yesterday, they concluded it was not the White House, but are now convinced it is a CIA thing, so the CIA turnoff would . . .

PRESIDENT: Well, not sure of their analysis. I'm not going to get that involved. I'm (unintelligible).

HALDEMAN: No, sir. We don't want you to.

PRESIDENT: You call them in. Good. Good deal. Play it tough. That's the way they play it and that's the way we are going to play it.

HALDEMAN: Okay, we'll do it.

PRESIDENT: When you get in these people . . . when you get these people in, say: "Look, the problem is that this will open the whole, the whole Bay of Pigs thing, and the President just feels that"—ah, without going into details . . . don't, don't lie to them to the extent to say there is no involvement, but just say this is sort of a comedy of errors, bizarre, without getting into it—"the President believes that it is going to open the whole Bay of Pigs thing up again. And, because these people are plugging for, for keeps and that they should call the FBI in and say that we wish for the country, don't go any further into this case"—period!

In a short meeting in the afternoon, from 1:04 P.M. to 1:13 P.M., the President reiterated his advice to Haldeman:

. . . very bad to have this fellow Hunt, ah, you know, ah, it's, he, he knows too damn much and he was involved, we happen to know that. And that if it gets out that the whole, this is all involved in the Cuban thing, that it's a fiasco, and it's going to make the CIA look bad, it's going to make Hunt look bad, and it's likely to blow the whole, uh, Bay of Pigs thing which we think would be very unfortunate for the CIA and for the country at this time, and for American foreign policy, and he just better tough it and lay it on them. Isn't that what you . . .

HALDEMAN: Yeah, that's the basis we'll do it on and just leave it at that.
PRESIDENT: I don't want them to get any ideas we're doing it because our concern is political.
HALDEMAN: Right.
PRESIDENT: And at the same time, I wouldn't tell them it is not political.
HALDEMAN: Right.

PRESIDENT: I would just say, "Look, it's because of the Hunt involvement . . ."

At 2:20 P.M. Haldeman reported back that Helms and Walters had been in and that there was no problem with them. The scenario had been spelled out to the two CIA men. Said Haldeman, "So at that point Helms kind of got the picture. He said, 'We'll be very happy to be helpful, and we'll handle anything you want.' " He added that Walters was going to make a call on Gray. "That's the way we put it, that's the way it was left."

It will be recalled that our evidence showed that Walters did call on Gray and Gray agreed to call off the interrogations of Dahlberg and Ogarrio. But Gray's concern grew as the days passed, and finally he asked Walters to put the CIA "layoff" request in writing. Walters, however, had regained his capacity for indignation. In writing he told Gray there was no CIA involvement in the Watergate break-in. Gray ordered the interrogations. But the delay in the investigation had given the conspirators time to perfect a new cover-up scenario.

THE PRESIDENT'S STATEMENT did "clear" Haig and St. Clair, as they had told me it would: "Although I recognized that these tapes presented potential problems, I did not inform my staff or my counsel of it, or those arguing my case, nor did I amend my submission to the Judiciary Committee in order to include and reflect it. . . ."

The President had admitted much, kept hidden much more, and had shown little or no remorse. And there was every indication that he intended to keep fighting. "I am firmly convinced," the statement said, "that the record, in its entirety, does not justify the extreme step of impeachment and removal of a President. I trust hat as the Constitutional process goes forward, this perspective will prevail. . . ."

In the sordid history of the cover-up President Nixon had never more grossly miscalculated. Fizzing and sputtering, his core of support in the Congress dissolved like a seltzer wafer in a glass of water. And a majority of the American people, including many of those who had stuck by him through tavern arguments and town hall debates, succumbed to the hurt and anger of the betrayed.

He was still sidling around the truth, unwilling to face the facts and level with the American people. But with all of his circumvention of the truth he was no longer capable of offering what might appear to be a reasonable explanation for his wrongdoing. Still he persisted on his course. It was the action either of a man who had lost touch with reality, which I did not believe, or of one who viewed the public intelligence with profound contempt. Whatever vestiges of sympathy for him I had maintained now disappeared.

Calls for the Nixon resignation came from every quarter. Newspapers that had fought him and newspapers that had supported him demanded that he step down. Nationally syndicated columnists who had long defended him cried out that he had lied to them, as if it were a personal matter. The most powerful men in the House and Senate, men of both parties, called on him to resign. The ten Republican members of the House Judiciary Committee who had voted against the impeachment resolution joined in the chorus, including Charles Wiggins of California, whose strong defense of the President had won him national recognition as an advocate.

Haig called me on August 7 and said he wanted to meet with me the next day. He didn't say why, but I felt certain that the President had decided to resign.

I was to call him the next morning to arrange a meeting place.

Before I called Haig I met with several members of my staff in my apartment. Quite likely Haig would be seeking something on behalf of the President, and we decided that no agreement of any kind should be made. The others felt that Richard Nixon's future should not be a matter solely for my determination, but that the Congress should express itself on the point. Perhaps, it was suggested, we should not move against Nixon if Congress passed a resolution that it believed such a course was not advisable. Several members of Congress already had hinted at such a resolution, and Senator Edward Brooke of Massachusetts had announced he planned to introduce one.

I called Haig at the White House. He was with the President, but returned my call in about ten minutes. The White House, he said, was literally ringed with newspersons expecting a major development. "If you come here, they'll start speculating that the President wants some kind of trade-out arrangement with you." We talked it over. Finally it was decided that Haig's aide would pick me up a half-block from my apartment and drive me to Haig's home. Haig would drive home in his private automobile and the newspersons would assume he had gone for lunch.

He was waiting for me when I arrived at his home. He introduced me to Mrs. Haig and escorted me into the living room. Mrs. Haig, a charming woman, brought us tea and coffee, then left us to our talk.

I began it. "I think we should have a clear understanding, Al, that we're not going to reach any kind of agreements about the President at this meeting."

"I know that," he said. "That's not why I wanted to meet. The President is going to resign tonight, if you haven't guessed."

I nodded.

"Now, he's going to be taking his tapes and papers with him, Leon. There's no hanky-panky involved. Your office will have access to them if you need them. He's going to San Clemente tomorrow and the tapes and papers will be shipped out later."

I told Haig I wasn't in a position to say what we would need, but that the materials must be available to us. "Any failure along that line will mean court hearings," I warned.

"Well, the President and I both felt we owed it to you to let you know what's going to happen." I gathered from what he was saying that the President was deteriorating, physically and mentally. Haig's concern was plain to see as he talked about Nixon, and his face showed the strain under which he had been working. One of his most difficult problems, he said, was in making the Nixon family understand why the President had to resign.

Haig didn't say so but the Washington grapevine throbbed with the story that Haig had been holding the Administration together, and that it was he who had finally convinced Nixon that there was no benign alternative to resignation.

"I want you to know," he said, "that the President has no intention of pardoning Haldeman or Ehrlichman before he turns over affairs to Gerald Ford. Haldeman called me and I could tell that's what he wanted. And Ehrlichman tried the same thing with Rose Mary Woods. He wanted her to mention a pardon for him to the President." He sipped from his cup. "Another thing, Leon . . . under no circumstances is the President going to testify in that cover-up trial or any other proceeding. If necessary, he'll take the Fifth Amendment, in my opinion."

That led us into a short discussion about the impending trial, and Haig said, "I don't mind telling you

261

that I haven't the slightest doubt that the tapes were screwed with. The ones with gaps and other problems."

Back to the President: Haig said the resignation speech would be short, that it would not be rancorous, that Nixon would express appreciation to those who had supported him and assure those who had opposed him he held no animosity for them.

"Are you going to stay on and help Ford?" I asked.

"Yes, but I don't know how long. Certainly a number of weeks."

"I think that's wise, Al. This transition period will be a critical one, and the new President will need you."

He said there was a strong possibility of a coal strike in a couple of months. "And it looks like more trouble coming in the Middle East and, in all likelihood, an oil embargo. That's going to mean a shortage of fuel, and it's going to be a blow to the economy."

The conversation was near its end, so I asked Haig if congressional supporters of the President were going to pass a resolution that would, in effect, tell me not to move against him.

"Oh, yes! I think it will be passed within a day or two. With no difficulty."

We walked to the doorway. "I want you to know how much I appreciate your taking on the Special Prosecutor's job," he said. "I know how tough it's been."

"It's been a little strenuous," I said, "but yours has been even worse."

We parted with a strong handshake. "I hope to see you from time to time," I said, "but not in my present capacity." He gave my hand a solid squeeze.

There was a sadness in our parting. Both of us had been knee-deep in an unparalleled tragedy, and it had forged a strange kinship. As my car started to move away, Mrs. Haig appeared at the front door and, standing by her husband, waved good-bye.

Later that day our office prepared a statement for the news media, to be released at the proper time:

There has been no agreement or understanding of any sort between the President or his representatives and the Special Prosecutor relating in any way to the President's resignation.

The Special Prosecutor's Office was not asked for any such agreement or understanding and offered none. Although I was informed of the President's decision this afternoon, my office did not participate in any way in the President's decision to resign.

It would have been a good resignation speech for a President leaving office because of illness, or for one who had lost congressional support because of differences over policies. It was not the speech of a President who had violated his constitutional oath and duty by obstructing justice, by abusing the power of his office, by transforming the Oval Office into a mean den where perjury and low scheming became a way of life.

The nearest Richard Nixon came to an admission of guilt was a few words of contrition. "I regret deeply," he said, "any injuries that may have been done in the course of the events that led to this decision. I would say only that if some of my judgments were wrong, and some were wrong, they were made in what I believed at the time to be the best interest of the Nation. . . ."

Most of the rest of it was a look at the accomplishments of his Administration and the problems facing his successor.

Watching him on television, listening to him, I remembered how firmly General Haig had spoken when he had said that Congress would pass a resolution to halt any proceeding against Nixon.

Not after this speech, Al, I thought. He hasn't given Congress even a crumb of remorse to chew on.

THE TEN REPUBLICANS on the House Judiciary Committee who had voted against the impeachment resolution signed a minority report saying Nixon resigned after having "substantially confessed to the crime of obstructing justice." The report added:

> We know that it has been said—and perhaps some will continue to say—that Richard Nixon was "hounded from office" by his political opponents and media critics.
>
> We feel constrained to point out, however, that it was Richard Nixon who impeded the FBI's investigation of the Watergate affair by wrongfully attempting to implicate the Central Intelligence Agency.
>
> It was Richard Nixon who created and preserved the evidence of that transgression and who, knowing that it had been subpoenaed by this Committee and the Special Prosecutor, concealed its terrible import, even from his own counsel, until he could do so no longer.
>
> And it was a unanimous Supreme Court of the United States which, in an opinion authored by the Chief Justice whom he appointed, ordered Richard Nixon to surrender that evidence to the Special Prosecutor, to further the ends of justice. . . .

chapter fourteen

Indict or Pardon?

SENATOR JAMES EASTLAND called me. "Senator Hruska is with me in my office," he said. "Could you come over?"

"Can it wait?" I asked. "I'm going to the airport and it will crowd me."

"Well," he said, "Congress has recessed, and we won't be back for a while."

I told him I'd be over. Senator Eastland was a close, longtime friend of Richard Nixon. He also was chairman of the Senate Judiciary Committee and, as such, a member of the consensus group that could have insulated me against a peremptory discharge. He had supported me from the beginning of my tenure. He and Senator Hruska were waiting for me in his office. As always, Eastland looked like a statesman, a solid, durable man who knew how to use the great power he had accumulated.

He said he had just talked with Nixon, that Nixon had called from San Clemente. "He was crying," Eastland said. "He said, 'Jim, don't let Jaworski put me in that trial with Haldeman and Ehrlichman. I can't take any more.'" Eastland shook his head. "He's in bad shape, Leon." There was a touch of the pity he felt for Nixon in his voice, but not the slightest intimation that he was trying to twist my arm. He was simply telling me something about a man in whom we both, for differing reasons, had a deep interest.

Senator Brooke had withdrawn his plan for a resolution asking that no action be taken against Nixon because he considered the resignation speech an arrogant affront to the country. But others, in and out of Congress, were still calling for such a resolution. I asked Eastland if the consensus group had any plans in that direction. He said no decision had been reached. "We'll think on it," he said. "We'll be in touch."

But no one got in touch. Members of both houses of Congress went home for vacations or to work for reelection. There was still talk, however. Senator Scott, the minority leader who earlier had complained that the White House had "suckered" him by getting him to defend Nixon on the basis of edited tape transcripts, now said, "The nation has its pound of flesh [the resignation]. It doesn't need the blood that goes with it." Others called for equal justice, meaning that Nixon should be indicted and tried along with the other conspirators. Among them was Chesterfield Smith, outgoing president of the American Bar Association. Opposing this was Vice President Nelson Rockefeller, who said Nixon already had been "hung" and shouldn't now be "drawn and quartered."

The polls were indefinite. Shortly before the resignation, a majority polled was opposed to special consideration for Nixon; several days after the resignation a majority polled opposed further investigation of him. The telegrams, mailgrams, letters, and telephone calls to my office—some 9,500 of them—favored criminal action against Nixon by 3½ to 1.

Columnists and cartoonists depicted me as a lonely man, deserted by Congress and the President, left to deal with a heavy burden. To them I was in a position of being damned if I did or damned if I didn't prosecute Nixon. Experts of various kinds were interviewed about "Jaworski's dilemma." Various courses of action were recommended, some bordering on the exotic.

It was all interesting, and I was touched by the concern, but the chief question occupying my mind was this: could Richard Nixon receive a fair trial? That was the true dilemma.

An estimated 92 million persons viewed the televising of the House Judiciary Committee proceedings, and every newspaper of any size reported in detail every item of proof of Nixon's participation in Watergate-related wrongdoing. Every American willing and able to read and listen knew that the Committee had voted a bill of impeachment. Capping that, when the June 23, 1972, tape recording was made public, numerous Republican Committee members who had defended Nixon went on live television, not only to say they were changing their vote but also to state flatly that they had concluded he was guilty of obstruction of justice. Then followed a few days of headlines on whether Nixon should resign, with Congressmen and others calling on him to do so, and the Committee standing 38 to 0 in favor of impeachment on the charge of obstruction of justice.

When Nixon resigned, the nation was told from shore to shore that he had done so to avoid certain impeachment. The news columns and airwaves were filled with inculpatory comments regarding his guilt, his ignominy and disgrace, and of its historically unprecedented nature. To the media, Nixon had, for all practical purposes, admitted guilt with his resignation.

What if this man, no longer a sitting President, were to be indicted for obstruction of justice? Like any other citizen, and regardless of his resignation and the unprecedented accusations of guilt, he was presumed to be innocent in the eyes of the law until proven guilty according to judicial standards. The grand jury, I knew, would indict him in a minute. But could he receive a fair trial, his constitutional right?

We had ample time to decide whether to prosecute; I had concluded that if Nixon were to be indicted, it would come only after the jury had been sequestered in the cover-up trial. To indict prior to that would mean an indefinite delay in the trial.

I called on such members of my staff as cared to express themselves on whether prosecution should be attempted. Almost all of the lawyers expressed themselves in one form or another and, without exception, they favored the return of an indictment.

There were, however, variations on the theme. And few of them had looked forward to the complexities *beyond* indictment, the procedural problems, the impact on the nation, the international reaction. We could not return an indictment just for the sake of indicting someone. For me to indict Nixon would mean that I expected to bring him to trial; that had to be the yardstick in the exercise of judgment.

Some staff members wanted to indict *and* prosecute. Some wanted to indict and signal President Ford that a pardon was in order . . . if Nixon would admit his guilt. That thought had some merit, but I saw little likelihood of Nixon making a clean breast.

George Frampton, who had so skillfully written the final version of our "road map," prepared a memorandum which, in a sense, represented the thoughts of most of the others. He had as much knowledge of the evidence against Nixon as anyone because of his undivided work as a member of the Watergate Task Force. His memorandum read:

Viewed broadly, the creation of a Special Prosecutor was a unique and extra-constitutional reaction by our constitutional system to preserve its integrity in the face of an emergency where those in control of the administration of justice were themselves charged with subverting it. It has always seemed to me that inherent in creation of this constitutionally precarious institution are unique

268

risks of failure. To avoid these risks we have hewed to a very few fundamental principles. These are: that we will pursue charges of wrong-doing to a conclusion wherever they lead, without regard to political influence or considerations but with regard only to the truth; that we will do our utmost as lawyers and human beings to make "just" decisions, however unpopular or misunderstood they may be, while recognizing the infirmity of any one view (or even a majority view) of what is just; that we will be scrupulous in conduct of our investigations and trials; and that in every matter we will proceed upon well-settled and established precedent and principles of law and practice.

This last—consistent adherence to precedent, to well-established legal and justice principles—has been especially critical because it has been the primary source of public credibility for an office that in its birth derived no credibility from the Constitution or history.

By these lights, perhaps unfortunately, I fear that history may yet judge this venture a failure should your decision be to "call it a day" and not indict former President Nixon.

As I understand it, three factors could be advanced to justify a decision not to prosecute: (1) public sentiment that Mr. Nixon has suffered enough and a concomitant feeling that the country must get on to other things, prosecution possibly leading to public divisiveness; (2) some feeling that the President did not initiate or mastermind the coverup but rather fell or was led into assisting the principal actors; (3) a fear that Mr. Nixon could not receive a fair trial.

My concern is not so much that the countervailing factors supporting prosecution outweigh those listed above, but that history will ultimately find each of the above factors illusory and thus judge harshly any reliance upon them.

To begin with the third justification, it seems to me that reliance on prejudicial pre-trial publicity to avoid prosecution altogether would be widely perceived (and stamped by history) as a resort to a completely novel legal theory—and thereby judged a "cop-out." Despite two years of intensive publicity concerning the Watergate actions of the defendants in *United States* v. *Mitchell, et al.,* we have argued that settled legal precedents support proceeding to trial at this time. These same precedents envision even more stringent safeguards than those employed in the *Mitchell* case before attempting to pick a jury in any prosecution of Mr. Nixon (e.g., a substantial continuance, change of venue, etc.). The Constitution indisputably contemplates prosecution of a former President even after impeachment. There is no precedent for dismissal of an indictment on publicity grounds, much less for a decision not to indict at all. If prejudicial publicity is invoked to support a decision not to prosecute, I fear history will say that when we came to Mr. Nixon we threw out our consistent course of reliance upon settled law and principles—a course that took us through such previously uncharted seas as prosecution of the President's top aides and litigation over Presidential tape recordings—and in the end by so doing exposed the arbitrary and manipulable character of the notion of "adherence to legal principles" from which the institution of Special Prosecutor derived so much of its credibility.

Similarly, I wonder if history would not judge harshly the entire work of the Special Prosecutor's office should you decide not to prosecute based on public sentiment that Mr. Nixon has suffered enough. The action you recommended to the grand jury in March was firmly grounded in the shared constitutional understanding of how our system deals with misconduct by a sitting President. Now, however, there is no established framework—no publicly-accepted set of criteria—within which to make your decision except the traditional one of a prosecutor. Familiar factors of prosecutorial discretion, of course, uniformly dictate prosecution here. To go outside the traditional compass on which we have relied so heavily for credibility in the past and to try to make a decision based on a mixture of perceived public sentiment and long-range public policy choices *could* result in a decision history would judge wise. But the risk that history would not only judge the decision wrong but, in light of it, view skeptically all we have done here would, it seems to me, be vastly increased. Those capable of making a "political" decision on this issue—the Congress, political leaders, President Ford—have not done so. Neither they nor the country can expect you now to abandon *your* mandate and responsibilities to the administration of justice in order to assume *their* burden.

More important in this regard, I wonder if ten years from now history will endorse the notion that Mr. Nixon has "suffered enough." The powerful men around him have also lost their jobs and been disgraced, but many of them will have lost their liberty and livelihood. Mr. Nixon, on the other hand, will continue to be supported in lavish style with a pension and subsidies at taxpayers' expense until his death. He may re-enter public life, however morally crippled. The prospect of Mr. Nixon publishing his memoirs (and thereby adding several million dollars to his net worth) should remind us that unlike his aides who are convicted of crimes Mr. Nixon will have the "last say" about his own role in Watergate if he is not prosecuted. This is why, in my view, it is important (absent a full admission of guilt) to have some definitive resolution of Mr. Nixon's Watergate actions. The House Committee's massive volumes may or may not be viewed by history as "conclusive" of Mr. Nixon's commission of crimes. What *is* certain is that if he is not prosecuted, after the vivid memory of impeachment proceedings fades away and after there is no more Special Prosecutor, Mr. Nixon in his writing and speaking will have the final opportunity to defend and justify his own role in Watergate as proper, constitutional and in the national interest—and to argue that only the political hysteria of the times brought about his downfall. (Mr. Nixon will undoubtedly argue, for instance, that the fact that he was not prosecuted demonstrated that there was insufficient evidence that he had actually committed any crime.)

With regard to the nature of Mr. Nixon's participation in Watergate, I doubt history would accept the idea that his role was peripheral and could be distinguished from those of his aides who were prosecuted. Mr. Nixon's role was an active one when his personal participation was essential to the conspiracy and the fact is that the central purpose of the coverup was to advance Mr. Nixon's own interests, not those of his aides. Again, we have relied on time-tested evidentiary considerations in making prosecutorial decisions in the case of others under investigation. I fear history would view us harshly were we to apply a completely new and unprecedented standard to Mr. Nixon as a basis for no prosecution.

In sum, I fear history will judge reliance upon any of these three justifications for *not* prosecuting Mr. Nixon as a departure from the close adherence to well-founded legal principles that we have thought important to sustain the precarious nature of the institution of Special Prosecutor—and that such historical judgment could prejudice history's view of all the work of the institution.

Who could say these arguments were not persuasive? Henry Ruth, for whom my admiration has never wavered, summed up what appeared to be all reasonable arguments pro and con on the issue. He left it to me to indict or not indict, of course, but concluded his brilliant memorandum thusly:

> . . . I know of few decisions as difficult as this one must be personally. Indictment of an ex-President seems so easy to many of the commentators and politicians. But in a deep sense that involves tradition, travail and submerged disgust, somehow it seems that signing one's name to the indictment of an ex-President is an act that one wishes devolved upon another but one's self. This is true even where such an act, in institutional and justice terms, appears absolutely necessary.
>
> I do not think that the political system can "walk away" from this one. As I outlined above, one can make a strong argument for leniency, and if President Ford is so inclined, I think he ought to do it early rather than late. For this reason, if you decide to recommend indictment, I think it fair and proper to notify Jack Miller [Herbert J. Miller, Nixon's new lawyer] and the White House sufficiently in advance so that pardon action could be taken before indictment. The timing is also justified in pragmatic terms inasmuch as any signifi-

cant Watergate action, such as a pardon for Mr.
Nixon, should postdate jury sequestration in the
coverup case. This is especially true if, as I think
necessary, a pardon action were accompanied by
an acknowledgement by Mr. Nixon of conspira-
torial participation.

I do not favor further talks with the Congressional leadership group listed in our charter as
necessary for consultation by the President before
dismissal of the Office of the Special Prosecutor.
The next two months of Congressional campaigning would doom what I would consider the required thoughtful decision process of Congressional action in this area. Even if a unanimous
request came from the eight leaders (and 6–2
seems the most outside possibility of agreement)
for no prosecution, each of the person's reasons
would be different and the conclusion of this
leadership group may not reflect any consensus
among the House and Senate as a whole.

If indictment is to be forthcoming, you and I
agree that it should be separate from the existing
coverup indictment and should be promulgated (if
the grand jury agrees) after jury sequestration in
the coverup case. Of course, an indictment ought
to follow only after the usual negotiations and presentations from defense counsel and only if those
negotiations do not produce a reason for nonin-
dictment that follows previous office policy.

As to any plea, which I consider highly unlikely, a one-count, section 1503 plea would be
sufficient in my mind and I would have to think
much more whether it might not be proper to join
in a recommendation to the court for leniency.
That is a possibility in my mind if I can think
through the possible existence of factors differing
from those that negated such a recommendation

274

for persons such as Krogh and Segretti and lesser figures who have already served prison time.

If you decide to recommend indictment to the grand jury, I think that the office presentation to the jury should include all the pros and cons of such an action. And I think it clear if you decide against an indictment recommendation, the matter must still be taken to the grand jury. This is true even if your reasons revolve around great doubts on the publicity issue. I see no indication from the cases [studied] that publicity questions are for other than the court to resolve, and this would hold true, I believe, even if you felt forced to agree with a defendant's motion to dismiss because of the pre-trial publicity. In that situation, a court might want to appoint special counsel for *amicus curiae* presentation of the no-dismissal side of the pre-trial publicity question.

Finally, a personal note. I am sure that many persons feel that the staff of this office is so embittered by now, and so partisan, than any judgment as to Mr. Nixon's fate cannot be suggested impartially.

Having returned from vacation after the resignation, I find from my own discussions with the staff that this alleged condition is just not a fact. True, there was bitterness about obstructive acts as each occurred. But this seemed to me focused upon our resultant inability to develop all the facts about the case, whatever those facts turned up. I find that there really is not a personal bitterness among the staff as to Mr. Nixon. Personally, I feel that he is a tragic figure, in deep loneliness and despair. I can appreciate what must be his bewilderment in that I can understand how, from his background, he must feel that he did what everyone else did and that his election mandate included much of what he did. I secure no enjoyment and little satisfaction from prosecution and, from my own background and beliefs, this prosecution business with its tragic consequences for individuals and their families and its aspects of playing "God" with people's futures is not a course of activity that I wish to pursue directly any longer than my sense of duty and responsibility requires. . . .

Then I received a memorandum from Herbert J. Miller, Jr., Nixon's attorney. I knew him as a capable attorney with much trial experience in criminal cases. At one time he had headed the Criminal Division of the Department of Justice. His memorandum, of course, was an argument against indictment of his client, and he based it on one issue: pretrial publicity. The memorandum was complete with references to legal precedents. We had studied these precedents, to be sure, and had concluded that in the main they did not preclude indictment. As Ruth had written in his memorandum: "I see no indication from the cases that publicity questions are for other than the court to resolve. . . ." Nevertheless, Miller's memorandum contained many of the thoughts that were disturbing me, and was persuasive enough to have a minor impact on some of the staff. It said:

Recent events have completely and irrevocably eliminated, with respect to Richard M. Nixon, the necessary premise of our system of criminal justice—that, in the words of Justice Holmes, ". . . the conclusions to be reached in a case will be induced only by evidence and argument in open court, not by any outside influence, whether of private talk or public print." *Patterson* v. *Colorado* (1905). As reiterated by the Court in *Turner* v.

Louisiana (1965): "The requirement that a jury's verdict 'must be based upon the evidence developed at trial' goes to the fundamental integrity of all that is embraced in the constitutional concept of trial by jury."

Never before in the history of this country have a person's activities relating to possible criminal violations been subjected to such massive public scrutiny, analysis and debate. The events of the past two years and the media coverage they received need not be detailed here, for we are sure the Special Prosecutor is fully aware of the nature of the media exposure generated. The simple fact is that the national debate and two-year fixation of the media on Watergate has left indelible impressions on the citizenry, so pervasive that the government can no longer assure Mr. Nixon that any indictment sworn against him will produce "a charge fairly made and fairly tried in a public tribunal free of prejudice, passion [and] excitement. . . ." *Chambers* v. *Florida* (1940).

Of all the events prejudicial to Mr. Nixon's right to a fair trial, the most damaging have been the impeachment proceedings of the House Judiciary Committee. In those proceedings neither the definition of the "offense," the standard of proof, the rules of evidence, nor the nature of the fact-finding body, were compatible with our system of criminal justice. Yet the entire country witnessed the proceedings, with their all-pervasive, multi-media coverage and commentary. And all who watched were repeatedly made aware that a committee of their elected Representatives, all lawyers, had determined upon solemn reflection to render an overwhelming verdict against the President, a verdict on charges time and again emphasized as constituting "high crimes and misdemeanors" for which criminal indictments could be justified.

All of this standing alone would have caused even those most critical of Mr. Nixon to doubt his chances of subsequently receiving a trial free from preconceived judgments of guilt. But the devastating culmination of the proceedings eliminated whatever room for doubt might still have remained as the entire country viewed those among their own Representatives who had been the most avid and vociferous defenders of the President (and who had insisted on the most exacting standards of proof) publicly abandon his defense and join those who would impeach him for "high crimes and misdemeanors."

None of this is to say, or even to imply, that the impeachment inquiry was improper, in either its inception or its conduct. The point here is that the impeachment process having taken place in the manner in which it did, the conditions necessary for a fair determination of the *criminal* responsibility of its subject under our principles of law no longer exist, and cannot be restored.

Even though the unique televised congressional proceedings looking to the possible impeachment of a President leave us without close precedents to guide our judgments concerning their impact on subsequent criminal prosecutions, one court has grappled with the issue on a much more limited scale and concluded that any subsequent trial must at minimum await the tempering of prejudice created by the media coverage of such events.

In *Delaney* v. *United States* (1st Cir. 1952), a District Collector of Internal Revenue was indicted for receiving bribes. Prior to the trial a subcommittee of the House of Representatives conducted public hearings into his conduct and related matters. The hearings generated massive publicity, particularly in the Boston area, including motion picture films and sound recordings, all of which "afforded the public a preview of the prosecution's case against Delaney without, however, the safeguards that would attend a criminal trial." Moreover, the publicized testimony "ranged far beyond matters relevant to the pending indictments." Delaney was tried ten weeks after the close of these hearings and was convicted by a jury. The Court of Appeals reversed, holding that Delaney had been denied his Sixth Amendment right to an impartial jury by being forced to "stand trial while the damaging effect of all that hostile publicity may reasonably be thought not to have been erased from the public mind."

The Court of Appeals did not suggest that the hearings were themselves improper. Indeed, the court emphatically stated that ". . . it was for the Committee to decide whether considerations of public interest demanded at that time a full-dress public investigation. . . ." But the court continued, "If the United States, through its legislative department, acting conscientiously pursuant to its conception of the public interest, chooses to hold a public hearing inevitably resulting in such damaging publicity prejudicial to a person awaiting trial on a pending indictment, then the United States must accept the consequence that the judicial department, charged with the duty of assuring the defendant a fair trial before an impartial jury, may find it necessary to postpone the trial until by lapse of time the danger of the prejudice may reasonably be thought to have been substantially removed."

The principle expounded by the court in *Delaney* is applicable here. Faced with allegations that the Watergate events involved actions by the President, the House of Representatives determined that not only was an impeachment inquiry required, but that the inquiry must be open to the public so that the charges and evidence in support thereof could be viewed and analyzed by the American people. We need not fault Congress in that decision. Perhaps—in the interest of the country—there was no other choice. But having pursued a course purposely designed to permit the widest dissemination of and exposure to the issues and evidence involved, the government must now abide by that decision which produced the very environment which forecloses a fair trial for the subject of their inquiry.

The foregoing view is not at all incompatible with the Constitution, which permits the trial of a President following impeachment—and therefore, some might argue, condones his trial after his leaving office. Nothing in the Constitution withholds from a former President the same individual rights afforded others. Therefore, if developments in means of communication have reached a level at which their use by Congress in the course of impeachment proceedings forever taints the public's mind, then the choice must be to forego their use or forego indictment following impeachment. Here, the choice has been made.

Further demonstration of the wholly unique nature of this matter appears in the public discussion of a pardon for the former President—which discussion adds to the atmosphere in which a trial consistent with due process is impossible.

Since the resignation of Mr. Nixon, the news media has been filled with commentary and debate on the issue of whether the former President should be pardoned if charged with offenses relating to Watergate. As with nearly every other controversial topic arising from the Watergate events, the media has sought out the opinions of both public officials and private citizens, even conducting public opinion polls on the question. A recurring theme expressed by many has been that Mr. Nixon has suffered enough and should not be subjected to further punishment, certainly not imprisonment.

Without regard to the merits of that view, the fact that there exists a public sentiment in favor of pardoning the former President in itself prejudices the possibility of Mr. Nixon's receiving a fair trial. Despite the most fervent disclaimers, any juror who is aware of the general public's disposition will undoubtedly be influenced in his judgment, thinking that it is highly probable that a vote of guilty will not result in Mr. Nixon's imprisonment. Indeed, the impact of the public debate on this issue will undoubtedly fall not only on the jury but also on the grand jury and the Special Prosecutor, lifting some of the constraints which might otherwise have militated in favor of a decision not to prosecute. Human nature could not be otherwise.

We raise this point not to suggest that the decision of whether to prosecute in this case cannot be reached fairly, but rather to emphasize that this matter—like none other before it and probably after it—has been so thoroughly subjected to extraneous and highly unusual forces that any prosecution of Mr. Nixon could not fairly withstand detached evaluation as complying with due process.

The Sixth Amendment guarantees a defendant trial by jury, a guarantee that has consistently been held to mean that each juror impaneled—in the often quoted language of Lord Coke—will be "indifferent as he stands unsworn." The very nature of the Watergate events and the massive public discussion of Mr. Nixon's relationship to them have made it impossible to find any array of jurymen who can meet the Sixth Amendment standard.

On numerous occasions the Supreme Court has held that the nature of the publicity surrounding a case was such that jurors exposed to it could not possibly have rendered a verdict based on the evidence. The most memorable of these was *Sheppard* v. *Maxwell* (1966), in which the Court, describing the publicity in the Cleveland metropolitan area, referred time and again to media techniques employed there—which in the Watergate case have been utilized on a nationwide scale and for a much longer period of time. The following excerpts from the Court's opinion are exemplary:

"Throughout this period the newspapers emphasized evidence that tended to incriminate Sheppard and pointed out discrepancies in his statements to authorities. . . ."

"On the sidewalk and steps in front of the courthouse, television and newsreel cameras were occasionally used to take motion pictures of the participants in the trial, including the jury and the judge. Indeed, one television broadcast carried a staged interview of the judge as he entered the courthouse. In the corridors outside the courtroom there was a host of photographers and television personnel with flash cameras, portable lights and motion picture cameras. This group photographed the prospective jurors during selection of the jury. After the trial opened, the witnesses, counsel, and jurors were photographed and televised whenever they entered or left the courtroom. . . ."

"The daily record of the proceedings was made available to the newspapers and the testimony of each witness was printed verbatim in the local editions, along with objections of counsel, and rulings by the judge. Pictures of Sheppard, the judge, counsel, pertinent witnesses, and the jury often accompanied the daily newspaper and television accounts. At times the newspapers published photographs of exhibits introduced at the trial, and the rooms of Sheppard's house were featured along with relevant testimony. . . ."

"On the second day of *voir dire* examination a debate was staged and broadcast live over WHK radio. The participants, newspaper reporters, accused Sheppard's counsel of throwing roadblocks in the way of the prosecution and asserted that Sheppard conceded his guilt by hiring a prominent criminal lawyer. . . ."

The prejudicial publicity in *Sheppard* commenced well before trial, even before charges were brought, and continued throughout the duration of the prosecution. Although Mr. Nixon has not been criminally tried, the press coverage of the impeachment proceedings and Watergate related criminal trials reflect obvious similarities to the *Sheppard* coverage.

The Sheppard murder was sensational and the media reacted accordingly. In the course they destroyed the state's ability to afford Sheppard a fair trial.

The sensation of Watergate is a hundredfold that of the Sheppard murder. But the media techniques remain the same and the destruction of an environment for a trial consistent with due process has been nationwide. The Supreme Court should not—upon an appeal by Mr. Nixon—have to recount for history the unending litany of prejudicial publicity which served to deprive the President of the rights afforded others.

The bar against prosecution raised by the publicity in this case defies remedy by the now common techniques of delaying indictment or trial, changing venue, or scrupulously screening prospective jurors. Although the court in *Delaney, supra,* could not envision a case in which the prejudice from publicity would be "so permanent and irradicable" that as a matter of law there could be no trial within the foreseeable future, it also could not have envisioned the national Watergate saturation of the past two years.

Unlike others accused of involvement in the Watergate events, Mr. Nixon has been the subject of unending public efforts "to make the case" against him. The question of Mr. Nixon's responsibility for the events has been the central political issue of the era. As each piece of new evidence became public it invariably was analyzed from the viewpoint of whether it brought the Watergate events closer to "the Oval Office" or as to "what the President knew and when he knew it." The focus on others was at most indirect.

In short, no delay in trial, no change of venue, and no screening of prospective jurors could assure that the passions aroused by Watergate, the impeachment proceedings, and the President's resignation would dissipate to the point where Mr. Nixon could receive the fair trial to which he is entitled. The reasons are clear. As the Supreme Court stated in *Rideau* v. *Louisiana* (1963):

"For anyone who has ever watched television the conclusion cannot be avoided that this spectacle, to the tens of thousands of people who saw and heard it, in a very real sense *was* . . . the trial. . . . Any subsequent court proceedings in a community so pervasively exposed to such a spectacle could be but a hollow formality."

Not only has the media coverage of Watergate been pervasive and overwhelmingly adverse to Mr. Nixon, but nearly every member of Congress and political commentator has rendered a public opinion on his guilt or innocence. Indeed for nearly two years sophisticated public opinion polls have surveyed the people as to their opinion on Mr. Nixon's involvement in Watergate and whether he should be impeached. Now the polls ask whether Mr. Nixon should be indicted. Under such conditions, few Americans can have failed to have formed an opinion as to Mr. Nixon's guilt of the charges made against him. Few, if any, could—even under the most careful instructions from a court—expunge such an opinion from their minds so as to serve as fair and impartial jurors. "The influence that lurks in an opinion once formed is so persistent that it unconsciously fights detachment from the mental processes of the average man." *Irvin* v. *Dowd* (1961). And as Justice Robert Jackson once observed, "The naïve assumption that prejudicial effects can be overcome by instructions to the jury . . . all practicing lawyers know to be unmitigated fiction."

The media accounts of Watergate, the political columnists' debates, the daily televised proceedings of the House Judiciary Committee, the public opinion polls, the televised dramatizations of Oval Office conversations, the newspaper cartoons, the "talk-show" discussions, the letters-to-the-editor, the privately placed commercial ads, even bumper stickers, have totally saturated the American people with Watergate. In the process the citizens of this country—in uncalculable numbers—from whom a jury would be drawn have formulated opinions as to the culpability of Mr. Nixon.

Those opinions undoubtedly reflect both political and philosophical judgments totally divorced from the facts of Watergate. Some are assuredly reaffirmations of personal likes and dislikes. But few indeed are premised only on the facts. And absolutely none rests solely on evidence admissible at a criminal trial. Consequently, any effort to prosecute Mr. Nixon would require something no other trial has ever required—the eradication from the conscious and subconscious of every juror the opinions formulated over a period of at least two years, during which time the juror has been subjected to a day-by-day presentation of the Watergate case as it unfolded in both the judicial and political arena.

Under the circumstances, it is inconceivable that the government could produce a jury free from *actual* bias. But the standard is higher than that, for the events of the past two years have created such an overwhelming likelihood of prejudice that the absence of due process would be inherent in any trial of Mr. Nixon.

It would be forever regrettable if history were to record that this country—in its desire to maintain the appearance of equality under law—saw fit to deny to the former President the right of a fair trial so jealously preserved to others through the constitutional requirements of due process of law and of trial by impartial jury.

But with all the advice, all the suggestions, with all the study I did myself, I knew in my own mind that if an indictment were returned and the court asked me if I believed Nixon could receive a prompt, fair trial as guaranteed by the Constitution, I would have to answer, as an officer of the court, in the negative.

If the question were then asked as to how long it would be before Nixon could be afforded his constitutional rights, I would have to say in fairness that I did not know.

chapter fifteen

The Pardon

WHILE I WAS studying the memoranda from the staff and seeking to determine the proper course of action, President Ford held a nationally televised press conference, his first since taking office, on August 28, 1974. Reporters, of course, were still interested in Nixon's future, and questioning of the President went in that direction.

QUESTION: Mr. President, aside from the Special Prosecutor's role, do you agree with the Bar Association that the laws apply equally to all men, or do you agree with Governor Rockefeller that former President Nixon should have immunity from prosecution, and, specifically, would you use your pardon authority, if necessary?

ANSWER: Well, let me say at the outset that I made a statement in this room in the few months [sic] after the swearing-in, and on that occasion I said the following: that I had hoped that our former President, who brought peace to millions, would find it for himself. Now, the expression made by Governor Rockefeller, I think, coincides with the general view and the point of view of the American people. I subscribe to that point of view, but let me add in the last ten days or two weeks I have asked for prayers for guidance on this very important point. In this situation I am the final authority. There have been no charges made, there has been no action by the courts, there has been no action taken by any jury, and until any legal process has been undertaken, I think it is unwise and untimely for me to make any commitment.

QUESTION: You are saying, sir, that the option of a pardon for former President Nixon is still an option that you will consider, depending on what the courts will do?

ANSWER: Of course, I make the final decision. Until it gets to me, I make no commitment one way or the other. But I do have the right as President of the United States to make the decision.

QUESTION: And you are not ruling it out?

ANSWER: I am not ruling it out. It is an option and a proper option for any President.

QUESTION: Do you feel the Special Prosecutor can in good conscience pursue cases against former top Nixon aides as long as there is the possibility that the former President may not also be pursued in the courts?

ANSWER: I think the Special Prosecutor, Mr. Jaworski, has an obligation to take whatever action he sees fit in conformity with his oath of office, and that should include any and all individuals.

QUESTION: Mr. President, you have emphasized here your option of granting a pardon to the former President.

ANSWER: I intend to.

QUESTION: You intend to have that option. If an indictment is brought, would you grant a pardon before any trial took place?

ANSWER: I said at the outset that until the matter reaches me, I am not going to make any comment during the process of whatever charges are made.

Like many others, I couldn't determine exactly what the President had meant in his replies to the reporters. I told some of the top members of the staff, however, that I certainly would not ask the grand jury to indict Nixon if President Ford intended to pardon him. Philip Lacovara, my counsel, recommended that I get in touch with the White House and ascertain the President's intention. If Ford was going to pardon Nixon, Lacovara recommended that I urge it be done immediately.

I really didn't need Lacovara's note to spur me in the direction of the White House, but I had no plan to urge anyone at the White House to do anything. I simply wanted to know where I stood. On September 4 I met with Philip Buchen, President Ford's counsel.

I told Buchen that Ford's statements at the press conference had put me in a peculiar situation. "It sounded like he was saying that any action I might take against Nixon would be futile."

Buchen said Ford wanted my opinion on how long it would be before Nixon could be given a fair trial if he were indicted. And the President wanted to know the areas of investigation involving Nixon's activities. Buchen didn't ask me for any recommendations and I offered none. I delivered him a letter that same day which said:

You have inquired as to my opinion regarding the length of delay that would follow, in the event of an indictment of former President Richard M. Nixon, before a trial could reasonably be had by a fair and impartial jury as guaranteed by the Constitution.

The factual situation regarding a trial of Richard M. Nixon within constitutional bounds is unprecedented. It is especially unique in view of the recent House Judiciary Committee inquiry on impeachment, resulting in a unanimous adverse finding to Richard M. Nixon on the Article involving obstruction of justice. The massive publicity given the hearings and the findings that ensued, the reversal of judgment of a number of the members of the Republican Party following release of the June 23 tape recording, and their statements carried nation-wide, and finally, the resignation of Richard M. Nixon, require a delay, before selection of a jury is begun, of a period from nine months to a year, and perhaps even longer. This judgment is predicated on a review of the decisions of the United States Courts involving prejudicial pre-trial publicity.

The Government's decision to pursue impeachment proceedings and the tremendous volume of television, radio and newspaper coverage given thereto, are factors emphasized by the Courts in weighing the time a trial can be had. The complexities involved in the process of selecting a jury and the time it will take to complete the process, I find difficult to estimate at this time.

The situation regarding Richard M. Nixon is readily distinguishable from the facts involved in the case of *United States* v. *Mitchell, et al.* The defendants in the Mitchell case were indicted by a grand jury operating in secret session. They will be called to trial, unlike Richard M. Nixon, if indicted, without any adverse finding by an investigatory body holding public hearings on its conclusions. It is precisely the condemnation of Richard M. Nixon already made in the impeachment process that would make it unfair to the defendants in the case of *United States* v. *Mitchell, et al.,* for Richard M. Nixon now to be joined as a co-conspirator, should it be concluded that an indictment of him was proper.

The *United States v. Mitchell, et al.* trial will within itself generate new publicity, some undoubtedly prejudicial to Richard M. Nixon. I bear this in mind when I estimate the earliest time of trial of Richard M. Nixon under his constitutional guarantees, in the event of indictment, to be as indicated above.

It so happened that just the day before I had received from Henry Ruth a list of areas of investigation in which Nixon may have been involved. There were ten of them, including tax deductions relating to the gift of pre-presidential papers, the misuse of IRS information, and misuse of the IRS through attempted initiation of audits of "enemies." In a note with the list, Ruth wrote: "None of these matters at the moment rises to the level of our ability to prove even a probable criminal violation by Mr. Nixon, but I thought you ought to know which of the pending investigations were even remotely connected to Mr. Nixon. Of course, the Watergate coverup is the subject of a separate memorandum." I attached a copy of the list to my letter to Buchen.

I reported to some staff members what had occurred, emphasizing that I had made no recommendation as to a pardon. The next day, September 5, Lacovara wrote me another memorandum. This time he urged me to recommend that a pardon, if in the offing, be a conditional one. Among the possible conditions was a provision that Nixon agree not to seek public office again. I sent Lacovara a memorandum the following day, September 6, pointing out that President Ford had not sought our advice or counsel on the matter of a pardon. "The President," I wrote, "has not undertaken to tell us how to prosecute, and I do not regard it proper to tell him how to pardon, if he has this in mind. . . ." Lacovara replied with a memorandum apologizing for having sent his initial memorandum without having thought through all the factors that might have been included in any discussion with Buchen.

I could not escape the conclusion that Ford had reached some decision on the matter, but I had no hard facts to back up my speculation.

Meanwhile, I had asked Judge Sirica to delay the cover-up trial from September 9 to September 30. Some of the defendants had asked for a delay on the basis of the publicity surrounding Nixon's resignation. It was my position that it was not necessary to consider the publicity issue since my office—and I assumed the defense—needed more time to transcribe and study the tapes Nixon had turned over to the judge to review for relevance to the case.

We also had moved to keep the remainder of the tapes in their White House vault. Haig, it will be recalled, had said the tapes would be shipped to Nixon in San Clemente. Shortly thereafter the White House announced that its legal office had concluded the Nixon tapes were his personal property and he could do with them as he wished. Before making a legal contest of it, talks were held with the White House lawyers and they agreed not to move the tapes until we could hold more substantial discussions on the matter. That satisfied the Special Prosecution Force for the moment. We had intervened just as a huge moving van was parked at the White House, ready to take the material to San Clemente.

FOUR DAYS AFTER MY MEETING with Buchen—it was Sunday, September 8—he called me at my apartment about 9:30 A.M. President Ford, he said, was going on television at 11 o'clock and announce the granting of a pardon to Richard Nixon. The pardon, he said, would cover all possible federal crimes Nixon may have committed while serving as President. I thanked him for calling. That was the extent of the conversation.

Jeannette and I had been planing to attend services at National Presbyterian Church and we left the apartment about 10:30. The President, of course, went on television while we were at worship. I could not concentrate on the sermon. My thoughts were a mixed bag. I could thank God, I thought, for clearing the atmosphere and for saving the nation from having Richard Nixon as President. But what were my obligations now? I knew one thing: I would have to examine the granting of the pardon from a legal standpoint and come to some judgment on whether it could be attacked.

Jeannette and I had hardly returned home from church before reporters from all the media swarmed into our lobby. When I didn't make an immediate appearance, they pitched camp to wait me out. I was too occupied with my thoughts to talk with them, and it was not the proper time to comment on Ford's action in any event. So Jeannette and I spent the afternoon and early evening in the apartment.

By dinnertime, however, we had tired of our self-imposed captivity. I called the desk clerk, a bright and friendly young man. Yes, he said, the lobby was still full of reporters and photographers. I told him we wanted to go to Harvey's for dinner and I didn't want to talk to the reporters.

"No problem," said the desk clerk. He came after us and took us down an elevator that opened on a hall near the kitchen. Through the kitchen we walked single file. Down to a basement we went. We walked past supplies and kitchen paraphernalia and then past garbage cans as we made our exit into an alley.

"Call me when you want to come back and I'll let you back in the same way," said the desk clerk.

We thanked him and walked down the alley to a side street and went on to Harvey's and our dinner. And, as the desk clerk had suggested, we returned the same way.

The next morning as I left for work a number of reporters were on hand again, but I had nothing to say to them. The pardon had drawn cries of outrage from the news media and other sectors and it appeared that President Ford would lose much of the support he had been granted as a "new broom." Some of the media saw the pardon as an undercutting and betrayal of the Special Prosecution Force.

When I did comment, I said I had not been consulted about the pardon. "It is a matter that was decided upon by the President on his authority under the Constitution." I said that Buchen had asked me when Nixon might come to trial if he were indicted and I had given him the best estimate I could give. But I emphasized that I gave Buchen no indication whether I intended to seek an indictment.

In his speech President Ford said he had been advised and was "compelled to conclude that many months and perhaps years will have to pass before Richard Nixon could hope to obtain a fair trial by jury in any jurisdiction of the United States under governing decisions of the Supreme Court."

Buchen, after the speech, read to reporters portions of my letter to him. In my opinion, he gave them the basics of the information I had given him. He did not read the portion where I noted that the huge amount of condemnatory publicity Nixon received from the impeachment proceedings would make it unfair to the cover-up defendants for him to be joined as a co-conspirator in the trial, if he were to be indicted. Buchen did this to conform to Judge Sirica's gag order on public discussion of the pending trial.

At one point Buchen told reporters: "President Ford has not talked with Mr. Jaworski, but I did report to President Ford the opinion of the Special Prosecutor about the delay necessary before any possible trial of the former President could begin."

QUESTION: Mr. Buchen, did Mr. Jaworski inform you that an indictment or indictments against former President Nixon were expected?

BUCHEN: No, he did not.

QUESTION: Was Mr. Jaworski ever consulted about this pardon, ever asked about this?

BUCHEN: No.

QUESTION: Did Jaworski agree to what was done today?

BUCHEN: He had no voice in it.

QUESTION: Do you know what his mood or sentiment was?

BUCHEN: You will have to ask him.

QUESTION: Why was he not consulted about what kind of action he contemplated against the former President before the pardon was issued?

BUCHEN: We didn't think that was relevant.

QUESTION: You assumed he would be prosecuted; is that right?

BUCHEN: We assumed that he may be prosecuted.

QUESTION: When was Jaworski told [about the pardon]?

BUCHEN: I called him about three-quarters of an hour before I knew the President was going to announce it so that he would know it.

QUESTION: Today?

BUCHEN: Yes.

QUESTION: What was his reaction?

BUCHEN: He thanked me for advising him in advance of his hearing it over the radio or TV.

QUESTION: And he did not object?

BUCHEN: He didn't. He didn't say anything one way or the other.

Because Buchen had omitted portions of my letter to him, President Ford used the omission to shed some of the heat the pardon had generated, according to news reports. He told congressional leaders, it was reported, that my letter would put the pardon in a more favorable light if only he could release all of it. Shortly thereafter Senator Scott, the Senate Minority Leader, implied to the media, it was reported, that the real explanation for the pardon could be found in my "secret" letter to Buchen. I had never sent Buchen a secret letter nor had I marked any parts of the September 4 letter as secret.

Rumors abounded that I was going to resign because of the pardon, and Doyle and his assistant, John Barker, were kept busy denying them. Lacovara, who had recommended on August 29 that I urge President Ford to grant an immediate pardon if he planned to issue one, did resign . . . on September 9, the day after the President's announcement. He had planned to resign, he wrote me, after the completion of the cover-up trial. Ford's decision, he wrote, had accelerated his intention to leave. He had performed well on the Special Prosecution Force, and his court presentations on unprecedented questions of law were notably distinguished. I told him so in a letter of reply.

NIXON DID NOT HELP President Ford with a statement he issued in accepting the pardon. He could see clearly now, Nixon said,

... that I was wrong in not acting more decisively and more forthrightly in dealing with Watergate, particularly when it reached the stage of judicial proceedings. ...

No words can describe the depths of my regret and pain at the anguish my mistakes over Watergate have cause the nation and the Presidency. ...

I know that many fair-minded people believe that my motivation and actions . . . were intentionally self-serving and illegal. I now understand how my own mistakes and misjudgments have contributed to that belief and seem to support it. ...

That the way I tried to deal with Watergate was the wrong way is a burden I shall bear for every day of the life that is left to me. ...

Still no admission of guilt. In the face of all the damning evidence, he would say only he had made mistakes. Accepting the pardon, however, amounted to an admission of guilt; one does not desire a pardon to hang on one's wall next to diplomas and awards of merit.

With no fanfare, the Special Prosecution Force made a thorough study to determine if the pardon were subject to an attack in court. We wanted to know if the pardon was invalid because it preceded any indictment or conviction. And we wanted to know if the President had bound himself through the Special Prosecutor's charter not to exercise his constitutional pardon powers when the exercise of that power would interfere with the independent judgment of the Special Prosecutor to decide whom to prosecute.

Before we could reach a determination, some members of Congress, editorial writers, and professors of law urged or demanded that I challenge the pardon. It was suggested that I do this by obtaining an indictment against Nixon and thus bring on a court test of the legality of the pardon. But I came to the conclusion that the President had a constitutional right to grant a pardon, regardless of his motives. I came to the further conclusion that granting the pardon did not affect the legal status of the prosecutions of the men in the cover-up case.

I had to withhold comment, however, because of the imminence of the cover-up case. So the sound and fury continued unabated. After the cover-up jury was sequestered, I made my conclusions public in a letter to Attorney General Saxbe:

. . . one of my responsibilities, not only as an officer of the court but as a prosecutor as well, is not to take a position in which I lack faith or which my judgment dictates is not supported by probable cause. The provision in the Constitution investing the President with the right to grant pardons, and the recognition by the United States Supreme Court that a pardon may be granted prior to the filing of charges are so clear, in my opinion, as not to admit of doubt. . . .

I have also concluded, after thorough study, that there is nothing in the charter and guidelines appertaining to the office of the Special Prosecutor that impairs or curtails the President's free exercise of the constitutional rights of pardon. . . .

Thus, in light of these conclusions, for me to procure an indictment of Richard M. Nixon for the sole purpose of generating a purported court test on the legality of the pardon would constitute a spurious proceeding in which I had no faith; in fact, it would be tantamount to unprofessional conduct and violative of my responsibility as prosecutor and officer of the court. . . .

Not long afterward the Supreme Court, in the case of *Maurice Schick* v. *George J. Reed, Chairman of the United States Board of Parole,* said: "We therefore hold that the pardoning power is an enumerated power of the Constitution and its limitations, if any, must be found in the Constitution itself. . . ."

Of course, there was no limitation to the pardoning power in the Constitution, as the legislators, editorialists, and professors of law could have ascertained. The Court also said: "Individual acts of clemency inherently call for discriminating choices because no two cases are the same. . . ." Six months after this decision, a nationally syndicated columnist was still criticizing my failure to attack the pardon.

And Lacovara, who had resigned in protest over the pardon, said in a radio interview: "I do believe, however, that if the issue were put to a court test, the courts would be likely to sustain the effectiveness of the pardon to Mr. Nixon, even if somehow—even if the granting of that pardon did constitute a breach of faith or a transgression of the commitments made to the Special Prosecutor. . . ."

When it became public knowledge that I did not intend to attack the pardon, we received a rash of mail. Some letters approved my stand, others decried it. One communication, a telegram, provided us all a chuckle. Florence Campbell, my secretary, was laughing when she placed it on my desk. It was from a young couple in the Middle West. Weeks earlier I had received a telegram from them when the Supreme Court had ruled in our favor on the tape question. They were so happy over the Supreme Court decision, they had wired, that they were naming their newborn son for me. The telegram just received was not a happy one, however. They were so upset over my decision not to attack the pardon that they were going to change their son's name immediately.

As we were preparing for the cover-up trial, John Ehrlichman subpoenaed Nixon as a defense witness. So did we. Ehrlichman needed Nixon for the trial, he said, because in unrecorded conversations with the former President he had been Nixon's conscience. Ehrlichman maintained that all during the period of the cover-up he was trying to get the truth out, and Nixon would confirm this. Nixon, he said, would testify that he told Ehrlichman, "I should have listened to you, John. . . ."

We subpoenaed Nixon because we thought at first that we would need him to verify the authenticity of the tapes. But James Neal, who was to prosecute, had a nagging hunch that Nixon, for one reason or another, would not appear for trial. So he set his team to hunting another means of establishing the tapes' authenticity, and the young lawyers found it in the law books. Recordings, they learned, are presumptively correct when they leave the hands of a co-conspirator provided certain facts can be established. Neal established the facts to Judge Sirica's satisfaction. Secret Service agents who had tended the tapes described how the recorders operated. It was shown that the tapes were taken from a co-conspirator, Nixon. It was shown that the tapes went directly from the White House to Judge Sirica and then to us—a chain of possession—and that they had not been altered. And Alexander Butterfield, the White House aide who had revealed the existence of the taping, testified that he had listened to the tapes and read our transcripts of them; the transcripts accurately identified the speakers, he said.

Nixon, in the meantime, was said to be very ill with phlebitis. His attorney said he couldn't travel and he couldn't testify. Judge Sirica sent a team of doctors to Southern California to examine him. They reported that

301

it would be dangerous for Nixon if he traveled to Washington and had to appear in Court. Ehrlichman then asked that the trial be delayed.

We argued that there was no way to tell how long the trial would have to be delayed; that Ehrlichman had offered no proof of what Nixon would testify to, such as an affidavit from the former President; that Nixon was a co-conspirator and that there was no showing in the recordings that he could help Ehrlichman.

Judge Sirica ruled that the trial would go on as scheduled.

We also decided not to try Gordon Strachan in the cover-up case, and charges against him eventually were dismissed. As Haldeman's aide and liaison man between the White House and CREEP, Strachan had played a minor but important role in the conspiracy. But before he was indicted, he had been granted immunity by the Senate Watergate Committee in exchange for his testimony. This meant we would have to develop our case against him at the trial without the use of the information he had given in his Committee testimony. We concluded we could do this—make the case without use of that information—and proved it in a showing before the court. But Neal calculated that Strachan's lawyers would be objecting repeatedly during the trial on the ground that some of the evidence was derived from immunized testimony, and thus impair our chances of convincing the others.

The trial began on October 1. It was in the good hands of Neal, Ben-Veniste, Volner, and other assistant prosecutors. I looked back at what we had accomplished, then looked ahead at the future. It was time I thought about going home to Texas.

chapter sixteen

Final Details

WITH THE JURY in the cover-up case chosen and sequestered, I could not see how I could make any significant contribution to the work ahead. For almost a solid year I had been confronted with decisions and legal problems of an unprecedented nature. Now I wanted to go home.

On October 12 I submitted a letter of resignation to Attorney General Saxbe. It read:

With the prosecution of *United States v. Mitchell, et al.* now in progress under the guidance of Associate Special Prosecutor James F. Neal and his assistants, the Watergate Special Prosecution Force is beginning to address itself to the completion of remaining investigations and to such prosecutions as are still to be conducted. The bulk of the work entrusted to the care of this office having been discharged, I am confident that such of our responsibilities as remain unfulfilled can well be completed under the leadership of another Special Prosecutor. A part of the unfinished matters relates to the area of the "milk fund" investigations, and as to these, I filed a letter of recusal shortly after becoming Special Prosecutor. Accordingly, after serving since November 5 of last year in this office, I tender my resignation effective October 25, 1974. . . .

When you testified at your nomination hearings,

you made it clear that you did not intend to interfere with the operation of my office and that you
would permit me to act independently and without
hindrance. You abided by this assurance and I
express to you my appreciation for having permitted me to proceed with my responsibilities as I
saw them.

I would appreciate receiving from you a communication accepting this resignation effective on
the date indicated.

He replied:

As you requested, I accept your resignation as
Special Prosecutor effective October 25, 1974. I do
so with great appreciation for the magnificent service you have rendered to the country. Your dedication and success in pursuing many difficult
problems and your great personal sacrifices de-
serve the praise of all Americans. . . .

The Watergate Special Prosecution Force has
aided immeasurably in achieving our shared goal
of restoring public confidence in the fair, effective
and impartial administration of the criminal laws.

In the coming days, I will be available to discuss
with you and your staff the outstanding issues
raised in your letter. You have my heartfelt
thanks and best wishes upon your return to private
life. . . .

With my letter of resignation, I also sent along an
interim report in which I made known my position on
the constitutionality and unassailability of the pardon
President Ford had granted Nixon. It read:

Two of the results achieved relate to the mandate directed to this office to investigate allegations

involving the President. Both are without precedent.

One is the extensive grand jury report on the involvement of Richard M. Nixon in Watergate coverup activities, prepared for the grand jury by this office and sent to the House Judiciary Committee last March, after successful litigation through the trial and appellate courts. While the grand jury report, which presented the chain of evidence in detail, has not been published, I am informed that it served as a major guide for the staff and members of the Committee in the development of the presentation leading to the Articles of Impeachment.

The second involved the successful litigation of a trial subpoena for tape recorded evidence in the hands of the President of the United States. The Supreme Court's unanimous decision supporting the subpoena for the Special Prosecutor compelled the former President to release, among others, the tape recording of June 23, 1973, which served as a forerunner to his resignation.

Although not appropriate for comment until after the sequestering of the jury in *United States v. Mitchell, et al.,* in view of suggestions that an indictment be returned against former President Richard M. Nixon questioning the validity of the pardon granted him, I think it proper that I express to you my views on this subject to dispel any thought that there may be some relation between my resignation and that issue.

As you realize, one of my responsibilities, not only as an officer of the court, but as a prosecutor as well, is not to take a position in which I lack faith or which my judgment dictates is not supported by probable cause. The provision in the Constitution investing the President with the right to grant pardons, and the recognition by the United States Supreme Court that a pardon may be granted prior to the filing of charges are so clear, in my opinion, as not to admit of doubt.

Philip Lacovara, then Counsel to the Special Prosecutor, by written memorandum on file in this office, came to the same conclusion, pointing out that: ". . . the pardon power can be exercised at any time after a federal crime has been committed and it is not necessary that there be any criminal proceedings pending. In fact, the pardon power has been used frequently to relieve federal offenders of criminal liability and other penalties and disabilities attaching to their offenses even where no criminal proceedings against the individual are contemplated."

I have also concluded, after thorough study, that there is nothing in the charter and guidelines appertaining to the office of the Special Prosecutor that impairs or curtails the President's free exercise of the constitutional right of pardon.

I was co-architect along with Acting Attorney General Robert Bork, of the provisions some theorists now point to as inhibiting the constitutional pardoning power of the President. The additional safeguards of independence on which I insisted and which Mr. Bork, on former President Nixon's authority, was willing to grant were solely for purposes of limiting the grounds on which my discharge could be based and not for the purpose of enlarging on the jurisdiction of the Special Prosecutor.

Hearings held by the Senate Judiciary Committee subsequent to my appointment make it clear that my jurisdiction as Special Prosecutor was to be no different from that possessed by my predecessor.

There was considerable concern expressed by some Senators that Acting Attorney General Bork, by supplemental order, inadvertently had limited the jurisdiction that previously existed. The hearings fully developed the concept that the thrust of the new provisions giving me the aid of the Congressional "consensus" committee were to insulate me from groundless efforts to terminate my employment or to limit the jurisdiction that existed. It was made clear, however, that there was no "redefining" of the jurisdiction of the Special Prosecutor as it existed from the beginning. There emerged from these hearings the definite understanding that in no sense were the additional provisions inserted in the Special Prosecutor's Charter for the purpose of either enlarging or diminishing his jurisdiction. I did stress, as I argued in the Supreme Court in *U.S.* v. *Nixon,* that I was given the verbal assurance that I could bring suit against the President to enforce subpoena rights, a point upheld by the Court. This, of course, has no bearing on the pardoning power.

I cannot escape the conclusion, therefore, that additional provisions to the Charter do not subordinate the constitutional pardoning power to the Special Prosecutor's jurisdictional rights. For me now to contend otherwise would not only be contrary to the interpretation agreed upon in Congressional hearings—it also would be, on my part, intellectually dishonest.

Thus, in the light of these conclusions, for me to procure an indictment of Richard M. Nixon for the sole purpose of generating a purported court test on the legality of the pardon, would constitute a spurious proceeding in which I had no faith; in fact, it would be tantamount to unprofessional conduct and violative of my responsibility as prosecutor and officer of the court.

Perhaps one of the more important functions yet to be discharged relates to our final report. It is contemplated that this report will be as all-encompassing as the authority granted this office permits, consistent with the prosecutorial function as delineated by the American Bar Association Standards for Criminal Justice. While this report will be cast in final form subsequent to my term as Special Prosecutor, I will be available to the authors for such contributions and consultations as they deem advantageous.

You are aware, of course, of the position this office has taken regarding access to former President Nixon's White House materials for all remaining investigations and prosecutions. Legislation now pending, if enacted, will solve the problem. If not enacted, I shall continue to be available, to whatever extent my successor desires, for counseling on reaching a solution to this problem so that all relevant materials will be forthcoming.

My Deputy, Henry Ruth, and most of the other members of the staff have worked together since the creation of the office. Mr. Ruth has a familiarity with all matters still under investigation as well as those still to be tried. He has been in charge of all "milk fund" matters, in view of my recusal. I trust that you will not mind my offering the suggestion that he be given consideration to serve as my successor, thus permitting the unfinished matters to continue without interruption.

I had timed my resignation so that the cover-up jury, sequestered and without access to news related to the case, would not be influenced by the public comments

I had anticipated. They would not know I had resigned until the trial was over.

I was surprised and gratified at the amount of editorial comment on my resignation, and at the remarks from those in public life for whom I had affection and regard. To be sure, *all* of the editorial comment was not laudatory. The New York *Times* savaged me in an editorial which said:

> After nearly a year of exemplary performance as Special Watergate Prosecutor, Leon Jaworski is leaving office under conditions that border on desertion of duty. Too many strands of the legal tangle left by the Nixon Presidency remain unraveled to justify Mr. Jaworski's assertion that his task is largely finished now that the jury in the Watergate coverup trial has been chosen and sequestered. Indeed, some of the statements made by the Special Prosecutor in his letter of resignation will contribute to making Watergate's final unraveling difficult, if not impossible.
>
> He was appointed in the wake of the "Saturday Night Massacre" in circumstances requiring exceptional integrity, independence and legal professionalism. Mr. Jaworski supplied that and more. He took over a deeply shaken staff, kept it together and moved ahead almost without missing a step.
>
> Under his leadership, major prosecutorial decisions were made which—with the large exception of permitting former Attorney General Richard G. Kleindienst to plead guilty to a misdemeanor—seemed judicious and appeared to serve the overriding interest of bringing to public knowledge and prosecution the perpetrators of the most serious crimes of the Nixon Administration. He persevered all the way to the Supreme Court in his quest for tapes and documents relating to the

coverup and thus was a major factor in terminating Mr. Nixon's Presidency.

But Mr. Jaworski has been unwilling to challenge the validity of the Nixon pardon or use the advantages of his office to the fullest in preparing for Congress the complete report of Mr. Nixon's malfeasance in office. In his emphatic letter to Attorney General Saxbe declining to test the legality of the pardon, Mr. Jaworski struck a note of certitude on a very dubious proposition. It is not at all clear that his charter is not broad enough to test Mr. Ford's use of the pardoning power. It is at least arguable that the President's act was an unwarranted intrusion on the Special Prosecutor's authority and subject to legal challenge.

Mr. Jaworski's reluctance to report to Congress on a completed investigation of Mr. Nixon is an even more dubious position. It is quite clear that he is required to submit a final report to Congress and there appears to be no reason whatsoever— other than Mr. Jaworski's reluctance to do so—to exclude from that report all of the details of the Special Prosecutor's investigations of Mr. Nixon's conduct.

Having taken those positions, Mr. Jaworski has created an atmosphere in which a decision by his successor to take either of those actions is bound to be highly controversial. And, in withdrawing at this stage of the investigation, Mr. Jaworski has made highly unlikely the selection of someone of a stature similar to his own or that of Archibald Cox, the original Watergate Special Prosecutor. Although Henry Ruth, Mr. Jaworski's deputy and preferred successor, is a man of ability and integrity, his appointment would not replace the moral authority which Mr. Jaworski built up during his tenure and which he squandered by his untimely resignation.

While Mr. Jaworski deserves the nation's thanks for the job he did, there can be no applause for the jobs he left undone or for the manner in which he failed to do them. The plain fact is that the job he was appointed to do is not yet done and he considerably reduced the likelihood that it ever will be. . . .

Several major newspapers chided the *Times* for skinning me, among them the San Francisco *Chronicle*:

. . . the best evidence that Jaworski acquitted himself brilliantly is that the first of the so-called "Watergate trials" has now been underway for a week before Judge Sirica. In admonishing the jurors to reserve judgment until all the evidence is before them, Judge Sirica said: "I don't know of any case I've been connected with in 47 years— 30 years as a lawyer and 17 years I've been on the bench—that I consider more important than this case. Not because of the names of the people involved, but because of the importance of the issues involved."

His [Jaworski's] critics fault him for not challenging President Ford's pardon of Nixon. He said simply that he felt Mr. Ford had full legal authority to do what he did, and testing this by a lawsuit would be "intellectually dishonest . . . tantamount to unprofessional conduct."

We are persuaded not only by Jaworski's views, but by the comment of Judge Sirica about the importance of the trial now in progress. Although there is no question that many Americans would have Mr. Nixon pursued, Mr. Ford's pardon re-

311

mains a fait accompli, and there is nothing to be gained in following cold trails.

The real arena is the courtroom. The opening statements of the prosecuting and defense lawyers suggest that little or nothing is going to go unconcealed. What one side fails to disclose, the other is almost certain to bring out.

In the language of courtroom lawyers, Jaworski "locked up the case" before he stepped out. His job was done. The entire scandal of Watergate has now entered a new phase. . . .

THE SPECIAL PROSECUTION FORCE also was criticized for what some saw as a lack of vigor in prosecuting corporations for making illegal campaign contributions. The question was asked: "Of the hundreds of major corporations why were only twenty corporations and twenty-four corporate officers prosecuted?"

It is likely that some officers of major corporations made illegal corporate contributions to the 1972 presidential campaign and avoided detection and prosecution, but in the estimate of the staff members who supervised the campaign contributions investigations, there weren't many.

The Special Prosecution Force, assisted by the FBI, investigated every substantial allegation or lead that could be obtained. Contributions records to both the Republican and Democratic presidential candidates were combed. Virtually every substantial contribution, by cash or check, from persons having identifiable connections with major corporations, was investigated. Contributors and fund-raisers were questioned. In many instances personal and corporate financial records were subpoenaed and examined. In every case in which a substantial corporate contribution to the 1972 presidential campaign was uncovered, a prosecution was brought.

312

Much was learned from these investigations. It was clear that, even though relatively few major federal prosecutions had been brought in the past, almost all corporate officials were well aware of the illegality of contributing corporate money to candidates for federal office. As a result, most did not make such contributions, motivated, if not by principle, at least by fear of being caught.

As a device to remain within the letter of the law a number of major corporations simply "encouraged" their officers to contribute from personal funds. A considerable amount of investigative attention was devoted to trying to obtain evidence of coercive practices in these patterns of corporate official giving, but without success.

Even where the amount of money contributed by an officer bore a suspiciously direct relationship to salary level, the corporate officers denied any express understanding of "ear-marking" a percentage of salary for political contributions. In a number of instances, corporate officials resorted to more transparent devices, such as reimbursement of corporate official contributors by phony "bonuses" or "expense accounts." In those instances where such evidence was obtained, prosecutions were brought.

As with any investigation of criminal conduct, some escaped detection. It was not feasible as a matter of sound prosecutive policy or effective use of investigative resources to do a detailed financial examination of every corporation and corporate officer. The Special Prosecution Force had to base its investigations on leads or evidence of "suspicious" contributions, and work from that. In one or two instances, strong suspicion remained that contributions purportedly from corporate officers' personal funds were in fact, in some indirect fashion, reimbursed from corporate monies. But suspicion could not take the place of evidence.

And lacking evidence, prosecutions could not be brought.

The question also was posed of why were there not more prosecutions of the political fund-raisers or candidates who received such contributions? The answer was that the statute, 18 U.S.C. 610, required that the recipient either *know* of the corporate source of political contributions, or receive such money in "reckless disregard" of whether the funds come from corporate sources or not.

The experience of our investigations demonstrated the virtual impossibility of proving such knowledge by the recipient. The corporate officials making the contribution, not surprisingly, did not tell the recipient that the money was corporate. Customarily, the contributions were delivered "from your friends at X Co." Our investigations further revealed that the recipients of such contributions were well aware of the provisions of 18 U.S.C. 610, and were quick to deny knowledge of the corporate source of the funds, usually stating that they presumed the contributions were from the personal funds of the officers of the corporation. Of course, in many instances investigated by the office that was the case; the contributions were from personal funds of officers and no violation of 18 U.S.C. 610 was established.

In two instances—the case of Maurice Stans, former Secretary of Commerce and Nixon's chief fund-raiser, and Jack Chestnut, Hubert Humphrey's campaign manager—prosecutions were brought against recipients of contributions made in violation of 18 U.S.C. 610. In the case of Chestnut, there was direct evidence that he knew that the money came from a corporation, Associated Milk Producers, Inc. Maurice Stans pleaded guilty to two counts of receiving corporate contributions in violation of 18 U.S.C. 610—$40,000 from the Goodyear Tire and Rubber Co. and $30,000 from the

Minnesota Mining and Manufacturing Co. Those two counts were charged on the "reckless disregard" theory and against a background of circumstantial evidence of Stans's receipt of large corporate cash contributions from officials of other companies.

In two other instances our investigation was able to establish that the defendants in fact knew the money came from corporate sources, but there was not sufficient evidence to establish that the committees and candidates who ultimately received the money were aware of the corporate source.

In the instances of other fund-raisers and candidates who received contributions which turned out to come from corporate sources, the amounts and numbers of such contributions were smaller and did not present direct evidence, as in the Chestnut case, or strong circumstantial evidence, as in the Stans case. It is of course much more difficult to argue that a $500 or $1,000 cash contribution should awaken suspicion as to a possible corporate source, than it is to make the same argument as to one or more $100,000 cash contributions. It was these practical realities of proof and political contribution practices that dictated the number of prosecutions brought. Even so, these relatively few cases brought by the Special Prosecution Force against recipients of illegal corporate contributions represented the first such federal prosecutions ever brought under this statute.

From the outset an overriding policy consideration of the Special Prosecution Force was to have the maximum deterrent effect on the practice of illegal corporate contributions to presidential candidates and political committees. The "volunteer policy" of pleading guilty served this end. It resulted in many more convictions than would otherwise have been the case. Perhaps more important, these Special Prosecution Force prosecutions opened the door for extensive investigation by the SEC and the IRS, and congressional investigations and stock-holder's actions which, in later months, laid more fully before the public the scope of the hitherto-concealed corporate abuses.

One of the most difficult decisions in formulation of the volunteer policy was whether to bring felony or mis-demeanor charges. The evidence in almost all instances would have supported the felony charge, but on balance it seemed fair to charge the volunteers with the mis-demeanor violation. Among the factors leading to this policy decision were (1) a desire, in the interest of general deterrence, to encourage many corporate viola-tors to come forward; (2) a recognition that felony charges had not been vigorously enforced in the past, particularly as to corporate officers, and we had to establish, by our prosecutive policies, a bridge between those past policies and hoped-for future policies of sterner enforcement; (3) a recognition that misde-meanor convictions, subjecting the individual defen-dants to fines and up to one year of imprisonment, pro-vided ample sentencing latitude to any judge disposed to impose a jail sentence; (4) a recognition that if the Special Prosecution Force had to follow the route of exhaustive investigation, absent the cooperation of cor-porate officials, evidence would be much more difficult to obtain and fewer prosecutions would result.

As the work of the Campaign Contributions Task Force progressed, it became clear that some "volun-teers" were more voluntary than others. The early volunteers had heard of "Rose Mary's List" and feared they might be on it. Rose Mary Woods, Nixon's secre-tary, had kept a list of those who had made large contributions to Nixon's campaign before April 7, 1972 —the effective date of a new campaign law which re-quired that contributions be reported publicly. The exis-tence of the list was initially disclosed in a civil suit brought against CREEP's finance committee. The Special Prosecution Force obtained a copy.

With the thought of the list being in our hands, the early volunteers decided to confess rather than construct a "cover story." The later volunteers confessed belatedly after our investigations had commenced. A few corporations decided not to volunteer and were prosecuted.

In the judgment of those of the Special Prosecution Force who directed the Campaign Contributions investigations, the "volunteer" policy achieved its desired impact. For the first time in the history of federal prosecutions, one after another, prominent heads of giant U.S. corporations pleaded guilty to making illegal corporate contributions. The prosecutions and the chain of disclosures set in motion by the convictions undoubtedly would prove to be a deterrent to that kind of illegal corporate conduct in the future.

In extenuation of the errant conduct of corporate officers, illegal campaign contributions had been a "way of life" through a number of administrations and no prior note had been taken of these violations. And, in the Nixon years, his fund-raisers' solicitations were often accompanied with the implied threat that the corporation that failed to contribute would not be aided with its business problems at the Washington level. Such coercion was despicable.

THERE WAS SOME SPECULATION, particularly in Texas, that I had resigned in order to be out of the Special Prosecutor's office before John Connally came to trial. He had been indicted on two counts of accepting an illegal payment, one count of conspiracy to commit perjury and obstruct justice, and two counts of making a false declaration to a grand jury.

There was not a grain of truth in the speculation. Connally's indictments grew out of the investigation of the Associated Milk Producers, Inc. (AMPI), the country's largest organization of dairy farmers. The organization and several of its ranking officers either pleaded guilty or were tried and found guilty of making illegal political contributions in the hundreds of thousands of dollars. Also investigated were reports that the Administration's decision to raise milk price supports in 1971 was prompted by AMPI's commitment of funds for the 1972 campaign.

Harold Nelson, former AMPI general manager, while pleading guilty to the felony charge of conspiracy to make corporate contributions, also pleaded guilty to approving a payment, to be made through a third party, to Connally, then Secretary of the Treasury. The third party was Jake Jacobsen, a Texas lawyer retained by AMPI. Jacobsen was indicted for making an illegal payment to a public official, Connally, and pleaded guilty to the charge. It was Connally's contention that the payment was never made.

It will be recalled that I disqualified myself in all aspects of the milk fund investigation almost immediately upon assuming the Special Prosecutor's job. I did this because my law firm was representing the Independent Milk Producers in an anti-trust suit against AMPI. I had no idea then that either Jacobsen or Connally would become involved. Later, when it appeared that criminal action might be taken against Jacobsen, I noted another disqualification. I pointed out that I should not serve in any matter relating to him because of our long acquaintance which began when he was Assistant Attorney General of Texas. During President Johnson's administration I also had contacts with Jacobsen, primarily at the suggestion of the President; Jacobsen was then serving as one of LBJ's assistants.

Connally and I had never been close friends. Indeed, I had supported Price Daniel when he and Connally had contested for the Texas governorship. After that race, which Connally won, we formed a friendly acquaintanceship. During his last term as Governor, Connally asked me to serve as chairman of the Governor's Committee on Public Education. I was working on several national commissions at the time, and I undertook to get him to appoint someone else. He was insistent that I take the assignment and eventually I accepted it.

When Connally left the Governor's office and came to Houston to practice law, we saw very little of each other. The references in the news columns that we were close friends were erroneous, although I always held him in high regard.

After Connally's appearance before the grand jury in Washington, I promptly called attention to my disqualification and at no time did I participate in the investigation or the action that was taken. The progress of matters was left entirely to Ruth and his assistants. I did ask Ruth to proceed with caution. It appeared that Connally was a likely candidate for the Republican nomination for President and I did not want him tarnished by news reports that he was under investigation until the matter was completed and a decision had been made as to whether the investigation should be closed or action should be taken. Although Connally made two appearances before the grand jury and visited the Special Prosecutor's office with his counsel, the appearances were handled in such manner as to avoid any publicity. When he visited our offices, I did not see him. I did not talk with him at all throughout this period of time, nor did I see or talk with Jacobsen.

In time, following Connally's second appearance before the grand jury and the conducting of further investigation, a decision was reached by Ruth and the assistant prosecutors in charge that an indictment against him should be returned. I was not aware of what had been said in his grand jury testimony and was unfamiliar with all of the other aspects of the investigation. Ruth told me, however, that he had gone to the Criminal Division of the Department of Justice and submitted the entire testimony to that division for evaluation. It had been concluded by that division, as well as by Ruth, than an indictment needed to be returned.

I was aware of plans to have Connally address the State Bar of Texas in San Antonio. I suggested to Ruth that if indictments involving Connally were contemplated, they should be deferred until the address had been made. Then it was announced that Connally's son was to be married and that Connally was to be the best man. I told Ruth of this and he decided to withhold the indictment until the wedding was over.

When the indictment finally came through, some Connally devotees suggested that I should have exerted some influence to restrain Ruth and his associates from proceeding with the indictment, despite my disqualification. This was an absurd, even unfair, attitude. But because of the talk along this line and because a reporter for the *Wall Street Journal* had gone to Houston to get comments about it, I dealt with the subject in an address I made to the Men's Forum of The Houston Club prior to Connally's trial. In that address I said:

I have commented on some decisions that were difficult. Now just a few comments about one that presented no difficulty to me—yet seems not to be a course acceptable to some. When I first assumed my duties in Washington, I looked over the list of companies and individuals under investigation to determine whether I was disqualified to make decisions as to any of these because of a conflict of interest. There were a few, involving allegedly illegal campaign contributions, that fell in this category. Prominent among them were matters under investigation relating to alleged illegal milk fund contributions and allied matters. I filed a written recusal in these investigations within a short period after taking my oath of office, pointing out the reasons for the disqualification. This was an *easy* decision because any other course would have been improper and dishonorable. To disqualify in such instances involves not only respect for a rule of law but a moral issue as well. The Standards of the American Bar Association, relating to the prosecution function, provide that "A prosecutor should avoid *the appearance or reality* of a conflict of interest with respect to his official duties." It further points out that the prosecutor's failure to do so may well constitute unprofessional conduct.

Once a disqualification is filed, that official is in honor bound—in fact, required by law—to disassociate himself completely from whatever investigations, discussions and decisions that may be involved. It would also be unprincipled and dishonorable for him, after disqualification, to undertake to influence any action or decision with respect to such matters.

Should any thoughtful person have any difficulty in understanding that the administration of justice would become tainted, in fact, prostituted, if this were not the course of conduct to follow? I would not think that this poses any question leaving room for doubt, yet recently I noted some indication to the contrary, either by misguided individuals or by some who seek to misguide.

Connally was tried on two counts of accepting illegal payments, and was acquitted. The other counts against him were dismissed. Still the talk continued. Some of it, I felt certain, was because Connally was a member of a large Houston law firm, and many persons naturally assumed some rivalry between that firm and mine.

The *Texas Monthly,* a respected journal, covered the Connally trial and offered some observations on the criticism that had been leveled at me.

Shortly after his arrival . . . Jaworski issued two recusal memoranda [the article said] . . . one withdrawing himself from "all aspects of the Dairy Industry Investigation" because his law firm represented another dairy co-op in a suit against AMPI; the other withdrawing from "all matters relating to" Jake Jacobsen because of a "long-standing acquaintance" with him. At that point, of course, Connally and Jake were still friends, still on the same side—Connally was even sending Jake copies of his grand jury testimony. And that was the last Jaworski saw of Connally's case.

Which was as it should be. It's all very easy now, in the comfortable serenity of hindsight, to say Jaworski should have done this or that. Some of Connally's friends think Jaworski should have told his staff, "Now this guy has a heck of a reputation and you'd better proceed with care." Less circumspect Connally supporters think he should have just derailed the investigation entirely. Alternatively, Connally's enemies can argue that Jaworski should have stayed with it if for no other reason than Jaworski is too able a lawyer to walk into court with as sorry a case as his former underlings had. Or, possibly, if Jaworski had the same low opinion of Jacobsen as most of Jake's other "long-standing acquaintances" seemed to have, then Jaworski should have warned his staff to be leery of dealing with such a man.

But all of these "shoulds," in the final analysis,

would simply amount to privileged tinkering with the judicial machinery. And that, we know, is *exactly* what brought Watergate down around us in the first place—what Jaworski was supposed to be rooting out, not encouraging. No, if there is any finger-pointing or blame-fixing to be done for such a weak case being brought to trial—if there's even any called for—then the responsible parties could be found among a select group of reporters and politicians.

Connally was given a clean bill of health according to the American system of justice. I felt relieved that the matter had been disposed of. If errors were made by those who were in charge of the investigation and the prosecution, they were not made with the intent of being oppressive or unjust. They were made in the spirit of letting our system of justice operate without seeking or granting favor. I wrote Connally a note telling him I was personally relieved that his ordeal was over and that I hoped that he and his wife would receive the peace and contentment to which they were entitled.

chapter seventeen

Haunting Memories

Bringing the Watergate cover-up conspirators to trial—and convicting them—was a major accomplishment of the Special Prosecution Force . . . and a triumph for the American people and our system of justice.

While the trial was in its preliminary stage, John Wilson, attorney for H. R. Haldeman, called my office and left a question with my secretary: "If Judge Sirica is willing, will Mr. Jaworski meet with me in the judge's chamber late this afternoon . . . say about four-thirty?"

I made arrangements to meet as requested. Fifteen minutes before the meeting, however, I met with Neal. It seemed likely to me that Wilson, at this late stage, wanted to bargain for a guilty plea for Haldeman. Neal said this was true. Wilson had indicated to him, Neal said, that if we were willing to accept a single felony plea from Haldeman and dismiss other charges, Haldeman would be willing to testify against Ehrlichman and in all other matters known to him. Neal added, "Wilson thinks, and I agree with him, that if Haldeman pleads, John Mitchell will cave in."

Neal and I talked it over a little more. He said he unqualifiedly supported such a plea arrangement with Haldeman. I took this thought with me into the meeting in Judge Sirica's chambers.

The judge greeted Wilson and me, and Wilson immediately began an explanation of the deal he wanted to make for Haldeman. "But," he told the judge, "before I enter a plea, I want to know, on behalf of my client, what your reaction would be as far as a sentence is concerned."

Without hesitation, Judge Sirica said, "Haldeman will have to take his chances on that."

Wilson sought to keep the conversation going, trying a number of times to get the judge to give some hint of the length of sentence Haldeman could expect. Each time the judge waved the query aside, repeating, "He'll have to take his chances. . . ."

Wilson finally gave up. "Well," he said, "I just wanted to see if there was some intimation I could take back to my client."

The meeting adjourned, the trial continued, and Neal, Ben-Veniste, Volner, and the other assistant prosecutors conducted the case brilliantly. Neal's summation will take its place in legal history. He showed how a trial lawyer can fully grasp the evidence, complex as some of it might be, and make his points to the jury with clarity and certitude. Neal demolished the "scenarios" constructed in the Oval Office. Early he said:

There has been some effort here to beguile you by stating over and over again that this nearly half million dollars paid to the original Watergate defendants was attorney fees, family support, income replacement and bail. And so what is the big problem?

The Government agrees that the use to which this money was put was attorney fees, income replacement, family support and bail. But we say most emphatically . . . that that does not answer the question; that simply poses it. The question is,

what was the motive or intent behind the payments?

One billion dollars, or one trillion dollars paid
for family support, income replacement, attorney
fees, bail, is not an offense. It is fine if it is motivated purely by charitable or humanitarian purposes and nothing else. But one red cent paid
to keep somebody from talking and divulging information to the appropriate authorities, whether
it is a red cent for attorney fees or a red cent
for a haircut, is obstruction of justice. . . .

As you have heard, the money was paid in
absolute secrecy. Communications were made from
phone booths to phone booths. Code names were
used and coded messages were sent. Cash, that
non-fundable commodity, was always used. The
bundles of cash were left in phone booths, in
lockers in airports, on ledges in hotels, and in the
dead of night in mail boxes out in Potomac,
Maryland.

The drops of money were made, ladies and
gentlemen, so that the persons delivering the
money and the persons receiving the money never
saw each other.

Doesn't that impress you as a rather extraordinary effort to conceal humanitarian or charitable
impulses? On the other hand, these efforts were
necessary if there was a conspiracy to keep people
from talking. . . .

On Neal went, recounting the evidence against
Mitchell, against Haldeman, Ehrlichman, Mardian, and
Parkinson. He had used as witnesses the former colleagues of the accused—Dean, Kalmbach, LaRue,
Magruder, Krogh, and Hunt. But uniquely in the history
of litigation, he had used the tapes; the jurors had
heard the conversations. And as the tapes brought on

the downfall of Richard Nixon, they sealed the convictions of all the defendants save Parkinson, who was found not guilty. Ehrlichman was found guilty of four of the five counts against him and was sentenced to serve two and a half to eight years in prison. Haldeman was found guilty on all five counts against him and received the same sentence. Mitchell also received the same sentence; he was found guilty on five of the six counts against him. Mardian was found guilty on one count of conspiracy to obstruct justice and was sentenced to serve ten months to three years in prison. All appealed their convictions.

As THE TRIAL drew to its conclusion, my last days in office were busy ones; there were the conferences with staff members in an effort to be of maximum assistance in channeling to eventual conclusion whatever matters remained. They were pleasant days but tinged with a special kind of sadness. Without exception, the members of the staff found a way of dropping by my office to say goodbye. We had been a team whose individual members had for each other both affection and respect.

James Doyle and his assistant, John Barker, took me to Dulles Airport, where I was to catch a plane for Austin (I was going from Austin to the ranch, where Jeanette was awaiting me). We drove to the airport in the Special Prosecutor's car—my last official ride. Barker sat in the front seat by the driver; Doyle was beside me in the back. We recalled that it had been Doyle and Barker who had met me at Dulles Airport when I arrived in Washington to take on my assignment. From somewhere in the car, Doyle—with a flourish—produced a small bottle of white wine. He pulled the cork, this wise and cheerful man, and, passing the bottle around, we three drank to the memory of the past with all its anguishes and triumphs.

On my arrival at Dulles Airport a year earlier, I

had been surrounded by an army of newspersons, all wanting a crack at the new Special Prosecutor. Doyle and Barker had "rescued" me and taken me to my office.

On this last day we waited alone for the plane to take me back to Texas.

MY REFLECTIONS OF WATERGATE center on the tapes: how they haunted Richard Nixon. From July, 1973, when Alexander Butterfield publicly revealed their existence, until his resignation, Nixon was absorbed in extricating himself from their grip. Before that, Nixon and his cohorts safely spun a fabric of lies and deceptions. After their existence was confirmed, he held innumerable sessions with his staff and others, seeking escape. He devoted not only long hours of the day to this problem, but spent many hours at night rehashing the day's conversations. There were boat trips on the Potomac to discuss the matter, trips to Florida and San Clemente, automobile trips with his close friend, Bebe Rebozo.

Listening and relistening to the tapes, I was amazed at the inordinate amount of time they consumed. I often wondered how Nixon was able to concentrate even briefly on the matters of state that begged for his attention. There he was in the Oval Office, day after day, night after night, scheming, plotting and finally sacrificing his staff and others, one by one, so as to save himself. It was a sordid, frightening drama.

The natural assumption is that Nixon taped his conversations because he wanted them for his memoirs —as vile and mean as many of those conversations were. But when Butterfield revealed the tapes' existence, why did not Nixon immediately destroy them? If he had done so, saying the conversations dealt with national security and matters highly embarrassing to members of his cabinet, to individuals in Congress and others, a majority of Americans would have accepted his word. Despite all the criticism such a desperate act would create, I believe he would have survived and remained in office.

But Nixon did not destroy the tapes because it never occurred to him that legal action might force him to surrender them. During 1972, and perhaps during the early part of 1973, he thought the tapes possessed extraordinary monetary value. He hoped to realize a fortune from them. And his background showed him to be a man greedy for both money and power. I am confident that he felt secure in his claim of executive privilege. And when that claim was jeopardized by the actions of the Special Prosecutor's office, it was too late.

Then there was the vindictive side of the President. As the tapes were to disclose, Nixon was not alone in these feelings. During a conversation with Haldeman and Dean on September 15, 1972—the day Nixon congratulated Dean for keeping the scandal away from the White House—they talked of their "enemies" and what they would do to them. They were particularly vexed at Attorney Edward Bennett Williams, who represented the Washington *Post*. Said Haldeman: "The Bureau ought to go into Edward Bennett Williams and let's start questioning that son-of-a-bitch. Keep him tied up for a couple of weeks." And Nixon said, "Yeah, I hope they do . . ."

Later Dean was explaining that there was some bitterness at CREEP over Watergate between the people on the finance committee and the political committee, and that it could cause trouble.

NIXON: They're all in it together.
DEAN: That's right.
NIXON: They should just behave and, and, recognize this, this is, again, this is war. We're getting

329

a few shots. It'll be over. Don't worry. I wouldn't want to be on the other side right now. Would you? I wouldn't want to be in Edward Bennett Williams' position after this election.

DEAN: No. No.

NIXON: None of these bastards—

DEAN: He, uh, he's done some rather unethical things that have come to light already, which in—again, Richey has brought to our attention.

NIXON: Yeah.

HALDEMAN: Keep a log on all that.

DEAN: Oh, we are, on these. Yeah.

NIXON: Yeah.

HALDEMAN: Because afterwards that is a guy . . .

NIXON: We're going after him.

HALDEMAN: That is a guy we've got to ruin.

DEAN: He had, he had an *ex parte*—

NIXON: You want to remember, too, he's an attorney for the Washington *Post*.

DEAN: I'm aware of that.

NIXON: I think we are going to fix that son-of-a-bitch. Believe me. We are going to. We've got to, because he's a bad man.

Dean explained that he had been keeping notes on people who were proving to be less than friends. "Great!" said Nixon—and Dean continued: "Because this is going to be over some day and they're—we shouldn't forget the way some of them have treated us."

NIXON: I want the most, I want the most comprehensive notes on all of those that have tried to do us in. Because they didn't have to do it.

DEAN: That's right.

NIXON: They didn't have to do it. I mean, if the thing had been a close—uh, they had a very close election everybody on the other side would understand this game. But now they are doing this quite deliberately and they are asking for it and they are going to get it. And this, this—we have not used the power in this first four years, as you know.

DEAN: That's right.

NIXON: We have never used it. We haven't used the Bureau and we haven't used the Justice Department, but things are going to change, and they're going to get it right—

DEAN: That's an exciting prospect.

NIXON: It's got to be done. It's the only thing to do.

The discussion turned to the Washington *Post,* which had broken the first stories about the cover-up. Said Nixon: "The main thing is, the *Post* is going to have damnable, damnable problems out of this one. They have a television station."

DEAN: That's right, they do.

NIXON: And they're going to have to get it [the license] renewed.

HALDEMAN: They've got a radio station, too.

NIXON: Does that come up [for re-licensing] too? The point is, when does it come up?

DEAN: I don't know. But the practice of non-licensees filing on top of licenses has certainly gotten more active in the area.

NIXON: And it's going to be goddamn active here.

From time to time the tapes reflected Nixon's disappointment that the Watergate bugging, which caused so much trouble, produced nothing of value to CREEP and the White House. He returned to this theme in a conversation with Dean.

NIXON: You know, that must, must be an indication of the fact that we had goddamn poor pickings. Because naturally anybody, either Chuck or Bob, were always reporting to me about what was going on. If they ever got any information they would certainly have told me that we got some information, but they never had a goddamn thing to report. What was the matter? Did they never get anything out of the damn thing?

DEAN: I don't think they ever got anything.

NIXON: A dry hole?

DEAN: That's right.

NIXON: Jesus Christ!

The tapes also showed Nixon's changing moods as the cover-up conspiracy began to break apart. On March 22, 1973—the day after Dean reviewed the situation with him—Nixon was talking with Dean, Haldeman, Ehrlichman, and Mitchell, and his faith in the cover-up was still strong. He gave them a pep talk. He said: "We all know what it is. Embarrassing goddamn thing and so forth. But my view is some of it will come out. We will survive. That's the way it is. That's the way you've got to look at it. . . ."

By April 16 he was squirming. He knew that Dean had been talking to the Justice Department but he didn't know what Dean had said. He attempted to make Dean rethink the long conversations of March 21 when they had discussed payoff money and clemency for the Watergate burglars. He was trying to minimize the things he said. Most of the time, on most of the points, Dean politely corrected him. Nixon obviously was talking for his tape machine; Dean was unaware of the taping, but he apparently sensed something was amiss.

At one point Dean told Nixon he was "incapable"

of going before investigative bodies and lying under oath. Nixon, suddenly all sanctimony, said: "That's right. Thank God. Don't ever do it, John. Whatever you do, tell the truth. That is the thing that you're gonna . . . I have told everybody around here, 'Goddamn it, tell the truth!' 'Cause all they do, John, is compound it. That son-of-a-bitch Hiss would be free today if he hadn't lied about that, John. If he had said, if he had just said . . . he didn't have . . . he could have just said, 'I . . . look, I knew Chambers and, yes, as a young man I was involved with some Communist activities but I broke it off many years ago.' And Chambers would have dropped it. But, if you are going to lie, you go to jail for the lie rather than the crime. . . ."

Two weeks later he fired Dean—for telling the truth to the Justice Department.

LOOKING BACK, one can trace Nixon's downfall from the day he was elected President in 1968. The extreme narrowness of Nixon's margin of victory over Hubert Humphrey was traumatic. Humphrey had emerged from the shambles of the Chicago convention far behind in the polls. But during the campaign, struggling on a financial shoestring, he gained votes as Nixon lost them. When the polls closed Humphrey was almost even in the popular vote. No wonder, then, that Nixon and his aides were willing to do almost anything to crush the opposition in 1972.

The landslide victory over George McGovern in November, 1972, was the next step in Nixon's undoing. Now his hold on power was firm. The bombing of Cambodia occurred just after the election, in the latter days of December, 1972. By January, 1973, the tapes showed that Nixon had begun to bristle over every criticism of the bombing. He vehemently denounced everyone who failed to give him strong support, cursing those who had been close friends for years.

In phone calls at night with Colson he was particularly bitter. But the significant part of these conversations was his references to his 62 percent of the vote in the election. After denigrating some person, he would ask Colson, "Does not this fellow realize that I have a mandate at the hands of the American people?" It was clear that he had interpreted the vote as a grant of *unlimited* power, and he left no doubt that he intended to use it.

I had thought Nixon would make a good and strong President. I was mistaken. He became petty and arrogant, determined to use the powers of his office as he pleased—whether right or wrong. His arrogance made him contemptuous of the public. And this was a tragic mistake, because an aroused public had a mighty impact on the course of events after Watergate. It will be recalled that in my first meeting with General Haig he made no effort to conceal his fears of the public's reaction to the "Saturday Night Massacre." He described that reaction to me as "almost revolutionary." According to him, things were "coming apart."

I would never have been appointed Special Prosecutor but for the fact that the public would not have allowed the selection of someone biased in Nixon's favor. I was not the ideal selection from Nixon's standpoint, but someone like me had to be chosen—even at the cost of giving the new Special Prosecutor more independence than Archibald Cox had, thereby providing assurance that another "Saturday Night Massacre" would not occur.

In the end, Nixon was forced to resign because the people had lost confidence in him. He had lied too often. The members of the House Judiciary Committee realized this, and that is why they concluded unanimously that he had been guilty of obstructing justice.

Even some of his devotees were appalled at his brazen falsehoods when their accumulative weight broke through politically partisan barriers.

I learned that the real guardians of our institutions of government are the very citizens he held in contempt.

I think now of two men, two of Nixon's staunchest supporters, Senator Barry Goldwater of Arizona and Dwight Chapin, the White House aide who headed the "Dirty Tricks" division of the Administration's political espionage program. The evidence against young Chapin was overwhelming, but never once did he seriously consider plea bargaining. To have pleaded guilty would have been a betrayal of the man he most admired. Because in Chapin's view Nixon could do no wrong, Chapin had done no wrong in serving him. He was the first White House figure to go to trial and be convicted. He left the courthouse praising Nixon and convinced of his own innocence. It took months of prison confinement to change his mind. In a letter to Judge Gerhard Gesell, who had sentenced him, Chapin wrote that he accepted his punishment "with a keen sense of awareness that I would not be here if, indeed, I had not done something wrong." Nixon has not yet admitted as much.

Senator Goldwater, it was reported, wept at Nixon's resignation; he later visited him in San Clemente. But time went by, and Nixon not only failed to show signs of repentance but indicated in various ways he was regaining some of the arrogance his resignation had diminished. He went to China in February, 1976, as a private citizen and, while there, made statements some interpreted as derogating the statesmanship of President Ford and Secretary of State Henry Kissinger. Goldwater was asked his opinion. He said, "I don't think Mr. Nixon's visit to China did anything . . . I don't think the average American has enough respect for Mr. Nixon any more to really believe that what he's doing is in anybody's interest but Mr. Nixon's. . . ."

THE TAPES! The teachings of right and wrong were forgotten in the White House. Little evils were permitted to grow into great evils, small sins escalated into big sins. In the hours and hours of tape-recorded conversations to which I listened, not once was there a reference to the Glory of God, not once a reference to seeking spiritual guidance through prayer. Our Lord was mentioned, yes, but on each pitiable occasion His name was taken in vain. If only there had been an occasional prayer for help, an occasional show of compassion! Why was there not just a simple statement such as: "May we hold our honor sacred. . . ." How different might have been the course of government if there had been an acknowledgment of God as the source of right instead of a denial of Him in a seemingly unending series of ruthless actions.

The founders of this nation would have been stunned by the revelations of Watergate. But they would have been especially proud of the judiciary they had created. There was a trial judge who did not accept distortions of the truth. There was an appellate court that acted with decisiveness and dispatch to meet the first challenge by President Nixon opposing the release of the tapes. The same trial court and the same appellate court, without delay, decided that a crucial grand jury report should be transmitted to the House Judiciary Committee. And that trial court overruled the President's claim of executive privilege in response to a subpoena *duces tecum* in a situation involving criminal wrongdoing. The Supreme Court, in the interest of expediting justice, bypassed the Court of Appeals and then boldly and with a minimum of delay laid to rest the troublesome problems that beset the nation.

Suppose the trial judge had been indifferent to his

full responsibilities? Suppose the Court of Appeals had not come to grips forthrightly with the unprecedented question posed in the transmission of the grand jury report to the House Judiciary Committee? And suppose the Supreme Court had not measured up courageously and judiciously to the traumatic issues that confronted all three branches of government and the nation as a whole?

The result would have been a chapter in our history books charging that our courts were ineffective and indolent. Respect for the administration of justice, at a time when suspicion lurked in the minds of the young, would have received a serious setback. Men in high places, whose sentences have become final, would have escaped the arm of the law. Had the grand jury report not been transmitted, the House Judiciary Committee hearings on Articles of Impeachment would have been so slow in proceeding, and perhaps so long delayed, that efforts to arrive at effective action could well have been temporized and eventually frustrated. Finally, had not the Supreme Court fearlessly met the issues on the subpoenaed tape recordings, there would have been no end to the ordeal the nation was experiencing, and the wounds of doubt and disillusion might never have been healed.

From Watergate we learned what generations before us have known: our Constitution works. And during the Watergate years it was interpreted again so as to reaffirm that no one—absolutely no one—is above the law.

appendix a

Status Report of Cases

The following were charged with offenses stemming from events following the break-in at Democratic National Committee Headquarters on June 17, 1972:

Charles W. Colson. Indicted on March 1, 1974, on one count of conspiracy to obstruct justice (18 USC Section 371) and one count of obstruction of justice (18 USC Section 1503). Pleaded not guilty March 9, 1974. Indictment dismissed by government June 3, 1974, after guilty plea in Fielding break-in case.

John W. Dean III. Pleaded guilty on October 19, 1973, to an information charging one count of violation of 18 USC Section 371, conspiracy to obstruct justice. Sentenced August 2, 1974, to a prison term of one to four years. Began term September 3, 1974. Released January 8, 1975, pursuant to order reducing sentence to time served.

John Ehrlichman. Indicted on March 1, 1974, on one count of conspiracy to obstruct justice (18 USC Section 371), one count of obstruction of justice (18 USC Section 1503), one count of making false statements to agents of the FBI (18 USC Section 1001), and two counts of making a false statement to a grand jury (18 USC Section 1623). Pleaded not guilty March 9, 1974. Section 1001 count dismissed by judge. Found guilty on all other counts January 1,

338

1975. Sentenced February 21, 1975 to serve 2½ to 8 years in prison. Conviction under appeal.

Harry R. Haldeman. Indicted on March 1, 1974, on one count of conspiracy to obstruct justice (18 USC Section 371), one count of obstruction of justice (18 USC Section 1503), and three counts of perjury (18 USC Section 1621). Pleaded not guilty March 9, 1974. Found guilty on all counts January 1, 1975. Sentenced February 21, 1975, to serve 2½ to 8 years in prison. Conviction under appeal.

Fred C. LaRue. Pleaded guilty on June 28, 1973, to an information charging one count of violation of 18 USC Section 371, conspiracy to obstruct justice. Sentenced one to three years, all but six months suspended. Sentence reduced by court to six months total. Entered prison April 1, 1975. Released August 15, 1975.

Jeb S. Magruder. Pleaded guilty on August 16, 1973, to an information charging one count of violation of 18 USC Section 371, conspiracy to unlawfully intercept wire and oral communications, to obstruct justice and to defraud the United States. Sentenced on May 21, 1974, to a prison term of 10 months to four years. Began term June 4, 1974. Released January 8, 1975, pursuant to order reducing sentence to time served.

Robert Mardian. Indicted on March 1, 1974, on one count of conspiracy to obstruct justice (18 USC Section 371). Pleaded not guilty March 9, 1974. Found guilty January 1, 1975. Sentenced February 21, 1975 to serve 10 months to three years. Conviction under appeal.

John Mitchell. Indicted on March 1, 1974, on one count of conspiracy to obstruct justice (18 USC Section 371), one count of obstruction of justice (18 USC Section 1503), two counts of making a false statement to a grand jury (18 USC Section 1623), one count of perjury (18 USC Section 1621), and one count of making a false statement to an agent of the FBI (18 USC Section 1001). Section 1001 count was dismissed by judge. Pleaded not guilty March 9, 1974. Found guilty on all other counts January 1, 1975. Sentenced February 21, 1975 to serve 2½ to 8 years in prison. Conviction under appeal.

Kenneth W. Parkinson. Indicted on March 1, 1974, on one count of conspiracy to obstruct justice (18 USC Section 371) and one count of obstruction of justice (18 USC Section 1503). Pleaded not guilty March 9, 1974. Acquitted January 1, 1975.

Herbert L. Porter. Pleaded guilty on January 28, 1974, to an information charging a one-count violation of 18 USC Section 1001, making false statements to agents of the FBI. Information had been filed January 21, 1974. Sentenced on April 11, 1974, to a minimum of five months and maximum of 15 months in prison, all but 30 days suspended. Served April 22 to May 17, 1974.

Gordon Strachan. Indicted on March 1, 1974, on one count of conspiracy to obstruct justice (18 USC Section 371), one count of obstruction of justice (18 USC Section 1503), and one count of making a false statement to a grand jury (18 USC Section 1623). Pleaded not guilty March 9, 1974. Case severed September 30, 1974. Charges dismissed on motion of Special Prosecutor March 10, 1975.

FIELDING BREAK-IN

The following were charged with offenses stemming from the September 3–4, 1971, break-in at the Los Angeles office of Dr. Lewis Fielding.

Bernard L. Barker. Indicted on March 7, 1974, on one count of conspiracy to violate civil rights (18 USC

Section 241). Pleaded not guilty March 14, 1974. Found guilty July 12, 1974. Suspended sentence. Three years probation. Conviction under appeal.

Charles W. Colson. Indicted on March 7, 1974, on one count of conspiracy to violate civil rights (18 USC Section 241). Indictment dismissed after Colson pleaded guilty on June 3, 1974, to an information charging one count of obstruction of justice (18 USC Section 1503). Sentenced June 21, 1974 to serve one to three years in prison and fined $5,000. Term started July 8, 1974. Released January 31, 1975, pursuant to order reducing sentence to time served.

Felipe DeDiego. Indicted on March 7, 1974, on one count of conspiracy to violate civil rights (18 USC Section 241). Pleaded not guilty March 14, 1974. Indictment dismissed by judge on May 22, 1974. U.S. Court of Appeals overturned dismissal on April 16, 1975. Special Prosecutor moved to dismiss charges May 19, 1975.

John D. Ehrlichman. Indicted on March 7, 1974, on one count of conspiracy to violate civil rights (18 USC Section 241), one count of making a false statement to agents of the FBI (18 USC Section 1001), and three counts of making a false statement to a grand jury (18 USC Section 1623). Pleaded not guilty on March 9, 1974. On July 12, 1974, Ehrlichman was found guilty on all charges, except one of the counts of making a false statement to a grand jury. On July 22, Judge Gerhard Gesell entered an acquittal on the Section 1001 charge. On July 31, 1974, he was sentenced to concurrent prison terms of 20 months to five years. Conviction under appeal.

Egil Krogh, Jr. Indicted on October 11, 1973, on two counts of violation of 18 USC Section 1623, making false statement to a grand jury. Pleaded not guilty October 18, 1973. Indictment dismissed January 24, 1974, after Krogh pleaded guilty on November 30,

1973, to an information charging one count of violation of 18 USC Section 241, conspiracy to violate civil rights. Sentenced on January 24, 1974, to a prison term of two to six years, all but six months suspended. Began sentence February 4, 1974. Released June 21, 1974.

G. Gordon Liddy. Indicted on March 7, 1974, on one count of conspiracy to violate civil rights (18 USC Section 241). Pleaded not guilty March 14, 1974. Found guilty July 12, 1974. Sentenced July 31, 1974 to a prison term of one to three years, sentence to run concurrently with sentence in *U.S.* v. *Liddy et al.* Released on bail October 15, 1974, pending appeal after serving twenty-one months. Bail revoked January 13, 1975. Conviction under appeal.

Eugenio Martinez. Indicted on March 7, 1974, on one count of conspiracy to violate civil rights (18 USC Section 241). Pleaded not guilty March 14, 1974. Found guilty July 12, 1974. Received a suspended sentence and three years probation on July 31, 1974. Conviction under appeal.

CAMPAIGN ACTIVITIES AND RELATED MATTERS

The following individuals entered pleas of guilty to misdemeanor non-willful violations of 18 USC Section 610, the federal statute prohibiting corporate campaign contributions.

Raymond Abendroth Time Oil Corp.	October 23, 1974	$2,000 fine[1]
James Allen Northrop Corp.	May 1, 1974	$1,000 fine
Richard L. Allison Lehigh Valley Co-operative Farmers	May 17, 1974	$1,000 fine[2]

[1]. Charged with two counts.
[2]. Fine suspended.

Orin E. Atkins Ashland Petro- leum Gabon	November 13, 1973	$1,000 fine[8]
Russell De Young Goodyear Tire and Rubber Co.	October 17, 1973	$1,000 fine
Ray Dubrowin Diamond Inter- national Corp.	March 7, 1974	$1,000 fine
Harry Heltzer Minnesota Mining and Manufactur- ing Co.	October 17, 1973	$500 fine
Charles N. Huseman HMS Electric Corp.	December 3, 1974	$1,000 fine
William W. Keeler Phillips Petroleum Co.	December 4, 1973	$1,000 fine
Harding L. Lawrence Braniff Airways	November 13, 1973	$1,000 fine
William Lyles Sr LBC & W Inc.	September 17, 1974	$2,000 fine[4]
H. Everett Olson Carnation Co.	December 19, 1973	$1,000 fine
Claude C. Wild Jr Gulf Oil Corp.	November 13, 1973	$1,000 fine
Harry Ratrie Ratrie, Robbins and Schweitzer, Inc.	January 28, 1975	Suspended sentence
Augustus Robbins III Ratrie, Robbins and Schweitzer, Inc.	January 28, 1975	Suspended sentence

[8]. Pleaded no contest to charges.
[4]. Charged with two counts.

The following individuals entered pleas of guilty to misdemeanor non-willful violations of 18 U.S.C. Section 2 and 610, aiding and abetting an illegal campaign contribution:

Francis X. Carroll	May 28, 1974	Suspended sentence
Norman Sherman	August 12, 1974	$500 fine
John Valentine	August 12, 1974	$500 fine

The following corporations entered pleas of guilty to violations of 18 U.S.C. Section 610, illegal campaign contribution:

American Airlines	October 17, 1973	$5,000 fine
Ashland Oil Inc.	December 30, 1974	$25,000 fine [5]
Ashland Petroleum Gabon Inc.	November 13, 1973	$5,000 fine
Braniff Airways	November 12, 1973	$5,000 fine
Carnation Company	December 19, 1973	$5,000 fine
Diamond International Corp.	March 7, 1974	$5,000 fine
Goodyear Tire and Rubber Company	October 17, 1973	$5,000 fine
Greyhound Corp.	October 8, 1974	$5,000 fine
Gulf Oil Corp.	November 13, 1973	$5,000 fine
Lehigh Valley Co-operative Farmers.	May 6, 1974	$5,000 fine
Minnesota Mining and Manufacturing Co.	October 17, 1973	$3,000 fine
National By-Products Inc.	June 24, 1974	$1,000 fine
Phillips Petroleum Co.	December 4, 1973	$5,000 fine

---

[5]. Charged with five counts.

344

| Time Oil Corp. | October 23, 1974 | $5,000 fine[6] |
| Ratrie, Robbins and Schweitzer, Inc. | January 28, 1975 | $2,500 fine |

The following corporations entered pleas of guilty to violations of 18 U.S.C. Section 611, illegal campaign contributions by government contractor:

| LBC & W Inc. | September 17, 1974 | $5,000 fine |
| Northrop Corporation | May 1, 1974 | $5,000 fine |

The following individual and corporation entered pleas of not guilty to an information filed October 19, 1973, charging four counts of misdemeanor non-willful violation of 18 U.S.C. Section 610, illegal campaign contribution. Both were acquitted on July 12, 1974, in U.S. District Court Minneapolis, Minnesota:
Dwayne O. Andreas
    Chairman of the Board, First Interoceanic Corp.
First Interoceanic Corp.

The following related matters were under the jurisdiction of the Watergate Special Prosecution Force:
American Shipbuilding Company. Pleaded guilty August 23, 1974, to one count of conspiracy (18 USC Section 371) and one count of violation of 18 USC Section 610, illegal campaign contribution. Fined $20,000. Charges were filed April 5, 1974.
Associated Milk Producers. Pleaded guilty on August 1, 1974, to one count of conspiracy (18 USC Section 371) and five counts of violation of 18 USC Section 610, illegal campaign contribution. Fined $35,000.
Tim M. Babcock. Pleaded guilty on December 10, 1974, to an information charging a one-count vio-

---

[6]. Charged with two counts.

lation of 2 USC Section 440, making a contribution in the name of another person. Sentenced to one year in prison and fined $1,000, with all but four months of the prison sentence suspended. Sentence under appeal.

Jack L. Chestnut. Indicted December 23, 1974, on one count of willful violation of 18 USC Section 610, aiding and abetting an illegal campaign contribution. Pleaded not guilty January 6, 1975. Found guilty May 8, 1975 after jury trial by Office of U.S. Attorney for Southern District of New York. Sentenced June 26, 1975, to serve four months in prison and fined $5,000. Conviction under appeal.

John B. Connally. Indicted on July 29, 1974, on two counts of accepting an illegal payment (18 USC Section 201[g], one count of conspiracy to commit perjury and obstruct justice (18 USC Section 371) and two counts of making a false statement to a grand jury (18 USC Section 1623). Pleaded not guilty August 9, 1974. Judge severed last three counts for separate trial. Found not guilty on first two counts April 17, 1975. Remaining counts dismissed April 18, 1975, on motion of Special Prosecutor.

Harry S. Dent, Sr. Pleaded guilty on December 11, 1974, to an information charging a one-count violation of the Federal Corrupt Practices Act (2 USC Sections 242 and 252). Sentenced to one month unsupervised probation.

DKI for '74. Pleaded guilty on December 13, 1974, to an information charging a violation of 2 USC Sections 434[a] and [b] and 441, failure to report receipt of contributions and failure to report names, addresses, occupations and principal places of business of the persons making such contributions. Suspended sentence.

Jack A. Gleason. Pleaded guilty on November 15, 1974, to an information charging a one-count violation of the Federal Corrupt Practices Act, (2 USC Section 252). Suspended sentence.

Jake Jacobsen. Indicted on February 21, 1974, on one count of violation of 18 USC Section 1623, making false statement to a grand jury. Indictment dismissed by Chief Judge George L. Hart May 3, 1974. Indicted July 29, 1974, on one count of making an illegal payment to a public official (18 USC Section 201[f]). Pleaded guilty August 7, 1974. Sentencing deferred.

Thomas V. Jones. Pleaded guilty on May 1, 1974, to an information charging a one-count violation of 18 USC Sections 2 and 611, willfully aiding and abetting a firm to commit violation of statute prohibiting campaign contributions by government contractors. Fined $5,000.

Herbert W. Kalmbach. Pleaded guilty on February 25, 1974, to a one-count violation of the Federal Corrupt Practices Act (2 USC Section 242[a] and 252[b]) and one count of promising federal employment as a reward for political activity and support of a candidate (18 USC Section 600). Sentenced to serve six to eighteen months in prison and fined $10,000 on the first charge. On the second charge, Kalmbach was sentenced to serve six months in prison, sentence to run concurrent with other sentence. Began term July 1, 1974. Released January 8, 1975. Sentence modified to time served.

John H. Melcher, Jr. Pleaded guilty April 11, 1974, to an information charging a one-count violation of 18 USC Sections 3 and 610, being an accessory after the fact to an illegal corporate campaign contribution. Fined $2,500.

Harold S. Nelson, former general manager, Associated Milk Producers Inc. Pleaded guilty on July 31, 1974, to a one-count information charging conspiracy to violate 18 USC Section 201[f] (illegal payment to governmental official), 18 USC Section 610 (illegal campaign contribution), and 18 USC Section 371. Sentenced November 1, 1974, to serve four months in prison and fined $10,000. Term began November 8, 1974. Released February 21, 1975.

David L. Parr, former special counsel, Associated Milk Producers Inc. Pleaded guilty on July 23, 1974, to a one-count information charging conspiracy to violate 18 USC Section 610, illegal campaign contribution. Sentenced November 1, 1974, to serve four months in prison and fined $10,000. Term began November 8, 1974. Released February 21, 1975.

Stuart H. Russell. Indicted December 19, 1974, on one count of conspiracy to violate 18 USC Section 610, illegal campaign contribution (18 USC Section 371), two counts of aiding and abetting a willful violation of 18 USC Section 610, illegal campaign contribution (18 USC Section 2 and 610). Pleaded not guilty. Found guilty in San Antonio, Texas, July 11, 1975. Sentenced in August 1975, to a prison term of two years. Conviction under appeal.

Maurice Stans. Pleaded guilty March 12, 1975, to three counts of violation of the reporting sections of the Federal Election Campaign Act of 1971, 2 USC, Sections 434[a] and [b], 441; and two counts of violation of 18 USC Section 610, accepting an illegal campaign contribution. Fined $5,000 on May 14, 1975.

George M. Steinbrenner III, Chairman of the Board, American Shipbuilding Co. Indicted April 5, 1974, on one count of conspiracy (18 USC Section 371), five counts of willful violation of 18 USC Section 610, illegal campaign contribution, two counts of aiding and abetting an individual to make a false statement to agents of the FBI (18 USC Sections 2 and 1001), four counts of obstruction of justice (18 USC Section 1503), and two counts of obstruction of a criminal investigation (18 USC Section 1510). Pleaded not guilty April 19, 1974. On August 23, 1974, Steinbrenner pleaded guilty to the count of the indictment charging a violation of 18 USC Section 371, conspiracy to violate 18 USC Section 610, and an information charging one count of violation of 18 USC Sections 3 and 610, being an accessory after the fact to an illegal campaign contribution. He was fined $15,000 on August 30, 1974. The remaining counts of the indictment were dismissed.

Wendell Wyatt. Pleaded guilty on June 11, 1975, to a one-count information charging violation of the reporting provisions of the Federal Election Campaign Act (18 USC Section 2[b] and 2 USC Sections 434 [a] and [b] and 441). Fined $750 on July 18, 1975.

DIRTY TRICKS, ITT AND OTHER MATTERS

Dwight L. Chapin. Indicted on November 29, 1973, on four counts of violation of 18 USC Section 1623, making false statement to a grand jury. He pleaded not guilty December 7, 1973. One count was dismissed by judge at conclusion of prosecution case. Found guilty on two of three remaining counts on April 5, 1974. Sentenced May 15, 1974, to serve 10 to 30 months in prison. Began sentence August 10, 1975. Appeal denied.

Richard G. Kleindienst. Pleaded guilty on May 16, 1974, to an information charging a one-count violation of 2 USC Section 192, refusal to answer pertinent questions before a Senate Committee. Sentenced June 7, 1974, to a prison term of 30 days and fined $100. Sentence suspended.

George A. Hearing.* Indicted by federal grand jury in Orlando, Fla., May 4, 1973, on two counts of fabricating and distributing illegal campaign literature (18

---

* Matter not under jurisdiction of Special Prosecutor.

USC Sections 612). Pleaded guilty May 11, 1973. Sentenced to a prison term of one year on June 15, 1973. Released March 22, 1974.

Edward L. Morgan. Pleaded guilty November 8, 1974, to an information charging one count of conspiracy to impair, impede, defeat and obstruct the proper and lawful governmental functions of the Internal Revenue Service (18 USC Section 371). Sentenced to serve two years in prison, all but four months suspended. Began term January 6, 1975. Released April 23, 1975.

Howard E. Reinecke. Indicted April 3, 1974, on three counts of perjury (18 USC Section 1621). One count dropped by government on July 9, 1974; one count dismissed by judge at conclusion of government's case on July 22, 1974. Found guilty on remaining count July 27, 1974. Received suspended 18-month sentence on October 2, 1974. Conviction reversed on appeal.

Donald H. Segretti. Indicted May 4, 1973, in Orlando, Fla., on two counts of distribution of illegal campaign literature (18 USC Sections 612 and 321). Pleaded not guilty. Indictment superceded by an August 24, 1973, indictment unsealed September 17, 1973. The new indictment charged four counts of conspiracy (18 USC Section 371) and three counts of distribution of illegal campaign literature (18 USC Section 612). Pleaded guilty October 1, 1973, to last three counts. Sentenced November 5, 1973 to serve six months in prison. Began term on November 12, 1973. Released March 25, 1974.

G. Gordon Liddy. Indicted March 7, 1974, on two counts of refusal to testify or produce papers before Congressional Committee (2 USC Section 192). Pleaded not guilty March 14, 1974. Found guilty on both counts May 10, 1974. Suspended six-month sentence.

Frank DeMarco, Jr. Indicted February 19, 1975, on one count of conspiracy to defraud the United States and an agency thereof by impairing, impeding, defeating and obstructing the proper and lawful governmental functions of the Internal Revenue Service (18 USC Section 371), one count of making a false statement to agents of the Internal Revenue Service (18 USC Section 1001), and one count of obstruction of an inquiry before a Congressional Committee (18 USC Section 1505). Judge ordered case transferred from Washington, D.C. Indicted July 29, 1975, on one charge of making a false statement to agents of the Internal Revenue Service (18 USC Section 1001). Defendant pleaded not guilty to all charges. Two charges were dismissed before trial; the others were dismissed during trial. Special Prosecutor appealed on first two counts.

Ralph G. Newman. Indicted February 19, 1975, on one count of conspiracy to defraud the United States and an agency thereof by impairing, impeding, defeating and obstructing the proper and lawful governmental functions of the Internal Revenue Service (18 USC Section 371); and one count of aiding and assisting in the preparation of a false document filed with a federal income tax return (26 USC Section 7206[2]). Judge ordered case transferred from Washington, D.C. Indicted August 15, 1975, on one count of making a false statement to agents of the Internal Revenue Service (18 USC Section 1001). Found guilty on all charges but one, and fined $10,000.

ORIGINAL WATERGATE DEFENDANTS

Bernard L. Barker. Indicted September 15, 1972, on seven counts of conspiracy, burglary, wiretapping and unlawful possession of intercepting devices (one count of 18 USC Section 371, two counts of 22 DC Code Section 1801[b], two counts of 18 USC Section 2511, two counts of 23 DC Code 543[a]). Pleaded guilty January 15, 1973. Sentenced November 9, 1973, to a prison term of 18 months to six years. Motion to withdraw guilty plea denied. Freed January 4, 1974, pending outcome of appeal. Appeal denied February 25, 1975. Sentence reduced by Judge John J. Sirica to time served.

Virgilio Gonzalez. Indicted September 15, 1972, on seven counts of conspiracy, burglary, wiretapping and unlawful possession of intercepting devices (one count of 18 USC Section 371, two counts of 22 DC Code Section 1801[b], two counts of 18 USC Section 2511, two counts of 23 DC Code 543[a]). Pleaded guilty January 15, 1973. Sentenced November 9, 1973, to a prison term of one to four years. Motion to withdraw guilty plea denied. Appeal denied February 25, 1973. Released on parole March 7, 1974.

E. Howard Hunt. Indicted September 15, 1972, on six counts of conspiracy, burglary, and wiretapping (one count of 18 USC Section 371, two counts of 22 DC Code Section 1801[b], three counts of 18 USC Section 2511). Pleaded guilty January 11, 1973. Sentenced November 9, 1973, to a prison term of 30 months to eight years and fined $10,000. Motion to withdraw guilty plea denied. Released on personal recognizance January 2, 1974, pending outcome of appeal. Appeal denied February 25, 1975. Reentered prison on April 25, 1975.

G. Gordon Liddy. Indicted September 15, 1972, on six counts of conspiracy, burglary, and wiretapping (one count of 18 USC Section 371, two counts of 22 DC Code Section 1801[b], three counts of 18 USC Section 2511). Convicted January 30, 1973, on all counts. Sentenced March 23, 1973, to a prison term of six years and eight months to 20 years and fined $40,000. Released on bail October 15, 1974. Appeal denied, re-entered prison February 16, 1975.

Eugenio R. Martinez. Indicted September 15, 1972, on seven counts of conspiracy, burglary, wiretapping and unlawful possession of intercepting devices (one count of 18 USC, Section 471, two counts of 22 DC Code Section 1801[b], two counts of 23 DC Code 543[a], two counts of 18 USC Section 2511). Pleaded guilty January 15, 1973. Sentenced November 9, 1973, to a prison term of one to four years. Motion to withdraw guilty plea denied. Released on parole March 7, 1974. Appeal denied February 25, 1975.

James W. McCord, Jr. Indicted on September 15, 1973, on eight counts of conspiracy, burglary, wiretapping and unlawful possession of intercepting devices (one count of 18 USC Section 371, two counts of 22 DC Code Section 1801[b], three counts of 18 USC Section 2511, two counts of 23 DC Code Section 543 [a]). Convicted January 30, 1973. Sentenced November 9, 1973, to a prison term of one to five years. Conviction upheld by U.S. Court of Appeals. Entered prison on March 21, 1975. Released May 29, 1975, pursuant to order reducing sentence to time served.

Frank A. Sturgis. Indicted September 15, 1972, on seven counts of conspiracy, burglary, wiretapping and unlawful possession of intercepting devices (one count of 18 USC Section 371, two counts of 22 DC Code Section 1801[b], two counts of 18 USC Section 2511, two counts of 23 DC Code Section 543 [a]). Pleaded guilty January 15, 1973. Sentenced November 9, 1973, to a prison term of one to four years. Motion to withdraw guilty plea denied. Released by court order on January 18, 1974, pending outcome of appeal. Parole Board announced on March 25, 1974, that parole would commence on termination of appeal bond. Appeal denied February 25, 1975.

MITCHELL-STANS TRIAL IN NEW YORK

The following indictments were handed up by a federal grand jury in New York on May 10, 1973, some two weeks before the Watergate Special Prosecution Force began its operations. Although technically under the jurisdiction of the Special Prosecutor, the cases were tried by the office of the U.S. Attorney for the Southern District of New York.

John Mitchell. Indicted on May 10, 1973, on one count of conspiracy to obstruct justice (18 USC Section 371), three counts of endeavoring to obstruct justice (18 USC Sections 1503, 1505, 1510, and 2), six counts of making false statement before a grand jury (18 USC Section 1623). Pleaded not guilty May 21, 1973. Acquitted April 28, 1974.

Maurice Stans. Indicted on May 10, 1973, on one count of conspiracy (18 USC Section 371), three counts of endeavoring to obstruct justice (18 USC Sections 1503, 1505, 1510 and 2), and six counts of making false statement to a grand jury (18 USC Section 1623). Pleaded not guilty May 21, 1973. Acquitted April 28, 1974.

Robert Vesco. Indicted on May 10, 1973, on one count of conspiracy to obstruct justice (18 USC Section 371) and three counts of endeavoring to obstruct justice (18 USC Sections 1503, 1505, 1510, and 2). Presently a fugitive, living outside the United States. Charges pending.

Harry Sears. Indicted on May 10, 1973, on one count of conspiracy to obstruct justice (18 USC Section 371) and three counts of endeavoring to obstruct justice (18 USC Sections 1503, 1505, 1510 and 2). Granted immunity from prosecution in return for testimony at trial. Charges dismissed March 17, 1975.

appendix b

Staff List

* Ruth served as Deputy Special Prosecutor from July, 1973, to October, 1974.

Stephen G. Breyer	June, 1973–June, 1974 (intermittent).
Rose S. Bryan	July, 1973–October, 1975 (intermittent).
Florence L. Campbell	June, 1973–October, 1975.
Verona Canty	July, 1973–January, 1975.
Richard A. Carter	August, 1974–May, 1975.
Robert M. Chideckel	August, 1973– August, 1974.
Toni L. Childers	August, 1974–May, 1975.
Phyllis E. Clancy	September, 1973– October, 1975.
Joseph J. Connolly	June, 1973–May, 1974.
David J. Cook	January, 1974–May, 1974.
Richard J. Davis	July, 1973–August, 1975.
Barbara B. DeLeon	May, 1974–October, 1975
Judith A. Denny	August, 1973– October, 1975.
Albert P. Deschenes	May, 1975–July, 1975 (intermittent).
Michael J. Dickman	August, 1973– September, 1974.
Gayle A. Dicks	July, 1973–October, 1973.
Loretta L. Dicks	June, 1973– December, 1973.
Theresa A. Doramus	July, 1973– September, 1973.
James S. Doyle	June, 1973–May, 1975.
Elizabeth M. Dunigan	November, 1974– October, 1975.
Robin D. Edwards	January, 1974– August, 1975.
Ruby N. Edwards	March, 1974–April, 1974.
Linda L. Eiskant	January, 1974– October, 1975.
Robin A. Elliott	September, 1973– May, 1974.

Ellen M. Fahey	August, 1973–October, 1975.
Carl B. Feldbaum	July, 1973–October, 1975.
Allison Finn	November, 1974–July, 1975.
Jonathan A. Flint	August, 1974–January, 1975.
Hamilton P. Fox, III	July, 1973–December, 1974.
George T. Frampton, Jr	June, 1973–February, 1975.
Nona J. Funk	August, 1973–September, 1973.
John B. Galus	October, 1973–August, 1975.
Marcellus Gant	February, 1975–July, 1975.
Kenneth S. Geller	July, 1973–October, 1975.
Maureen E. Gevlin	July, 1973–October, 1975.
William J. Gilbreth	April, 1975–August, 1975 (intermittent).
Sidney M. Glazer	July, 1973–September, 1974
Ann B. Goetcheus	October, 1973–July, 1975.
Gerald Goldman	June, 1973–April, 1975.
Mary E. Graham	July, 1973–October, 1975.
Stephen E. Haberfeld	June, 1973–December, 1974.
Lawrence A. Hammond	August, 1973–July, 1974.
Elizabeth A. Harvey	May, 1974–October, 1975.
Henry L. Hecht	June, 1973–October, 1975.
Philip B. Heymann	May, 1973–June, 1975 (intermittent).
Paul R. Hoeber	August, 1973–June, 1974.
Cheryl O. Holmes	October, 1973–October, 1975
Jay S. Horowitz	August, 1973–October, 1975.

Dixie J. Housman	June, 1973–March, 1974.
Archibald B. Hughes	January, 1975–February, 1975.
Lawrence Iason, II	June, 1973–February, 1975.
Dianna Ingram	September, 1973–August, 1975.
Janet Johnson	June, 1973–July, 1973.
Marian M. Johnson	August, 1973–May, 1975.
Susan E. Kaslow	July, 1973–October, 1975.
Sherry F. Kaufman	May, 1974–March, 1975.
David H. Kaye	June, 1973–December, 1974.
John G. Koeltl	August, 1973–November, 1974.
Peter M. Kreindler	June, 1973–October, 1975.
Rosanne Kumins	May, 1973–August, 1973.
Philip A. Lacovara	July, 1973–September, 1974.
Louis B. Lapides	August, 1974–May, 1975.
Cynthia F. Law	May, 1974–February, 1975.
Michael L. Lehr	December, 1974–October, 1975.
Don Loeb	January, 1974–August, 1975 (intermittent).
Gloria L. Lowe	June, 1974–October, 1975.
Rosalyn L. Lowenhaupt	July, 1974–October, 1974.
Eugene C. Lozner	December, 1973–April, 1974.
Ilona L. Lubman	February, 1974–June, 1974.
Paula J. Lusby	August, 1973–January, 1974.
John P. Lydick	April, 1975–October, 1975.
Daniel F. Mann	August, 1973–October, 1975.

Francis J. Martin	June, 1973–October, 1975.
Thomas J. Martorelli	January, 1974–May, 1974.
Linda S. Mayes	June, 1973–October, 1974.
Thomas F. McBride	May, 1973–October, 1975.
William H. Merrill	June, 1973– September, 1974.
Paul R. Michel	April, 1974–August, 1975.
Yolanda D. Molock	September, 1973– August, 1975.
Betty J. Monroe	July, 1973–October, 1975.
Pamela D. Morris	June, 1973–October, 1975.
Scott W. Muller	October, 1974–June, 1975 (intermittent).
Stanley Nalesnik	August, 1974–May, 1975.
James F. Neal	May, 1973–January, 1975 (intermittent).
Shirah Neiman	July, 1975–October, 1975.
Jo Ann Nelson	August, 1974–May, 1975.
Linda D. Noonan	September, 1973– September, 1975.
Robert L. Palmer	July, 1973–October, 1974.
Anthony J. Passaretti	June, 1974–May, 1975.
Mark B. Peabody	August, 1974– October, 1975.
Julia M. Pfeltz	June, 1973– November, 1974.
Donna J. Phillips	July, 1974– December, 1974 (intermittent).
Charles A. Pidano, Jr	September, 1973– August, 1974.
Charles W. Pitcher, Jr	September, 1973– August, 1975.
Jean R. Pyles	July, 1973–April, 1974.
James L. Quarles, III	June, 1973–June, 1975.
Barbara J. Raney	October, 1973– September, 1975.

Ann J. Reines	May, 1974–August, 1975 (intermittent).
Peter F. Rient	May, 1973–October, 1975.
Patricia A. Robertson	August, 1974–May, 1975.
Cynthia J. Robinson	October, 1973–July, 1975.
Renee M. Robinson	August, 1973– August, 1975.
Judith H. Rollenhagen	July, 1973–August, 1974.
Patricia Ronkovich	June, 1973– September, 1975 (intermittent).
Daniel N. Rosenblatt	April, 1974–October, 1975.
Thomas P. Ruane	July, 1973–October, 1975.
Charles F. Ruff	July, 1973–July, 1975.
Jon A. Sale	September, 1973– August, 1975.
Susan L. Sauntry	October, 1974– November, 1974 (intermittent).
Meriam I. Schroeder	September, 1973– August, 1974.
Monica Schuster	October, 1973–May, 1974.
Linda E. Schwarz	September, 1973– October, 1975.
Charles S. Scott	January, 1974–May, 1974.
Audrey M. Snell	June, 1973– September, 1975.
Joseph N. Sprowl, Jr	January, 1974–May, 1974.
Barbara A. Stagnaro	July, 1973–October, 1975.
Jay B. Stephens	November, 1974– October, 1975.
Hazel D. Stewart	September, 1973– October, 1975.
Theresa M. Strong	September, 1973– May, 1975.
Mark A. Surette	August, 1974–May, 1975.

Lois M. Swann	October, 1973–March, 1974.
Susanne D. Thevenet	July, 1973–September, 1975.
Karen I. Thompson	June, 1973–April, 1975.
Mark R. Thompson	September, 1973–January, 1975.
Christine M. Thren	August, 1975–October, 1975.
Frank M. Tuerkheimer	December, 1973–June, 1975.
Richard D. Van Wagenen	April, 1975–July, 1975.
Jill W. Volner	July, 1973–April, 1975.
James Vorenberg	May, 1973–October, 1975 (intermittent).
Richard D. Weinberg	July, 1973–April, 1975.
Suzanne L. Westfall	July, 1973–January, 1975.
Audrey J. Williams	July, 1973–March, 1975.
Michael Y. Williams	July, 1973–October, 1975.
Sally G. Willis	June, 1973–October, 1975.
Roger M. Witten	June, 1973–December, 1974.
William F. Woods	August, 1974–October, 1975.
Tyrone C. Wooten	October, 1973–May, 1974.
Gilbert A. Wright	July, 1973–August, 1973.
Pamela Wright	July, 1973–October, 1975.
Carol A. Zorger	June, 1973–March, 1975 (intermittent).

FEDERAL PROTECTIVE SERVICE:

The following officers were detailed from the General Services Administration, Federal Protective Service, and provided security protection for the Watergate Special Prosecution Force:

Lt. James M. Hairston	June, 1973–October, 1975.
Lt. Edward B. King	June, 1973–April, 1974.
Lt. O. H. Lewis	June, 1973–October, 1975.
Johnny L. Augustus	June, 1973–October, 1975.
James M. Banks	June, 1973–October, 1975.
Lindsay L. Boomer	July, 1973–October, 1975.
Russell F. Curry	July, 1973–October, 1975.
Joel D. Davies	June, 1973–October, 1975.
Jimmy Dickson	June, 1973–October, 1975.
James O. Highsmith	June, 1973–October, 1975.
Willie Hilliard	June, 1973–October, 1975.
Wilbert L. Lofton	June, 1973–October, 1975.
Joseph F. Maisner	August, 1973– October, 1975.
John E. McFarland	June, 1973–October, 1975.
Richard A. McGriff	June, 1973–October, 1975.
James F. Moore	July, 1973–October, 1975.
Waymon Stewart	June, 1973–October, 1975.
Thomas C. Watson	June, 1973–October, 1975.
John C. Wright	August, 1973–April, 1975.

Index

366

pre-trial publicity as prejudicial to, 270, 275, 276-86, 291, 295-96
public vs. private character of, 64
repentance lacking in, 335
resignation called for, 259
resignation of, 260-63, 266, 267, 290-91, 293, 305-06, 334-35
"road map" and, 118-19, 121, 122-23, 125-26, 142-43, 151
Supreme Court decision and, 237-38, 244-46
taping by, 16-17, 328-29, 332
testifying of, 100-01
as unindicted co-conspirator, 157-59, 161, 196-98, 200-01, 212-28, 231-32
vindictive side of, 329-31
Watergate cover-up and, 16, 23, 24, 30, 51-52, 115, 116-18, 135, 137, 139-43, 154-55, 210-11, 212-28, 247-48, 250-58, 272-73, 292, 305, 328-33
Watergate preoccupation vs. executive role of, 160, 328
wiretap project and, 82
Nixon family, 261
Novak, Robert, 70

O'Brien, Lawrence, 85, 135
Ogarrio, Manuel, 133-34, 252, 258
Olson, H. Everett, 343

pardon:
Ford and, 268, 271, 273, 288-98, 304, 305-06, 310, 311-12
Nixon's acceptance of, 297-98
validity of, as question, 294, 296, 298-99, 304, 305, 306, 307, 310, 311

Parkinson, Kenneth W., 129, 135, 326, 340
Parr, David L., 348
Pentagon Papers case, 16, 27-28, 37, 39, 79-80, 81
Petersen, Henry, 24-25, 135, 216, 221, 224-25, 227-28
Plumbers, 36-39, 130, 133, 251
Plumbers case (*see also* Fielding break-in), 20, 26, 36-43, 79-81
national security contentions in, 21, 22-23, 24, 25, 31, 34, 35, 42-43, 158
Plumbers Task Force, 15, 22-23, 35, 74, 158
Political Espionage Task Force, 18, 47
Pope, Alexander, 130
Porter, Herbert L., 135, 340
Powell, Lewis F., Jr., 231
Powers, Samuel, 62
Providence *Journal,* 65

Ratrie, Harry, 343
Rebozo, Bebe, 328
Rehnquist, William H., 195, 230, 231
Reinecke, Howard E., 350
Republican presidential candidates, investigation of contributions to, 312-13
Richardson, Elliott, 2, 80-81
"road map," 118-19, 120-27, 142-43, 150, 151, 268
Robbins, Augustus, III, 343
Rockefeller, Nelson, 266, 288
Rodino, Peter, 110, 114, 115, 245-46
Rogers, William P., 197
Roosevelt, Franklin D., 60
Rose, H. Chapman (Chappy), 66-69
"Rose Mary's List," 316-17
Ruckelshaus, William, 2, 76, 79-80, 83

369